SPEAK THAI WITH CONFIDENCE!

ESSENTIAL THAI

PHRASEBOOK & DICTIONARY

Revised Edition

> **Sàwàt dii khâ.**
> Hello!

> **Khun maa jàak pràthêht àrai khá.**
> Where are you from?

> **Phŏm pen khon á-meh-rí-kan khráp.**
> I'm American.

Jintana Rattanakhemakorn
Scot Barmé

TUTT
Tokyo | Rutlar

T0162931

Contents

Introduction

Welcome to the Tuttle Essential Language series, covering all the most popular Asian languages. These books are basic guides to communicating in the language. They're concise, accessible and easy to understand, and you'll find them indispensable on your trip abroad to get you where you want to go, pay the right prices and do everything you've been planning to do.

Each guide is divided into 14 themed sections and starts with a pronunciation table which explains the phonetic pronunciation to all the words and sentences you'll need to know, and a basic grammar guide which will help you construct basic sentences in your chosen language. At the end of the book is an extensive English–Thai dictionary.

Throughout the book you'll come across boxes with a 🖑 beside them. These are designed to help you if you can't understand what your listener is saying to you. Hand the book over to them and encourage them to point to the appropriate answer to the question you are asking.

Other boxes in the book—this time without the symbol—give listings of themed words with their English translations.

For extra clarity, we have put all phonetic pronunciations of the foreign language terms in bold italic.

This book covers all subjects you are likely to come across during the course of a visit, from reserving a room for the night to ordering food and drink at a restaurant and what to do if your car breaks down or you lose your money. With over 2,000 commonly used words and essential sentences at your fingertips you can rest assured that you will be able to get by in all situations, so let **Essential Thai** become your passport to learning to speak with confidence!

Pronunciation guide

Thai is a tonal language with 5 tones, meaning that a word with different tones has different, unrelated meanings. Hence the purpose of this section: firstly, to give you some idea as to how Thai is pronounced and, secondly, to show you how the tones work. Every Thai word throughout this book is displayed alongside its romanization and tonal marks in order to make learning easier for you. However, there is nothing better than hearing the sound by asking your Thai friend to give some assistance with both pronunciation and tone.

Consonants

The majority of Thai consonants has the same pronunciation as in English. Some of them may be difficult for English speakers. For example, the hard **p** sound is a cross between "p" and "b," while the hard **t** sound is a cross between "t" and "d."

The table below shows the Thai consonants and how they are pronounced in English, and examples of how those letters would sound if they are placed in a Thai word.

Consonant	Sounds like	Example
k	**g** as in "get"	กิน _kin_ "eat"
kh	**k** as in "kind"	คน _khon_ "person"
ng	**ng** as in "singing"	เงิน _ngern_ "money"
j	**j** as in "job"	ใจ _jai_ "heart"
ch	**ch** as in "chat"	ชื่อ _chûeh_ "name"
s	**s** as in "sun"	ซื้อ _súe_ "buy"
y	**y** as in "yes"	ยาว _yaow_ "long"
d	**d** as in "down"	เดือน _duean_ "month"
t	**t** as in "stone"	ตา _taa_ "eye"
th	**t** as in "tap"	ทำ _tham_ "do/make"
n	**n** as in "near"	นอน _naawn_ "sleep"
b	**b** as in "bear"	บ่าย _bàai_ "afternoon"
p	**p** as in "spot"	ปี _pii_ "year"
ph	**p** as in "pen"	พ่อ _phâw_ "father"

f	**f** as in "<u>f</u>all"	ฟ้า _f**á**a_ "blue"
m	**m** as in "<u>m</u>y"	แม่ _m**á**ae_ "mother"
r	**r** as in "<u>r</u>un"	เรา _**r**ao_ "we"
l	**l** as in "<u>l</u>ove"	แล้ว _l**á**ew_ "already"
w	**w** as in "<u>w</u>in"	วัน _**w**an_ "day"
h	**h** as in "<u>h</u>ow"	หัว _**h**ŭa_ "head"

Ending consonants

Thai has only eight ending consonant sounds. These eight sounds can be divided into two groups—stops and sonorants. Thai stop sounds are not voiced aloud and have a sudden stop once they are spoken in a word. In contrast, sonorants are pronounced softly and possible to sustain for some time.

There are three stop ending sounds and five sonorant sounds

Stop consonant	Sounds like	Example
k	**g** as in "ba<u>g</u>"	มาก _m**â**ak_ "very"
t	**t** as in "shou<u>t</u>"	ปิด _p**ì**t_ "to close/turn off"
p	**p** as in "ta<u>p</u>"	กับ _k**à**p_ "and/with"

Sonorant consonant	Sounds like	Example
ng	**ng** as in "ri<u>ng</u>"	ลอง _laawng_ "try"
n	**n** as in "fu<u>n</u>"	จาน _jaan_ "dish"
m	**m** as in "ti<u>me</u>"	ขม _kh**ŏ**m_ "bitter"
y	**y** as in "wh<u>y</u>"	สวย _s**ŭ**ay_ "beautiful"
w	**w** as in "no<u>w</u>"	แก้ว _g**â**aew_ "glass"

Consonant Clusters

There are eleven consonant cluster sounds in Thai, each of which clusters with **r**, **l** and **w** sounds. They are as follows:

   gr, gl, gw, khr, khl, khw, tr, pr, pl, phr, phl.

The sounds **l** and **r** are often used interchangeably in Thai or sometime can be dropped or omitted to a great extent, particularly in everyday street/casual talk. For example:

Formal speech	Informal speech
khrai (Who?) ใคร	*khai* ใค
plaa (a fish) ปลา	*paa* ปา
rian (to study) เรียน	*lian* เลียน

It is very common that some Thais cannot properly say **l** and **r**, specifically in some parts of the country, such as the North and North-East, where their dialects replace **r** ร with **h** ฮ. So many Thais lack **r** in their native tongue.

Vowels

Thai vowels are generally categorized into three groups: *single vowels, diphthongs* (combination of two vowels), and *extra vowels,* and they are separated into short and long forms. The term "long" and "short" refers to the duration that the vowel is pronounced, not the sound of the vowel. For example, in English you can say "nope" (shortly) or you draw out the vowel like "Nooooooo" while the word still has the same meaning. In Thai, on the other hand, you need to use the correct one, otherwise it can change the meaning of the word. For example, วัด *wàt* (short vowel) means "temple," but วาด *wàat* (long vowel) means "to draw."

1. Short vowels
There are nine 'short' vowels:

Vowel sound	Pronunciation	Example (Thai word)
<u>a</u>	**a** as in "c<u>u</u>t"	ปะ *pà* "patch"
<u>i</u>	**i** as in "s<u>i</u>t"	ติ *tì* "criticize"
<u>**ue**</u>	**u** as in "h<u>u</u>h"	หึ *hùe* "chuckle"
<u>**u**</u>	**u** as in "s<u>u</u>it"	จุ *jù* "contain"
<u>**e**</u>	**e** as in "w<u>e</u>t" (shorter)	เละ *lé* "mess"
<u>**ae**</u>	**ae** as in "c<u>a</u>t" (shorter)	แกะ *gàe* "sheep"
<u>**o**</u>	**o** as in "<u>o</u>nly" (shorter)	โละ *ló* "to get rid of"
<u>**aw**</u>	**aw** as in "p<u>o</u>t" (shorter)	เจาะ *jàw* "puncture"
<u>**oe**</u>	**er** as in "off<u>er</u>"	เยอะ *yóe* "a lot"

2. Long vowels

Each short vowel also has a long form as counterpart, by which you should stretch out the sound for an extra beat, e.g., "ohhhh" rather than "oh."

Vowel sound	Pronunciation	Example (Thai word)
aa	**ar** as in "jar"	มา *maa* "to come"
ii	**ee** as in "tree"	มี *mii* "to have"
ueh	**u** as in "umm" (longer)	หรือ *rǔeh* "or"
uu	**ue** as in "true"	ดู *duu* "to watch"
eh	**ay** as in "bay"	เจ *jeh* "Chinese vegetarian"
aeh	**air** as in "pair"	แต่ *tàeh* "but"
oh	**ol** as in "sold"	โทร *thoh* "phone call"
aw	**aw** as in "claw"	คอ *khaw* "neck"
oeh	**ur** as in "fur"	เจอ *joeh* "to meet"

3. Mixed vowels

There are three other mixed vowels, which combine two vowels together, such as **ia** (**ii** + **aa**), **ua** (**ou** + **aa**), **uea** (**ue** + **aa**), and the other three extra vowels: **am**, **ai** and **ao**.

Vowel sound	Pronunciation	Example (Thai word)
ia	**ear** as in "near"	เมีย *mia* "wife"
ua	**ure** as in "sure"	บัว *bua* "lotus"
uea	**ua** as in "dual" (longer)	เสือ *sǔea* "tiger"
am	**um** as in "drum"	ทำ *tham* "to do/make"
ai	**ye** as in "dye"	ไต้/ใต้ *tâi* "torch (set alight)/under"
ao	**ow** as in "cow"	เบา *bao* "light"

Tones

Thai has five tones: mid, low, falling, high and rising. The pitch of a particular word changes its meaning. For example, it can change the meaning from close to far, and from being pretty to being bad luck! In this book, each tone, except the mid tone, is represented by a symbol written above the vowel. Ask Thai people to help practicing the tones with you for a few minutes.

Pitch Level	Symbol	Example	Meaning
mid	no mark	ปา *paa*	"throw"
low	`	ป่า *pàa*	"forest, jungle"
falling	^	ป้า *pâa*	"aunt (mother's older sister)"
high	′	ป๊า *páa*	an informal term to call "father," derived from Chinese
rising	ˇ	ป๋า *pǎa*	an informal term to call "father," derived from Chinese

Pitch Level	Symbol	Example	Meaning
mid	no mark	ไมล์ *mai*	"mile"
low	`	ใหม่ *mài*	"new"
falling	^	ไม่ *mâi*	"no, not"
high	′	ไม้ *mái*	"wood"
rising	ˇ	ไหม *mǎi*	"silk"

Important Things to Note

The phrases in this book are straightforward once you've familiarized yourself with the romanized Thai. However, a few basic points concerning language usage and grammar need to be understood.

Basic grammar

Grammar is basically sentence or language "rules." Knowing a few basic rules will allow you to create and develop your communicative ability in the Thai language. The word order of Thai sentence is very simple. Basic sentences have the same order as in English. There are no articles like "a," "an," and "the." Also, there are no plural forms, and verbs are not conjugated in Thai, and Thai words never change form. We'll have a look at these separately.

1. Word order

The basic Thai sentence structure is "Subject + Verb + Object" as in English.

kháo châwp sàp-pà-rót   He/She likes pineapples.

In order to form a question, you add a short question word at the end of the sentence.

Khun phôut thai <u>dâi mái</u>   <u>Can</u> you speak Thai?

Khun chûeh <u>à-rai</u>   <u>What</u> is your name?

Note: No punctuation is used to indicate a question or the end of a Thai sentence.

2. Nouns

A noun can be a person or thing as well as people. As mentioned earlier, there is no distinction between the singular and plural forms. In order to indicate the number of things (or people, objects, etc.), you need to add a "classifier." Each object has a specific classifier word that should be used when you are stating the quantity of that object. A simple rule is "noun + number + classifier"

Noun + number + classifier

khâaw sìi jaan	rice +	four	+ dishes	four dishes of rice
náam sǎam khùat	water +	three	+ bottles	three bottles of water

3. Pronouns

Thai personal pronouns range from very formal through very casual to impolite (which should not be used in public), and there's distinct differences between male and female usage. Also, subject pronouns and object pronouns are the same (there's no difference between "I" and 'me' or "he/she" and "him/her"). The commonly used personal pronouns are:

English Pronoun	**Thai Pronoun**
I, me (for male speakers)	*phǒm*
I, me (for female speakers)	*chǎn*
you (polite)	*khun*
he, she, they	*khǎo*
we, us	*rao*

Note: Personal pronouns are often omitted in informal conversation, especially "I" and "You." In casual speech, it's very common to use a nickname to refer to yourself or a third person, rather than using a personal pronoun. Additionally, a kinship term like "mother" or "father" is often used to address people of different ages and also indicate respect for the older person by the younger.

4. Adjectives

Adjectives are words that describe nouns. The word order is unlike in English. Thai uses **noun + adjective** as in "house + white" = *bâan sǐi khǎaw*, and "cat + big" = *maew yài*. Also, Thai adjectives can function as the main verb in the sentence without any form of the verb "to be" and are placed after the nouns they are describing as the following examples.

The flower is beautiful.	=	Flower + beautiful *dàwk mái sǔay*
Thai food is delicious.	=	Thai food + delicious *aa-hǎan thai à-ròy*

5. Possessive adjectives

Possessive adjectives are always placed <u>after</u> the noun.

chǎn/phǒm I	*khǎwng-chǎn/khǎwng phǒm* my
khun you	*khǎwng-khun* your
khǎ he/she/they	*khǎwng-khǎo* his/her/their
rao we	*khǎwng-rao* our

Examples:

Krâwp-krua <u>khǎwng-chǎn</u> mii sìi khon	There are four people in my family.
Phâw khǎwng-khun tham-ngaan à-rai	What is your father's job?

6. Verbs

Thai verbs do not inflect their form and have only one simple form regardless of subject or tense. The Thai verb "to go" is never changed whether the subject is "I, you, he/she" or "they," and whether the action took place in the past, present or future. Instead, tenses are indicated mostly by using a "time-frame" or helping words at the beginning of or the end of the sentence.

In order to state the past and the future in Thai, you can use the following optional words.

- Using time, such as "now", "today", "yesterday", "tomorrow", "six o'clock", etc. For example,

<u>Mûea-waan-níi</u> rao rian phaa-sǎa thai	Yesterday we learned Thai language.
Tawn níi chǎn tham ahǎan	I'm now cooking.

- Using *láehw* แล้ว ("already") at the very end of the sentence to indicate that something was completed before or prior to the moment of speaking. For example,

Chǎn ìm <u>láehw</u>	I'm already full.
Phǒm àap-nám <u>láehw</u>	I already showered.

- Using *jà* จะ ("will") in front of verbs to indicate the future, and sometimes you can also include the time word to emphasize when it is going to happen in the future. For example,

Phŏm jà pai chiang mài	I'm going to Chiang Mai.
Phrûng níi phŏm jà pai chiang mài	Tomorrow I'm going to Chiang Mai.

7. Questions

There are two main types of question: **Wh-questions** and **Yes-No questions**. The word order for a question is different from that in English. In Thai, question words are located at the end of the sentence.

7.1 Wh-questions

Use a question word like *khrai* "Who," *à-rai* "What," *thîi-năi* "Where" *mûea-rài* "When," *tham-mai* "Why," *yang-ngai* "How," *thâo-rài* "How much." Here are some examples of questions you can ask.

<u>Who</u>'s working with you?	= *Khun tham-ngaan gàp <u>krai</u>*
<u>What</u> is your name?	= *Khun chûeh <u>à-rai</u>*
<u>Where</u> is the bathroom?	= *Hăwng-náam yòu <u>thîi-năi</u>*
<u>When</u> will you come home?	= *Khun jà glàp bâan <u>mûea-rài</u>*
<u>Why</u> are you crying?	= *Khun ráwng-hâai <u>tham-mai</u>*
<u>How</u> is your mother?	= *Mâe khăwng khun pen <u>yang-ngai</u>*
<u>How much</u> does this shirt cost?	= *Sêua tua níi <u>thâo-rài</u>*

There are some cases where question words are put at the beginning of the sentences. For example,

<u>Who</u> teaches Thai?	= *<u>Krai</u> săwn phaa-saă thai*

7.2 Yes-No questions

There are four ways to ask and answer with yes/no questions.

1. *Mái* ("Are/Is…?" / "Do/Does….?") can be interpreted as both a general question and an invitation or suggestion. It is

placed at the end of a sentence. To answer "yes" repeat the **verb** or **adjective**. For saying "no," put *mâi* (which mean "not") before the verb or adjective. For example,

Q:	Are you hungry?	*Khun hǐw mái*
Yes:	I'm hungry.	*Chǎn <u>hǐw</u>*
No:	I'm not hungry	*Chǎn <u>mâi hǐw</u>*

2. *Dâi-mái* ("Can..?") refers to (1) having the ability or skill to do something, and (2) having permission to do something. To answer "yes" say *dâi* (can/able to), for "no" respond with *mâi-dâi* (cannot/unable to). They are placed at the end of both question and answer sentences. For example,

Q:	Can you swim?	*Khun wâai náam <u>dâi-mái</u>*
Yes:	I can swim.	*Phǒm wâai náam <u>dâi</u>*
No:	I can't swim.	*Phǒm wâai náam <u>mâi-dâi</u>*

3. **Châi-mái** is asked to confirm an answer that's already expected. It is the equivalent of "aren't you?," "isn't it?" or "right?," and answered by repeating the verb or adjective or with **châi** ("yes")/**mâi-châi** ("no"). For example,

Q:	You're Anne, right?	*Khun chûeh Anne <u>châi-mái</u>*
Yes:	I am.	*<u>Châi</u>*
No:	I am not.	*<u>Mâi-châi</u>*

4. *Rúe-yang* ("Have you . . . yet?") is used to ask whether one has done something previously or has done something yet. To answer "yes" put *láehw* ("already") after the verb. To say "no," put **yang-mâi-dâi** ("not yet") before the verb.

Q:	Have you taken any medicine?	*Khun <u>gin</u> yaa <u>rúe-yang</u>*
Yes:	I've taken some already.	*Chǎn <u>gin</u> láehw*
No:	I haven't taken any yet.	*Chǎn <u>yang mâi-dâi</u> gin*

8. Polite sentence endings

Another key area of the Thai language is the use of gender-specific words known as polite particles. These are used at the end of an utterance to indicate politeness, respect and courtesy.

- Men will use the word *khráp* when asking or answering a question. It is a neutral ending for men to use in any situation.

- Women will say *khâ* (with a falling tone) when making a statement, command, and also using it alone as a polite way to answer "yes." But they will use *khá* (with a high tone) when asking a question.

Whenever using examples from this book (some of which don't include polite particles) please remember to use the appropriate gender-specific polite particles. In Thailand, it is always better to be polite and show great respect to someone you have just met or do not know well.

A final tip

Thai has an ever-increasing number of English loanwords, although they are pronounced in a distinctively Thai manner and may not even sound like English, e.g. "bill" (at a restaurant) becomes **bin**; "room service" *ruum soeh wít*; "computer" *khawm phiw tôeh* and so on. Many "brand names" are pronounced in the Thai way as well, e.g. "Fanta" is *faentâa*, and Pepsi is *páepsîi* in Thai. These are, of course, just a few examples of English loanwords in Thai, and you will probably hear more if you are in Thailand.

1. Greetings and Requests

It is usual in Thailand to "wai" (*wâi*) on meeting someone and when taking one's leave. The "wai" involves putting the hands together in a prayer-like gesture and bringing them up towards the tip of the nose or, in the case of greeting a significant or powerful individual, to the bridge of the nose. You "wai" a superior or an elderly person whom you respect, as well as monks. Thais generally "wai" their colleagues and bosses at work when they first meet them each day and on leaving at the end of the day. If someone "wais" you just a smile, and perhaps a nod of the head, is sufficient. It is perhaps better to avoid "wai-ing" others until you develop a good sense of Thai cultural practice. At that point the "wai" should come to you naturally.

Thais tend not to complain, at least face to face with someone, as westerners often do. If you wish to criticize something, it's often better to say nothing and just take things in your stride.

1.1 Greetings

Hello/Good morning, Khun James. (formal)	*sàwàt dii khun James* สวัสดี คุณเจมส์
Hello/Good morning, Khun Anitra.	*sàwàt dii khun Anitra* สวัสดี คุณอนิทรา
Hello, Somsri. (informal)	*sàwàt dii Somsri* สวัสดีสมศรี
Hi, Peter.	*sàwàt dii Peter* สวัสดีปีเตอร์
Hello/Good afternoon/ evening.	*sàwàt dii* สวัสดี

How are you?/ How are things?	*sàbaai dii mái/pen yang-ngai bâang* สบายดีไหม/เป็นยังไงบ้าง
Fine, thank you, and you?	*sàbaai dii khàwp khun; láehw khun lâ* สบายดี ขอบคุณ แล้วคุณล่ะ
Very well, and you?	*sàbaai dii; láehw khun lâ* สบายดี แล้วคุณล่ะ
In excellent health/ In great shape.	*sùk-khà-phâap dii yîam/khǎeng raehng dii* สุขภาพดีเยี่ยม/แข็งแรงดี
So-so.	*rûeai rûeai* เรื่อยๆ
Not very well.	*mâi khôi sàbaai* ไม่ค่อยสบาย
(It's) Not bad/ It's OK.	*kôr dii na* ก็ดีนะ
I'm going to leave.	*pai lá ná* ไปละนะ
I have to be going, someone's waiting for me.	*tâwng pai lá ná; mii khon raw yùu* ต้องไปละนะ มีคนรออยู่
See you soon.	*phóp kan reo reo níi ná* พบกันเร็วๆ นี้นะ
See you in a little while.	*dǐao phóp kan ná* เดี๋ยวพบกันนะ
Sweet dreams.	*fǎn dii ná* ฝันดีนะ
Good night.	*raatrii sàwàt* ราตรีสวัสดิ์
All the best.	*chôhk dii* โชคดี
Have fun.	*sànùk ná* สนุกนะ
Good luck.	*chôhk dii* โชคดี
Have a nice vacation.	*thîao hâi sànùk ná* เที่ยวให้สนุกนะ
Bon voyage/ Have a good trip.	*doehn thaang doey plàwt phai ná* เดินทางโดยปลอดภัยนะ
Thank you, the same to you.	*khàwp khun; khun dûai* ขอบคุณ คุณด้วย
Say hello to/Give my regards to… (formal)	*sòng khwaam khít thǔeng pai yang…* ส่งความคิดถึงไปยัง…
Say hello to… (informal)	*fàak sàwàt dii…* ฝากสวัสดี…

1.2 Asking a question

Key Vocabulary

ใคร *khrai* Who?
ที่ไหน *thîi năi* Where?
เท่าไร *thâorài* How much?
เมื่อไร *mûea rài* When?
ทำไม *tham mai* Why?

อะไร *àrai* What?
ยังไง *yang-ngai* How?
อันไหน *an năi* Which one(s)?
…ได้ไหม *dâi măi* Can/May I?

Who's that?	*nân khrai* นั่นใคร
Who is it?	*khrai ná* ใครน่ะ
Who's there?	*khrai yùu thîi nân* ใครอยู่ที่นั่น
(Pardon me) What did you say?	*àrai ná* อะไรนะ
What is there to see?	*mii àrai hâi duu* มีอะไรให้ดู
What category of hotel is it?	*rohng raehm kìi dao* โรงแรมกี่ดาว
Where's the bathroom?	*hâwng náam yùu thîi năi* ห้องน้ำอยู่ที่ไหน
Where are you going?	*khun jà pai năi* คุณจะไปไหน
Where are you from?	*khun maa jàak năi* คุณมาจากไหน
How far is that?	*klai khâeh năi* ไกลแค่ไหน
How long does that take?	*naan khâeh năi* นานแค่ไหน
How long is the trip?	*dern thaang naan thâorài* เดินทางนานเท่าไร
How much is this?	*nîi thâorài* นี่เท่าไร
What time is it?	*kìi mohng láehw* กี่โมงแล้ว
Which glass is mine?	*kâeo năi khăwng chăn* แก้วไหนของฉัน
When are you leaving?	*khun jà pai mûearài* คุณจะไปเมื่อไร
Do you know…?	*khun rúujàk…mái khá/khráp* คุณรู้จัก…ไหมคะ/ครับ
Do you know whether…?	*khun rúu mai wâa…* คุณรู้ไหมว่า…
Do you have…?	*khun mii…mái khá/khráp* คุณมี…ไหมคะ/ครับ

Do you have a…for me?	*khun mii...hâi chăn măi* คุณมี…ให้ฉันไหม
Do you have a vegetarian dish please?	*khun mii aahăan jeh măi* คุณมีอาหารเจไหม
I would like…	*chăn yàak...* ฉันอยาก…
I'd like a kilo of apples, please.	*chăn yàak dâi áeppôen nùeng kiloh* ฉันอยากได้แอปเปิลหนึ่งกิโล
Can/May I take this away?	*chăn ao nîi pai dâi măi* ฉันเอานี่ไปได้ไหม
Can I smoke here?	*chăn sùup burìi thîi nîi dâi măi* ฉันสูบบุหรี่ที่นี่ได้ไหม
Could I ask you something?	*khăw thăam arai nòi dâi măi* ขอถามอะไรหน่อยได้ไหม

1.3 Making a request

Could you…?	*chûai...nòi dâi măi* ช่วย…หน่อยได้ไหม
Could you come with me please?	*chuâi maa kàp chăn dâi măi* ช่วยมากับฉันได้ไหม
Could you please help me/give me a hand?	[FEMALE] *chuâi chăn nòi dâi măi* ช่วยฉันหน่อยได้ไหม
	[MALE] *chuâi phŏm nòi dâi măi* ช่วยผมหน่อยได้ไหม
Could you point that out to me/show me please?	*chuâi chíi hâi duu nòi dâi măi* ช่วยชี้ให้ดูหน่อยได้ไหม
Could you reserve/book some tickets for me, please?	*chuâi jawng tŭa hâi nòi dâi máii* ช่วยจองตั๋วให้หน่อยได้มั้ยi
Could you recommend another hotel?	*náe-nam rohng raehm ùehn hâi nòi dâi măi* แนะนำโรงแรมอื่นให้หน่อยได้ไหม

1.4 How to reply

Yes, of course	*dâi, nâeh nawn* ได้ แน่นอน
No, I'm sorry	*mâi dâi; sĭa jai dûai* ไม่ได้ เสียใจด้วย
Yes, what can I do for you?	*jà hâi chăn tham arai hâi khun* จะให้ฉันทำอะไรให้คุณ

Just a moment, please.	*sák khrûu ná* สักครู่นะ
No, I don't have time now.	*mâi dâi, tawn níi chǎn mâi mii wehlaa* ไม่ได้ ตอนนี้ฉันไม่มีเวลา
No, that's impossible.	*mâi nâa pen pai dâi* ไม่น่าเป็นไปได้
I think so too.	[FEMALE] *chǎn khít yàang nán mǔean kan* ฉันคิดอย่างนั้นเหมือนกัน
	[MALE] *phǒm khít yàang nán mǔean kan* ผมคิดอย่างนั้นเหมือนกัน
I agree.	[FEMALE] *chǎn hěn duâi* ฉันเห็นด้วย
	[MALE] *phǒm hěn duâi* ผมเห็นด้วย
I hope so too.	*chǎn wǎng wâa yàang nán dûai* ฉันหวังว่าอย่างนั้นด้วย
No, not at all.	*mâi loei/mâi châi loei* ไม่เลย/ไม่ใช่เลย
Absolutely not.	*mâi châi nâeh nawn* ไม่ใช่แน่นอน
No, no one.	*mâi mii khrai* ไม่มีใคร
No, nothing.	*mâi mii àrai* ไม่มีอะไร
That's right.	*thùuk láehw* ถูกแล้ว
Something's wrong.	*mii àrai phìt pàkàtì* มีอะไรผิดปกติ
I agree (don't agree).	*chǎn hěn dûai (mâi hěn dûai)* ฉันเห็นด้วย (ไม่เห็นด้วย)
Okay.	*Oh-kheh/tòk long* โอเค/ตกลง
It's fine/All right.	*mâi pen rai* ไม่เป็นไร
Perhaps/maybe.	*baang thii/àat jà* บางที/อาจจะ
I don't know.	*chǎn mâi rúu* ฉันไม่รู้

1.5 Thank you

Thank you.	*khàwp khun* ขอบคุณ
That's all right.	*mâi pen rai* ไม่เป็นไร
Thank you very much/ Many thanks.	*khàwp khun mâak* ขอบคุณมาก

Very kind of you.	*khun jai dii mâak* คุณใจดีมาก
My pleasure.	*dûai khwaam yin dii* ด้วยความยินดี
I enjoyed it very much.	*chăn sànùk mâak* ฉันสนุกมาก
Thank you for…	*khàwp khun sămràp...* ขอบคุณสำหรับ…
That was so kind of you.	*khun mii nám jai mâak mâak* คุณมีน้ำใจมากๆ

1.6 I'm sorry

Excuse me/pardon me/ sorry.	*khăw thôht* ขอโทษ
Sorry, I didn't know that…	*khăw thôht, chăn mâi rúu…* ขอโทษ ฉันไม่รู้…
I really do apologize.	*chăn khăw thôht jing jing* ฉันขอโทษจริงๆ
I'm sorry.	*sĭa jai dûai* เสียใจด้วย
I didn't mean it.	[FEMALE] *chăn mâi dâi tâng jai* ฉันไม่ได้ตั้งใจ
	[MALE] *phŏm mâi dâi tâng jai* ผมไม่ได้ตั้งใจ
It was an accident.	*man pen ùbatìhèht* มันเป็นอุบัติเหตุ
That's all right/Never mind/Don't worry about it.	*mâi pen rai* ไม่เป็นไร
Forget it.	*châang man thòe* ช่างมันเถอะ
It could happen to anyone.	*man àat kòeht kàp khrai kôr dâi* มันอาจเกิดขึ้นกับใครก็ได้

1.7 What do you think?

| Which do you prefer/ like best? | *khun yàak dâi/châwp an năi mâak thîi sùt* คุณ อยากได้/ชอบ อันไหนมากที่สุด |
| What do you think? | *khun khít wâa yang-ngai* คุณคิดว่ายังไง |

Don't you like dancing?	*khun mâi châwp tên ram rûeh* คุณไม่ชอบเต้นรำหรือ
I don't mind.	*chǎn mâi rangkìat* ฉันไม่รังเกียจ
Well done!/Great!/ Marvelous!	*kèng mâak* เก่งมาก!
Not bad!	*mâi leo* ไม่เลว!
We're in luck.	*pûak rao chôhk dii jing jing* พวกเราโชคดีจริงๆ
You're lucky	*khun chôhk dii* คุณโชคดี!
I'm (not) very happy with…	*chǎn (mâi) khôi phaw jai rûeang…* ฉัน (ไม่) ค่อยพอใจเรื่อง…
I'm glad that…	*chǎn dii jai thîi* ฉันดีใจที่…
I'm having a great time.	*chǎn kamlang sànùk mâak* ฉันกำลังสนุกมาก
I can't wait till tomorrow/ I'm looking forward to tomorrow.	*chǎn raw thǔeng phrûng níi mâi dâi/ chǎn jà raw wan phrûng níi* ฉันรอถึงพรุ่งนี้ไม่ได้/ฉันจะรอวันพรุ่งนี้
I hope it works out.	*chǎn wǎng wâa jà dâi phǒn* ฉันหวังว่าจะได้ผล
How awful/terrible!	*yâeh mâak* แย่มาก!
It's frightening/scary/ horrible!	*nâa klua* น่ากลัว
What a pity/shame!	*nâa sǒngsǎan* น่าสงสาร!
How disgusting!	*nâa rangkìat* น่ารังเกียจ!
What nonsense/How silly!	*mâi khâo rûeang* ไม่เข้าเรื่อง!
I don't like it/them.	*chǎn mâi châwp* ฉันไม่ชอบ
I'm bored to death.	*chǎn bùea jà tai* ฉันเบื่อจะตาย
I'm fed up.	*chǎn thon mâi wǎi láehw* ฉันทนไม่ไหวแล้ว
This is no good.	*mâi dii loei* ไม่ดีเลย
This is not what I expected.	*nîi mâi châi thîi chǎn khít wái* นี่ไม่ใช่ที่ฉันคิดไว้

2. The Basics

Numbers

ศูนย์ *sǔun* 0	ยี่สิบ *yîi sìp* 20
หนึ่ง *nùeng* 1	ยี่สิบเอ็ด *yîi sìp èt* 21
สอง *sǎwng* 2	ยี่สิบสอง *yîi sìp sǎwng* 22
สาม *sǎam* 3	สามสิบ *sǎam sìp* 30
สี่ *sìi* 4	สามสิบเอ็ด *sǎam sìp èt* 31
ห้า *hâa* 5	สามสิบสอง *sǎam sìp sǎwng* 32
หก *hòk* 6	สี่สิบ *sìi sìp* 40
เจ็ด *jèt* 7	ห้าสิบ *hâa sìp* 50
แปด *pàeht* 8	หกสิบ *hòk sìp* 60
เก้า *kâo* 9	เจ็ดสิบ *jèt sìp* 70
สิบ *sìp* 10	แปดสิบ *pàeht sìp* 80
สิบเอ็ด *sìp èt* 11	เก้าสิบ *kâo sìp* 90
สิบสอง *sìp sǎwng* 12	หนึ่งร้อย *nùeng rói* 100
สิบสาม *sìp sǎam* 13	(หนึ่ง) ร้อยหนึ่ง *(nùeng) rói nùeng, rói èt* 101
สิบสี่ *sìp sìi* 14	
สิบห้า *sìp hâa* 15	(หนึ่ง) ร้อยสิบ *(nùeng) rói sìp* 110
สิบหก *sìp hòk* 16	
สิบเจ็ด *sìp jèt* 17	(หนึ่ง) ร้อยยี่สิบ *(nùeng) rói yîi sìp* 120
สิบแปด *sìp pàeht* 18	สองร้อย *sǎwng rói* 200
สิบเก้า *sìp kâo* 19	สามร้อย *sǎam rói* 300

สี่ร้อย *sìi rói* 400

ห้าร้อย *hâa rói* 500

หกร้อย *hòk rói* 600

เจ็ดร้อย *jèt rói* 700

แปดร้อย *pàeht rói* 800

เก้าร้อย *kâo rói* 900

หนึ่งพัน *nùeng phan* 1,000

หนึ่งพันหนึ่งร้อย *nùeng phan nùeng rói* 1,100

สองพัน *sǎwng phan* 2,000

หนึ่งหมื่น *nùeng mùehn* 10,000

หนึ่งแสน *nùeng sǎehn* 100,000

หนึ่งล้าน *nùeng láan* 1,000,000

ที่หนึ่ง *thîi nùeng* 1st

ที่สอง *thîi sǎwng* 2nd

ที่สาม *thîi sǎam* 3rd

ที่สี่ *thîi sìi* 4th

ที่ห้า *thîi hâa* 5th

ที่หก *thîi hòk* 6th

ที่เจ็ด *thîi jèt* 7th

ที่แปด *thîi pàeht* 8th

ที่เก้า *thîi kâo* 9th

ที่สิบ *thîi sìp* 10th

ที่สิบเอ็ด *thîi sìp èt* 11th

ที่สิบสอง *thîi sìp sǎwng* 12th

ที่สิบสาม *thîi sìp sǎam* 13th

ที่สิบสี่ *thîi sìp sìi* 14th

ที่สิบห้า *thîi sìp hâa* 15th

ที่สิบหก *thîi sìp hòk* 16th

ที่สิบเจ็ด *thîi sìp jèt* 17th

ที่สิบแปด *thîi sìp pàeht* 18th

ที่สิบเก้า *thîi sìp kâo* 19th

ที่ยี่สิบ *thîi yîi sìp* 20th

ที่ยี่สิบเอ็ด *thîi yîi sìp èt* 21st

ที่ยี่สิบสอง *thîi yîi sìp sǎwng* 22nd

ที่สามสิบ *thîi sǎam sìp* 30th

ที่หนึ่งร้อย *thîi nùeng rói* 100th

ที่หนึ่งพัน *thîi nùeng phan* 1,000th

หนึ่งที, ทีหนึ่ง *nùeng thii, thii nùeng* once

สองที *sǎwng thii* twice

สองเท่า *sǎwng thâo* double

สามเท่า *sǎam thâo* triple

ครึ่ง *khrûeng* half

หนึ่งในสี่ *nùeng nai sìi* a quarter

หนึ่งในสาม *nùeng nai sǎam* a third

บาง/สองสาม *baang/sǎwng sǎam* some/a few

สองบวกสี่ เท่ากับ หก *sǎwng bùak sìi thâo kàp hòk* $2 + 4 = 6$

สี่ลบสอง เท่ากับ สอง *sìi lóp sǎwng thâo kàp sǎwng* $4 - 2 = 2$

สองคูณสี่ เท่ากับ แปด *sǎwng khuun sìi thâo kàp pàeht* $2 \times 4 = 8$

สี่หารด้วยสอง เท่ากับ สอง *sìi hǎan dûai sǎwng thâo kàp sǎwng* $4 \div 2 = 2$

เลขคู่ *lêhk khûu* even

เลขคี่ *lêhk khîi* odd

ทั้งหมด *tháng mòt* total

หกคูณเก้า *hòk khuun kâo* 6×9

2.2 Telling Time

What time is it?	*kìi mohng láehw* กี่โมงแล้ว
It's nine o'clock.	*kâo mohng cháo* เก้าโมงเช้า
It's five past ten.	*sìp mohng hâa naathii** สิบโมงห้านาที
It's a quarter past eleven.	*sìp èt mohng sìp hâa (naathii)* สิบเอ็ดโมงสิบห้า (นาที)
It's twenty past twelve.	*thîang yîi sìp (naathii)* เที่ยงยี่สิบ (นาที)
It's half past one.	*bàai mohng khrûeng* บ่ายโมงครึ่ง
It's twenty-five to three.	*bàai sǎwng mohng sǎam sìp hâa (naathii)* บ่ายสองโมงสามสิบห้า (นาที)
It's a quarter to four.	*bàai sǎam mohng sìi sìp hâa (naathii)* บ่ายสามโมงสี่สิบห้า (นาที)
It's ten to five.	*sìi mohng yen hâa sìp (naathii)* สี่โมงเย็นห้าสิบ (นาที)
It's midday (twelve noon).	*thîang wan* เที่ยงวัน
It's midnight.	*thîang khuehn* เที่ยงคืน
half an hour	*khrûeng chûamohng* ครึ่งชั่วโมง
What time?	*kìi mohng* กี่โมง
What time can I come by?	*chǎn maa dâi tawn kìi mohng* ฉันมาได้ตอนกี่โมง
At…	*tawn* ตอน…
After…	*lǎng* หลัง…
Before…	*kàwn* ก่อน…
Between…and…(o'clock)	*rá-wàang…kàp…(naalíkaa/mohng)* ระหว่าง…กับ…(นาฬิกา/โมง)
From…to…	*jàak…thǔeng…* จาก…ถึง…
In…minutes	*ìik…naathii* อีก…นาที
In an hour	*ìik nùeng chûamohng* อีกหนึ่งชั่วโมง

* Note: There is no special word for "quarter to" or "quarter past" the hour. Minutes past the hour are expressed by using the word *naathii* after giving the hour and sometimes it can be omitted in casual conversation.

In…hours	*iik…chûamohng* อีก...ชั่วโมง
a quarter of an hour	*sìp hâa naathii* สิบห้านาที
three quarters of an hour	*sìi sìp hâa naathii* สี่สิบห้านาที
too early/late	*reo pai/cháa pai* เร็วไป/ช้าไป
on time	*trong wehlaa* ตรงเวลา

Days and weeks

What day is it today?	*wan níi wan àrai* วันนี้วันอะไร
Today's Monday.	*wan níi wan jan* วันนี้วันจันทร์
Today's Tuesday.	*wan níi wan ang khaan* วันนี้วันอังคาร
Today's Wednesday.	*wan níi wan phút* วันนี้วันพุธ
Today's Thursday.	*wan níi wan phá rúe hàt* วันนี้วันพฤหัส
Today's Friday.	*wan níi wan sùk* วันนี้วันศุกร์
Today's Saturday.	*wan níi wan săo* วันนี้วันเสาร์
Today's Sunday.	*wan níi wan aa thít* วันนี้วันอาทิตย์
What's the date today?	*wan níi wan thîi thâorài* วันนี้วันที่เท่าไร
Today's the 24th.	*wan níi wan thîi yîi sìp sìi* วันนี้วันที่ยี่สิบสี่
Monday 3 November.	*wan jan thîi săam duean phrúetsacìkaayon* วันจันทร์ที่สามเดือนพฤศจิกายน
in the morning	*tawn cháo* ตอนเช้า
in the afternoon	*tawn bàai* ตอนบ่าย
in the evening	*tawn yen* ตอนเย็น
at night	*tawn klaang khuehn* ตอนกลางคืน
this morning	*cháo níi* เช้านี้
this afternoon	*bàai níi* บ่ายนี้
this evening	*yen níi* เย็นนี้

tonight	*khuehn níi* คืนนี้
last night	*mûea khuehn níi* เมื่อคืนนี้
this week	*sàpdaa níi* สัปดาห์นี้
next...	*...nâa* ...หน้า
in...days	*ìik...wan* อีก....วัน
in...weeks	*ìik...aa thít* อีก...อาทิตย์
...weeks ago	*...láai sàpdaa maa láehw* ...หลาย สัปดาห์มาแล้ว
day off	*wan yùt* วันหยุด

2.4 Months and years

next month	*duean nâa* เดือนหน้า
in...months	*ìik...duean* อีก .... เดือน
in...years	*ìik...pii* อีก...ปี
in January	*nai duean mákàraakhom* ในเดือนมกราคม
since February	*tâng tàeh duean kumphaaphan* ตั้งแต่เดือนกุมภาพันธ์
in spring	*nai ruéduu bai mái phlì* ในฤดูใบไม้ผลิ
in summer	*nai rúeduu ráwn* ในฤดูร้อน
in autumn	*nai rúeduu bai mái rûang* ในฤดูใบไม้ร่วง
in winter	*nai rúeduu nǎo* ในฤดูหนาว
2018	*pee khaw sǎw sǎwng phan sìp pàeht* ปี ค.ศ. สองพันสิบแปด
2019	*pee khaw sǎw sǎwng phan sìp kâo* ปี ค.ศ. สองพันสิบเก้า
the twentieth century	*sàttawát thîi yîi sìp* ศตวรรษที่ยี่สิบ
the twenty-first century	*sàttawát thîi yîi sìp èt* ศตวรรษที่ยี่สิบเอ็ด
last year	*pii thîi láehw* ปีที่แล้ว

2.5 What does that sign say?

น้ำร้อน/
น้ำเย็น
náam ráwn/
náam yen
hot water/
  cold water

ไฟฟ้าแรงสูง
fai-fáa raeng
  sǔung
high voltage

ให้เช่า
hâi châo
for rent/hire

โรงแรม
rong-raem
hotel

หยุด *yùt*
stop

ไม่ใช้แล้ว
mâi chái
  láehw
not in use

ผลัก *phlàk*
push

ดึง *dueng*
pull

ที่ขายตั๋ว
thîi khǎai tǔa
ticket office

ตำรวจ
tamrùat
police

ห้องน้ำ
hâwng-náam
bathroom(s)

ขาย *khǎai* for sale

เต็ม *tem* full

ไปรษณีย์ *praisànii*
post office

ไม่ว่าง *mâi wâang*
engaged/busy

ระวังสุนัขดุ
ráwang sùnǎk dù
beware of the dog

เบรคฉุกเฉิน
brèk chùk-chǒen
emergency brake

ที่แลกเปลี่ยน
thîi lâek-plìan
(a place to) exchange

คนเก็บเงิน
khon kèp ngoehn
cashier

ห้ามล่าสัตว์
hâam lâa sàt
No hunting

ห้ามตกปลา
hâam tòk plaa
No fishing

ขายหมดแล้ว
khǎai mòt láew
sold out

ทางเข้า (ฟรี)
thaang khâo (frii)
entrance (free)

ประชาสัมพันธ์
prà chaa-sǎmphan
information

ตารางเวลา *ta-raang wehlaa*
timetable

เสีย *sǐa*
out of order/broken

โรงพยาบาล
rohng phá-yaa-baan
hospital

สำนักงานบริการข้อมูล
นักท่องเที่ยว
sam nâk ngan bawríkaan khâw
  moon thâwng thîao
tourist information bureau

ปฐมพยาบาล
pàthǒm phá-yaa-baan
first aid

อุบัติเหตุและเหตุฉุกเฉิน
(โรงพยาบาล)
ùbatihèt láe hèt chùk-chǒen
  (rohng phá-yaa-baan)
accident and emergency
  (hospital)

บันไดหนีไฟ *ban-dai nǐi fai*
fire escape

บันไดเลื่อน *ban-dai lûen*
escalator

ทางออก(ฉุกเฉิน)
thaang awk (chùk-chǒen)
(emergency) exit

สียังไม่แห้ง
sǐi yang mâi hâeng
wet paint

ห้ามสูบบุหรี่ *hâam sùup bùrìi*
No smoking

คนเดินเท้า *khon durn tháo*
pedestrian

ทางเข้า
thaang khâo
entrance

ห้ามทิ้งขยะ
hâam thíng khàyà
No littering

กรุณาอย่าจับ
kàrúnaa yàa jàp
Please do not touch

อันตรายจากไฟ
antàraai jàak fai
fire hazard

(ไม่ใช่) น้ำดื่ม
(mâi châi) náam dùehm
(not) drinking water

จอง **jawng**
to reserve/to book

ห้องรับรอง
hâwng ráp rawng
waiting room

ตำรวจจราจร
tàmrûat ja ra jorn
traffic police

กรุณาอย่ารบกวน
kàrúnaa yàa róp-kuan
Please do not disturb

อันตรายต่อชีวิต
antàraai tòr chiiwít
danger to life

หน่วยดับเพลิง
nùai dàp phloeng
fire department

ตำรวจ (เทศบาล)
tàmrûat (thétsabaan)
(municipal) police

ปิด (วันหยุด/ปรับปรุง)
pìt (wan yùt/pràp prung)
closed (for holiday/
refurbishment)

2.6 Holidays

The most important public holidays in Thailand are the following: (those marked with a † change from year to year; also note if a public holiday falls on either a Saturday or Sunday the following Monday becomes a holiday):

January 1, New Year's Day **wan pii mài** วันปีใหม่

†March, Maka Puja **wan maakhá buuchaa** วันมาฆบูชา The day 1,250 of the Lord Buddha's disciples gathered to listen to his first sermon

April 6, Chakri Day **wan jàk-krii** วันจักรี The founding of the present dynasty in Bangkok in 1782

April 13-15, Songkran festival; Chiang Mai New Year festival **wan sǒngkraan** วันสงกรานต์ Days that are the hottest and driest of the year, celebrated with water throwing

May 7, Royal Ploughing Ceremony Day **wan phûeht mongkhon** วันพืชมงคล An auspicious Hindu-Brahman ceremony held at Sanam Luang (Pramane Ground) to marks the beginning of the rice-planting season

†June, Visakha Puja *wan wísǎakhà buuchaa* วันวิสาขบูชา A very important Buddhist holiday marking the birth, enlightenment and death of Buddha; candle-lit processions occur at Thai temples

July 28, the King's Birthday *Wan Chaloem Phra Chonmaphansa Phrabat Somdet Phra Vajira Klao Chao Yu Hua* วันเฉลิม พระชนมพรรษาพระบาทสมเด็จพระวชิรเกล้าเจ้าอยู่หัว Much of the celebrations are centered around the Grand Palace and along Ratchadamnoen Avenue in Bangkok

†July, Asalaha Puja *wan aasǎanhà buuchaa* วันอาสาฬหบูชา The beginning of the Buddhist lent. Every Thai Buddhist male spends at least three months as a monk. Lent is often the period chosen, as its three months occur over the rainy season when monks are to remain in their temples

†August, Buddhist Lent Day *wan khâo phansǎa* วันเข้าพรรษา When monks enter a "rains retreat", staying in their temples to strictly attend to religious duties

August 12, Mother's Day *wan mâeh* วันแม่

October 23, Chulalongkorn Day *wan piyá mahǎarâat* วันปิยมหาราช Celebrates the reign of King Chulalongkorn (r.1873–1910) who passed away on this day in 1910

†October, Ork Phansa *wan àwk phansǎa* วันออกพรรษา Marks the end of the rains retreat and the start of the *kathin* period when people present new saffron robes to the monks

November 26, Loi Krathong *wan loi krathong* วันลอยกระทง A beautiful Thai water festival offering the opportunity to see your cares and woes "float away" in a *krathong* made of leaves, a candle, some coins and flower petals

December 5, National Father's Day: Commemorates the birthday of King Bhumibol Adulyadej *wan chalǒehm phráchonmá phansǎa Phra Bat Somdet Phra Boromchanakathibet Maha Bhumibol Adulyadej Maharaj Borommanatbophit* วันคล้ายวันเฉลิม พระชนมพรรษาพระบาทสมเด็จพระบรมชนกาธิเบศร มหาภูมิพล อดุลยเดชมหาราช บรมนาถบพิตร

December 10, Constitution Day *wan rátthàthammánuun*
วันรัฐธรรมนูญ

December 25, Christmas Day *wan khrís(t)mâat* วันคริสต์มาส
Not a Thai festival, but many shops in the larger cities recognize
the celebration of Christmas for the traveler

December 31, New Year's Eve *wan sîn pii* วันสิ้นปี Celebrated
as the end of the year for most Thai matters (the old Thai New
Year is celebrated at Songkran)

3. Small Talk

3.1 Introductions

May I introduce myself?	[FEMALE] *chǎn khǎw náe-nam tua ehng* ฉันขอแนะนำตัวเอง
My name's…	[FEMALE] *chǎn chûeh…* ฉันชื่อ…
What's your name?	*khun chûeh àrai* คุณชื่ออะไร
May I introduce…?	[FEMALE] *chǎn khǎw náe-nam…* ฉันขอแนะนำ…
This is my wife.	[MALE] *nîi phanyaa khǎwng phǒm* นี่ภรรยาของผม
This is my husband.	[FEMALE] *nîi sǎamii khǎwng chǎn* นี่สามีของฉัน
This is my daughter.	[FEMALE] *nîi lûuk sǎow khǎwng chǎn* นี่ลูกสาวของฉัน
	[MALE] *nîi lûuk sǎow khǎwng phǒm* นี่ลูกสาวของผม
This is my son.	[FEMALE] *nîi lûuk chaai khǎwng chǎn* นี่ลูกชายของฉัน
	[MALE] *nîi lûuk chaai khǎwng phǒm* นี่ลูกชายของผม

This is my mother.	[FEMALE] *nîi mâeh khǎwng chǎn* นี่แม่ของฉัน [MALE] *nîi mâeh khǎwng phǒm* นี่แม่ของผม
This is my father.	[FEMALE] *nîi phâw khǎwng chǎn* นี่พ่อของฉัน [MALE] *nîi phâw khǎwng phǒm* นี่พ่อของผม
This is my fiancé.	[FEMALE] *nîi khûu mân chǎn* นี่คู่หมั้นฉัน
This is my friend.	*nîi phûean chǎn* นี่เพื่อนฉัน
How do you do?	*yin dii thîi dâi rúujàk* ยินดีที่ได้รู้จัก
Hi, pleased to meet you.	*sàwàt dii, yin dii thîi dâi phóp khun* สวัสดี ยินดีที่ได้พบคุณ
Where are you from?	*khun maa jàak prà-thêht àrai* คุณมาจากประเทศอะไร
I'm Amcrican.	[FEMALE] *chǎn pen khon á-meh-rí-kan* ฉันเป็นคนอเมริกัน [MALE] *phǒm pen khon á-meh-rí-kan* ผมเป็นคนอเมริกัน
I'm Australian.	[FEMALE] *chǎn pen khon áwt-sà-treh-lia* ฉันเป็นคนออสเตรเลีย [MALE] *phǒm pen khon áwt-sà-treh-lia* ผมเป็นคนออสเตรเลีย
I'm British.	[FEMALE] *chǎn pen khon ang-krìt* ฉันเป็นคนอังกฤษ [MALE] *phǒm pen khon ang-krìt* ผมเป็นคนอังกฤษ
I'm Canadian.	[FEMALE] *chǎn pen khon khae-naa-daa* ฉันเป็นคนแคนาดา [MALE] *phǒm pen khon khae-naa-daa* ผมเป็นคนแคนาดา
I'm Singaporean.	[FEMALE] *chǎn pen khon sing-khà-poh* ฉันเป็นคนสิงคโปร์ [MALE] *phǒm pen khon sing-khà-poh* ผมเป็นคนสิงคโปร์
What city do you live in?	*khun yùu mueang nǎi* คุณอยู่เมืองไหน

Have you been here long?	*khun maa thîi nîi naan láehw rǔeh* คุณมาที่นี่นานแล้วหรือ
A few days.	*sǎwng sǎam wan* สองสามวัน
How long are you staying here?	*khun jà yùu thîi nîi naan thâo-rài* คุณจะอยู่ที่นี่นานเท่าไร
We're (probably) leaving tomorrow.	*rao (khong) jà klàp phrûngníi* เราคงจะกลับพรุ่งนี้
We're (probably) leaving in two weeks.	*rao (khong) jà klàp ìik sǎwng aathít* เราคงจะกลับอีกสองอาทิตย์
Where are you staying?	*khun phák thîi nǎi* คุณพักที่ไหน
I'm staying in a hotel.	[FEMALE] *chǎn phák thîi rohng raehm* ฉันพักที่โรงแรม [MALE] *phǒm phák thîi rohng raehm* ผมพักที่โรงแรม
I'm staying in an apartment.	[FEMALE] *chǎn phák thîi àpháatmén* ฉันพักที่อพาร์ทเมนต์ [MALE] *phǒm phák thîi àpháatmén* ผมพักที่อพาร์ทเมนต์
I'm staying with friends.	[FEMALE] *chǎn phák kàp phûean* ฉันพักกับเพื่อน [MALE] *phǒm phák kàp phûean* ผมพักกับเพื่อน
I'm staying with relatives.	[FEMALE] *chǎn phák kàp yâat* ฉันพักกับญาติ [MALE] *phǒm phák kàp yâat* ผมพักกับญาติ
Are you here on your own?	*khun maa thîi nîi khon diao rǔeh* คุณมาที่นี่คนเดียวหรือ
I'm on my own.	*chǎn maa khon diao* ฉันมาคนเดียว
I'm with my partner.	[FEMALE] *chǎn maa kàp faehn* ฉันมากับแฟน [MALE] *phǒm maa kàp faehn* ผมมากับแฟน
I'm with my wife.	[MALE] *phǒm maa kàp phanyaa* ผมมากับภรรยา

I'm with my husband.	[FEMALE] *chăn maa kàp săamii* ฉันมากับสามี
I'm with my family.	[FEMALE] *chăn maa kàp khrâwp khrua* ฉันมากับครอบครัว [MALE] *phŏm maa kàp khrâwp khrua* ผมมากับครอบครัว
I'm with relatives.	[FEMALE] *chăn maa kàp yâat* ฉันมากับญาติ
I'm with a friend.	[FEMALE] *chăn maa kàp phûean* ฉันมากับเพื่อน
Are you married?	*khun tàeng-ngaan láehw rŭe yang* คุณแต่งงานแล้วหรือยัง
Are you engaged?	*khun mân láehw rúe yang* คุณหมั้นแล้วหรือยัง
Do you have a boyfriend/girlfriend?	*khun mii faehn rúe yang* คุณมีแฟนหรือยัง
I'm married.	*chăn tàeng-ngaan láehw* ฉันแต่งงานแล้ว
I'm single.	*chăn sòht* ฉันโสด
I'm not married.	*chăn yang mâi tàeng-ngaan* ฉันยังไม่แต่งงาน
I'm separated.	*chăn yâehk kan* ฉันแยกกัน
I'm divorced.	*chăn yàa láehw* ฉันหย่าแล้ว
I'm a widow.	[FEMALE] *chăn pen mâeh mâai* ฉันเป็นแม่ม่าย
I'm a widower.	[MALE] *phŏm pen phâw mâai* ผมเป็นพ่อม่าย
I live alone/with someone.	*chăn yùu khon diao/kàp khon ùehn* ฉันอยู่ คนเดียว/กับคนอื่น
Do you have any children?	*khun mii lûuk mái?* คุณมีลูกไหม
Do you have any grandchildren?	*khun mii lăan mái?* คุณมีหลานไหม
How old are you?	*khun aayú thâorài* คุณอายุเท่าไร
How old is she/he?	*khăo aayú thâo-rài* เขาอายุเท่าไร
I'm…(years old).	*chăn aayú…pii* ฉันอายุ…ปี

She's/he's…(years old).	*kháo aayú…pii* เขาอายุ...ปี
What do you do for a living?	*khun tham ngaan arai* คุณทำงานอะไร
I work in an office.	*chăn tham ngaan nai office* ฉันทำงานในสำนักงาน
I'm a student.	*chăn pen nákrian* ฉันเป็นนักเรียน
I'm unemployed.	*chăn wâang ngaan* ฉันว่างงาน
I'm retired.	*chăn kàsĭan láehw* ฉันเกษียณแล้ว
I'm a housewife.	*chăn pen mâeh bâan* ฉันเป็นแม่บ้าน
Do you like your job?	*khun châwp ngaan khun mái* คุณชอบงานคุณไหม
Mostly I do, but I prefer vacations.	*suàn yài chăn châwp, tàe chăn châwp pai thîao mâak kwàa* ส่วนใหญ่ฉันชอบแต่ฉันชอบไปเที่ยวมากกว่า

3.2 Pardon me, do you speak English?

I don't speak any...	[FEMALE] *chăn mâi phûut..* ฉันไม่พูด........
	[MALE] *phŏm mâi phûut...* ผมไม่พูด.......
I speak a little...	[FEMALE] *chăn phûut...nít nòi* ฉันพูด.....นิดหน่อย
	[MALE] *phŏm phûut...nít nòi* ผมพูด.....นิดหน่อย
Do you speak English?	*khun phûut phaasăa angkrìt dâi măi* คุณพูดภาษาอังกฤษได้ไหม
Is there anyone who speaks…?	*mii khrai phûut phaasăa…bâang măi* มีใครพูดภาษา...บ้างไหม
I beg your pardon/What?	*àrai ná* อะไรนะ
I (don't) understand.	*chăn (mâi) khâojai* ฉัน (ไม่) เข้าใจ
Do you understand me?	*khun khâojai chăn măi* คุณเข้าใจฉันไหม
Could you repeat that, please?	*chûai phûut ìik thii dâi măi* ช่วยพูดอีกทีได้ไหม

Could you speak more slowly, please?	*chûai phûut cháa cháa dâi măi* ช่วยพูดช้าๆ ได้ไหม
What does that mean?	*nân măi khwaam wâa àrai* นั่นหมายความว่าอะไร
What does that word mean?	*kham nán măi khwaam wâa àrai* คำนั้นหมายความว่าอะไร
Could you write that down for me, please?	*chûai khĭan hâi chăn dâi măi* ช่วยเขียนให้ฉันได้ไหม
Could you spell that for me, please?	*chûai sakòt hâi chăn dâi măi* ช่วยสะกดให้ฉันได้ไหม
Could you point that out in this phrase book, please?	*chûai chíi nai nangsŭeh níi hâi chăn dâi măi* ช่วยชี้ในหนังสือนี้ให้ฉันได้ไหม
Just a minute, I'll look it up.	*dĭao, chăn jà hăa hâi* เดี๋ยว ฉันจะหาให้
I can't find the word.	[FEMALE] *chăn hăa kham mâi joeh* ฉันหาคำไม่เจอ [MALE] *phŏm hăa kham mâi joeh* ผมหาคำไม่เจอ
I can't find the sentence.	[FEMALE] *chăn hăa prayòhk mâi joeh* ฉันหาประโยคไม่เจอ [MALE] *phŏm hăa prayòhk mâi joeh* ผมหาประโยคไม่เจอ
How do you say that in…?	*khun phûut yang-ngai nai phaasăa…* คุณพูดยังไงในภาษา…
How do you pronounce that?	*khun àwk síang yang-ngai* คุณออกเสียงยังไง

3.3 Starting/ending a conversation

Could I ask you something?	*khăw thăam àrai nòi dâi măi* ขอถามอะไรหน่อยได้ไหม
Could you help me please?	*chuâi chăn nòi dâi măi* ช่วยฉันหน่อยได้ไหม
Yes, what's the problem?	*dâi, mii panhăa àrai* ได้ มีปัญหาอะไร
What can I do for you?	*jà hâi chûai àrai* จะให้ช่วยอะไร

Sorry, I don't have time now.	*sǐa jai, tawn níi chǎn mâi mii wehlaa* เสียใจ ตอนนี้ฉันไม่มีเวลา
May I join you?	*chǎn pai dûai dâi mǎi* ฉันไปด้วยได้ไหม
Could you take a picture of me?	*chûai thài rûup hâi chǎn nòi dâi mǎi* ช่วยถ่ายรูปให้ฉันหน่อยได้ไหม
Could you take a picture of us?	*chûai thài rûup hâi rao nòi dâi mǎi* ช่วยถ่ายรูปให้เราหน่อยได้ไหม
I want to be alone.	[FEMALE] *chǎn yàak yùu khon diao* ฉันอยากอยู่คนเดียว [MALE] *phǒm yàak yùu khon diao* ผมอยากอยู่คนเดียว
Leave me alone.	[FEMALE] *khǎw chǎn yùu khon diao* ขอฉันอยู่คนเดียว [MALE] *khǎw phǒm yùu khon diao* ขอผมอยู่คนเดียว

 3.4   Chatting about the weather

Key Vocabulary

อากาศดี *aakàat dii* clear	ฝนตกปรอยๆ *fǒn-tòk proi proi* light rain	ลูกเห็บ *lûuk-hèp* hail
เย็นสบาย *yen sabai* (comfortably) cool	ฝนตกหนัก *fǒn-tòk nàk* a downpour/heavy rain	อบอ้าว *òb-âo* muggy
ลมแรง *lom raehng* strong winds	น้ำค้างแข็ง *náam-kháang khǎeng* frost/frosty	มรสุม *morasǔm* monsoon
พายุเฮอริเคน *phaa hurikhen* hurricane	ฝนตกเป็นบางแห่ง *fǒn-tòk pen baang hàeng* scattered showers	ฝนตกหนัก *fǒn-tòk nàk* heavy rain
ลมกรรโชก *lom kan-chôok* gusts of wind	(ลม) ปานกลาง/แรง/แรงมาก *(lom) paan klaang/raeng/raeng mâak* moderate/strong/very strong wind(s)	ฝนตก *fǒn-tòk* rain

วันแดดออก
wan dàet àwk
(a) sunny day

คลื่นความร้อน
khlûen khwaam-ráwn
heatwave

หมอก/หมอกจัด
màwk/màwk-jàt
fog/foggy

แดดออก
dàet àwk
sunny

มีน้ำค้างแข็งตอนกลางคืน
**mii náam-kháang-khǎeng
  tawn klaang khuehn**
overnight frost

ร้อนอบอ้าว/เปียกชื้น
ráwn òb-âo/pìak chúen
sweltering/muggy

ฟ้าใส/เมฆครึ้ม/ฝนจะตก
fáa sǎi/mêhk khrúem/fǒn jà tòk
clear skies/cloudy or overcast/
  it will rain

พายุ
phaayú
storm

ลม
lom
wind

อึดอัด
ùet-àt
stifling

Is the weather going to be good?	**aakàat jà dii khûen mái?** อากาศจะดีขึ้นไหม
Is the weather going to be bad?	**aakàat jà yâeh long mái?** อากาศจะแย่ลงไหม
Is it going to get colder?	**aakàat jà yen long mái?** อากาศจะเย็นลงไหม
Is it going to get hotter?	**aakàat jà ráwn khûen mái?** อากาศจะร้อนขึ้นไหม
What temperature is it going to be?	**unhàphuum jà thâorài** อุณหภูมิจะเท่าไร
Is it going to rain?	**fǒn jà tòk mǎi** ฝนจะตกไหม
Is there going to be a storm?	**jà mii phaayú mǎi** จะมีพายุไหม
Is it going to flood?	**náam jà thûam mǎi** น้ำจะท่วมไหม
Is it going to be humid?	**aakàat jà òp âo mǎi** อากาศจะอบอ้าวไหม
Is it going to be foggy?	**màwk jà long mǎi** หมอกจะลงไหม
Is there going to be a thunderstorm?	**jà mii fǒn fáa khánawng mǎi** จะมีฝนฟ้าคะนองไหม
The weather's changing.	**aakàat kamlang plìan** อากาศกำลังเปลี่ยน

It's going to be cold.	*aakàat jà yen* อากาศจะเย็น
What's the weather going to be like today?	*wan níi aakàat jà pen yang-ngai?* วันนี้อากาศจะเป็นยังไง
What's the weather going to be like tomorrow?	*phrung níi aakàat jà pen yang-ngai?* พรุ่งนี้อากาศจะเป็นยังไง
It's so hot today!	*wan níi ráwn jang* วันนี้ร้อนจัง
It's so cold today!	*wan níi nǎow/yen jang* วันนี้หนาว/เย็นจัง
Isn't it a lovely day?	*wan níi aakàat dii mâak* วันนี้อากาศดีมาก
It's so windy!	*lom raehng jang* ลมแรงจัง
What a storm!	*phaayú raehng jang* พายุแรงจัง
It's so foggy!	*màwk long jàt* หมอกลงจัด
Has the weather been like this for long?	*aakàat pen yàang níi naan láehw rǔeh* อากาศเป็นอย่างนี้นานแล้วหรือ
Is it always this hot here?	*thîi nîi ráwn yàang níi tàlàwt mái* ที่นี่ร้อนอย่างนี้ตลอดไหม
Is it always this cold here?	*thîi nîi nǎow yàang níi tàlàwt mái* ที่นี่หนาวอย่างนี้ตลอดไหม
Is it always this dry here?	*thîi nîi aakàat hâehng yàang níi tàlàwt mái* ที่นี่อากาศอย่างนี้ตลอดไหม
Is it always this humid here?	*thîi nîi aakàat òp âo yàang níi tàlàwt mái* ที่นี่อากาศอบอ้าวอย่างนี้ตลอดไหม

3.5 Hobbies

| Do you have any hobbies? | *khun mii ngaan adirèhk mǎi* คุณมีงานอดิเรกไหม |
| I like knitting. | [FEMALE] *chǎn châwp thàk níttìng* ฉันชอบถักนิตติ้ง
[MALE] *phǒm chậwp thàk níttìng* ผมชอบถักนิตติ้ง |

I like reading.	[FEMALE] *chăn châwp àan năngsŭeh* ฉันชอบอ่านหนังสือ [MALE] *phŏm châwp àan năngsŭeh* ผมชอบอ่านหนังสือ
I like photography.	[FEMALE] *chăn châwp thàai rûup* ฉันชอบถ่ายรูป [MALE] *phŏm châwp thàai rûup* ผมชอบถ่ายรูป
I enjoy listening to music.	*chăn châwp fang phlehng* ฉันชอบฟังเพลง
I like listening to Korean pop on my MP3 player.	*chăn châwp fang phleng póp kao-lii nai em-phi săam khăwng chăn* ฉันชอบฟังเพลงป๊อปเกาหลีในอิ๊มพี3 ของฉัน
I play the guitar.	[FEMALE] *chăn lên kiitâa* ฉันเล่นกีตาร์ [MALE] *phŏm lên kiitâa* ผมเล่นกีตาร์
I play the piano.	[FEMALE] *chăn lên pianoh* ฉันเล่นเปียโน [MALE] *phŏm lên pianoh* ผมเล่นเปียโน
I like the cinema.	*chăn châwp duu năng* ฉันชอบดูหนัง
I like traveling.	[FEMALE] *chăn châwp pai thîao* ฉันชอบไปเที่ยว [MALE] *phŏm châwp pai thîao* ผมชอบไปเที่ยว
I like playing sports.	[FEMALE] *chăn châwp lên kiilaa* ฉันชอบเล่นกีฬา [MALE] *phŏm châwp lên kiilaa* ผมชอบเล่นกีฬา
I like fishing.	[FEMALE] *chăn châwp tòk plaa* ฉันชอบตกปลา [MALE] *phŏm châwp tòk plaa* ผมชอบตกปลา

| I like going for a walk. | [FEMALE] *chǎn châwp pai doehn lên*
ฉันชอบไปเดินเล่น
[MALE] *phǒm châwp pai doehn lên*
ผมชอบไปเดินเล่น |

3.6 Invitations

Do you have any plans for today?	*wan níi jà tham àrai mái* วันนี้จะทำอะไรไหม
Do you have any plans for this afternoon?	*bàai níi jà tham àrai mái* บ่ายนี้จะทำอะไรไหม
Do you have any plans for tonight?	*khuehn níi jà tham àrai mái* คืนนี้จะทำอะไรไหม
Would you like to go out with me?	*khun yàak àwk pai thîao kàp chǎn mǎi* คุณอยากออกไปเที่ยวกับฉันไหม
Would you like to have lunch with me?	[FEMALE] *khun yàak pai kin aahǎan thîang kàp chǎn mǎi* คุณอยากไปกินอาหารเที่ยงกับฉันไหม [MALE] *khun yàak pai kin aahǎan thîang kàp phǒm mǎi* คุณอยากไปกินอาหารเที่ยงกับผมไหม
Would you like to have dinner with me?	[FEMALE] *khun yàak pai kin aahǎan yen kàp chǎn mǎi* คุณอยากไปกินอาหารเย็นกับฉันไหม [MALE] *khun yàak pai kin aahǎan yen kàp phǒm mǎi* คุณอยากไปกินอาหารเย็นกับผมไหม
Would you like to go dancing with me?	*khun yàak pai tên ram kàp chǎn mǎi* คุณอยากไปเต้นรำกับฉันไหม
Would you like to come to the beach with me?	*khun yàak pai chai thaleh kàp chǎn mǎi* คุณอยากไปชายทะเลกับฉันไหม
Would you like to come and see some friends with us?	*khun yàak pai hǎa phûean kàp rao mǎi* คุณอยากไปหาเพื่อนกับเราไหม

Would you like to come into town with us?	*khun yàak khâo mueang kàp rao măi* คุณอยากเข้าเมืองกับเราไหม
Shall we dance?	*pai tên kan măi* ไปเต้นกันไหม
Shall we sit at the bar?	*pai nâng thîi baa kan măi* ไปนั่งที่บาร์กันไหม
Shall we get something to drink?	*pai dùehm àrai kan măi* ไปดื่มอะไรกันไหม
Shall we go for a walk?	*pai doehn lên kan măi* ไปเดินเล่นกันไหม
Shall we go for a drive?	*pai khàp rót lên kan măi* ไปขับรถเล่นกันไหม
Yes, all right.	*pai tòklong* ไป ตกลง
Good idea.	*pen khwaam khít thîi dii* เป็นความคิดที่ดี
No, thank you.	*mâi pai khàwp khun* ไม่ไป ขอบคุณ
Maybe later.	*dĭao àat jà pai* เดี๋ยวอาจจะไป
I don't feel like it.	*chăn mâi rúusùek yàak pai* ฉันไม่รู้สึกอยากไป
I don't have time.	*chăn mâi mii wehlaa* ฉันไม่มีเวลา
I already have a date.	*chăn mii nát láehw* ฉันมีนัดแล้ว
I'm not very good at dancing.	[FEMALE] *chăn tên mâi kèng* ฉันเต้นไม่เก่ง [MALE] *phŏm tên mâi kèng* ผมเต้นไม่เก่ง
I'm not very good at volleyball.	[FEMALE] *chăn lên wawnlehbawn mâi kèng* ฉันเล่นวอลเลย์บอลไม่เก่ง [MALE] *phŏm lên wawnlehbawn mâi kèng* ผมเล่นวอลเลย์บอลไม่เก่ง
I'm not very good at swimming.	[FEMALE] *chăn wâai náam mâi kèng* ฉันว่ายน้ำไม่เก่ง [MALE] *phŏm wâai náam mâi kèng* ผมว่ายน้ำไม่เก่ง

3.7 Paying a compliment

You look great! — *khun tàeng tua sǔai jang*
คุณแต่งตัวสวยจัง

I like your car! — *chǎn châwp rót khun* ฉันชอบรถคุณ

You are very nice. — *khun pen khon dii mâak*
คุณเป็นคนดีมาก

You're a good dancer. — *khun tên ram kèng mâak*
คุณเต้นรำเก่งมาก

You're a very good cook. — *khun tham aahǎan kèng mâak*
คุณทำอาหารเก่งมาก

You're a good soccer player. — *khun lên fútbawn kèng mâak*
คุณเล่นฟุตบอลเก่งมาก

3.8 Intimate conversations

I like being with you. — *chǎn châwp yùu kàp khun*
ฉันชอบอยู่กับคุณ

I've missed you so much. — *chǎn khít thǔeng khun mâak*
ฉันคิดถึงคุณมาก

I dreamt about you. — *chǎn fǎn thǔeng khun* ฉันฝันถึงคุณ

I think about you all day. — *chǎn khít thǔeng khun tháng wan*
ฉันคิดถึงคุณทั้งวัน

I've been thinking about you all day. — *chǎn khít thǔeng khun talàwt wan*
ฉันคิดถึงคุณตลอดวัน

You have such a sweet smile. — *khun yím wǎan jang*
คุณยิ้มหวานจัง

You have such beautiful eyes. — *taa khun sǔai mâak*
ตาคุณสวยมาก

I'm very fond of you. — *chǎn châwp khun mâak*
ฉันชอบคุณมาก

I love you. — *chǎn rák khun* ฉันรักคุณ

I love you too. — *chǎn rák khun mǔeahn kan*
ฉันรักคุณเหมือนกัน

I don't feel as strongly about you.	*chăn mâi rúusùek arai mâak kàp khun* ฉันไม่รู้สึกอะไรมากกับคุณ
I already have a girlfriend/ boyfriend.	*chăn mii faehn láehw* ฉันมีแฟนแล้ว
I'm not ready for that.	*chăn yang mâi phráwm nai rûeang nán* ฉันยังไม่พร้อมในเรื่องนั้น
I don't want to rush into it.	*chăn yang mâi yàak rîip ráwn* ฉันยังไม่อยากรีบร้อน
Take your hands off me.	*ao mueh khun àwk pai* เอามือคุณออกไป
Okay, no problem.	*tòklong, mâi mii panhăa* ตกลง ไม่มีปัญหา
Will you spend the night with me?	*khun jà kháang kàp chăn mái khuehn níi* คุณจะค้างกับฉันไหมคืนนี้
I'd like to go to bed with you.	*chăn yàak jà nawn kàp khun* ฉันอยากจะนอนกับคุณ
Only if we use a condom.	*thâa rao chái thŭng yaang, thâo nán* ถ้าเราใช้ถุงยางเท่านั้น
We shouldn't take any risks.	*rao mâi khuan sìang* เราไม่ควรเสี่ยง
Do you have a condom?	*khun mii thŭng yaang mái* คุณมีถุงยางไหม
No? Then the answer's no.	*mâi mii rŭeh, thâa ngán mâi dâi* ไม่มีหรือ ถ้างั้นไม่ได้

3.9 Congratulations and condolences

Happy birthday.	*sùksăn wan kòeht* สุขสันต์วันเกิด
Many happy returns!	*khăw hâi mii khwaam sùk mâak mâak* ขอให้มีความสุขมากๆ
Please accept my condolences.	*khăw sadaehng khwaam sĭa jai dûai* ขอแสดงความเสียใจด้วย
My deepest sympathy.	*chăn sĭa jai yàang sùt súeng* ฉันเสียใจอย่างสุดซึ้ง

3.10 Arrangements

When will I see you again?	*chăn jà dai phôp khun iik mûea rài* ฉันจะได้พบคุณอีกเมื่อไร
Are you free over the weekend? (informal)	*khun wâang mái, săo aathít níi* คุณว่างไหมเสาร์อาทิตย์นี้
What's the plan, then?	*thâa ngán mii phăehn àrai* ถ้างั้นมีแผนอะไร
Where shall we meet?	*rao jà phóp kan thîi năi* เราจะพบกันที่ไหน
Will you pick me up?	[FEMALE] *khun jà maa ráp chăn măi* คุณจะมารับฉันไหม [MALE] *khun jà maa ráp phŏm măi* คุณจะมารับผมไหม
Will you pick us up?	*khun jà maa ráp rao măi* คุณจะมารับเราไหม
Shall I pick you up?	*chăn pai ráp khun, dee măi* ฉันไปรับคุณดีไหม
I have to be home by…	*chăn tâwng klàp bâan kàwn* ฉันต้องกลับบ้านก่อน…

3.11 Being the host(ess)

See also 4 Eating out

Can I offer you a drink?	*khun yàak dùehm àrai mái* [FORMAL] คุณอยากดื่มอะไรไหม *khun hĭu náam măi* [INFORMAL] คุณหิวน้ำไหม
What would you like to drink?	*khun yàak dùehm àrai* คุณอยากดื่มอะไร
Something non-alcoholic, please.	*àrai thîi mâi mii alcohol* อะไรที่ไม่มีแอลกอฮอล์
Would you like a cigarette/cigar?	*khun yàak sùup burìi/cigar măi* คุณอยากสูบ บุหรี่/ซิการ์ ไหม
I don't smoke.	*chăn mâi sùup* ฉันไม่สูบ

Can I take you home?	*chǎn pai sòng khun thîi bâan dâi mǎi* ฉันไปส่งคุณที่บ้านได้ไหม
Can I write to you?	*chǎn khǐan thǔeng khun dâi mǎi* ฉันเขียนถึงคุณได้ไหม
Can I call you?	*chǎn thoh hǎa khun dâi mǎi* ฉันโทรหาคุณได้ไหม
Will you write to me?	*khun jà khǐan thǔeng chǎn mǎi* คุณจะเขียนถึงฉันไหม
Will you call me?	*khun jà thoh hǎa chǎn mǎi* คุณจะโทรหาฉันไหม
Can I send you an email?/ Can I email you?	*chǎn sòng ii-mei hǎa khun dâi mǎi* ฉันส่งอีเมล์หาคุณได้ไหม
Can I have your address?	*khǎw thîi yùu khǎwng khun dâi mǎi* ขอ ที่อยู่ ของคุณได้ไหม
Can I have your phone number?	*khǎw boeh thohrásàp khǎwng khun dâi mǎi* ขอ เบอร์โทรศัพท์ ของคุณได้ไหม
Do you have an email address?	*khun mii ii-mei mǎi* คุณมีอีเมล์ไหม
Can I have your email address?	*khǎw ii-mei khǎwng khun dâi mǎi* ขออีเมล์ของคุณได้ไหม
Thanks for everything.	*khàwp khun sǎmràp thúk yàang* ขอบคุณสำหรับทุกอย่าง
It was a lot of fun.	*sànùk mâak* สนุกมาก
Say hello to…	*fàak sàwàt dii…* ฝากสวัสดี…
All the best/Good luck.	*chôhk dii* โชคดี
When will you be back?	*khun jà klàp maa ìik mûea-rài* คุณจะกลับมาอีกเมื่อไร
I'll be waiting for you.	*chǎn ja raw khun* ฉันจะรอคุณ

I'd like to see you again.	*chăn yàak phóp khun ìik*
	ฉันอยากพบคุณอีก
I hope we meet again soon.	*chăn wăng wâa rao jà phóp kan ìik reo reo níi*
	ฉันหวังว่าเราจะพบกันอีกเร็วๆ นี้
Here's our address. If you're ever in the United States…	*nîi thîi yùu khăwng rao, thâa khun pai àmehríkaa…*
	นี่ที่อยู่ของเรา ถ้าคุณไปอเมริกา…
You'd be more than welcome.	*chăn yindii tâwn ráp tem thîi*
	ฉันยินดีต้อนรับเต็มที่

4. Eating Out

Eating establishments

Many Thais "snack all day," and the noodle shops (*ráan kŭai tĭao*) and smaller eating places (*ráan aahǎan*) are open much of the day, and often late into the night. Restaurants (*ráan aahǎan*) usually open for lunch and dinner. In Bangkok, as in the west, there are specific restaurants for seafood (*aahǎan thaleh*), steak (*núea wua*), as well as international styles, the main being German (*yoehraman*), Italian (*itaalii*) and French (*faràngsèht*). A growing trend for snacking is in the coffee shop serving beautiful cakes (*ráan kaafaeh khǎi khanǒm khéhk*), and also at the donut parlors (*ráan khǎi dohnát*).

Mealtimes

Monks eat only twice in a day (early morning and just before midday), but on the whole, Thais eat three main meals (*sǎam múeh*) a day: **Breakfast** (*aahǎan cháo*) is eaten sometime between 5 and 8 a.m. Many Thais get up very early to go to work, and some give food to the monks on their dawn food round. Breakfast is often a rice porridge (*cóhk*), but can also be a rice dish. Some Thais like the western or *farang*-style breakfast of fried eggs (*khài dao*), grilled or fried frank-furters (*sâi kràwk thâwt*) and some toast (*khanǒm pang pîng*) with coffee (*kaafaeh*). **Lunch** (*aahǎan klaang wan*) is usually eaten at food shops/small restaurants near offices, or for students, in canteens at schools and universities. Some students and workers upcountry take their lunch in a food carrier (*pintoh*) packed with two or three dishes (*kàp khâo*), e.g. stir-fried chicken with bean sprouts (*kài phàt thùa ngâwk*) or stir-fried meat with ginger and vegetables (*núea phàt khĭng*), and some rice (*khâo sǔai*). **Dinner** (*aahǎan yen*) is eaten around 6 or 7 p.m., and often involves more "formal" Thai food, e.g. a soup, a curry dish or spicy salad, perhaps a fish dish and a range of Thai condiments. Most notable of Thai foods are the hot and spicy sour soup with prawns and mushrooms (**tôm yam kûng**); the various curries: red (**kaehng daehng**), green (**kaehng khǐao**), masuman (**mátsamàn**); and Pat Thai (**phàt thai**)—thin rice noodles with tofu, egg, meat and vegetables.

In restaurants

Because food is relatively cheap in Thailand, it's common for Thai families to eat out. The meal will often consist of many and various dishes from which the family or group shares. Thai restaurants range from the smaller inexpensive places serving common dishes, to interesting but sometimes expensive venues serving specialties or having particular gimmicks, e.g. waiters on roller skates or tables set around water. Additional charges may include service charge topped by the ubiquitous Value Added Tax (VAT) (**phasǐi muunlákhâa phôehm**).

4.1 At the restaurant

I'd like to reserve a table for seven o'clock, please.	**khǎw cawng tó sǎmràp tawn nùeng thûm khâ/khráp** ขอจองโต๊ะสำหรับตอนหนึ่งทุ่มค่ะ/ครับ
A table for two, please.	**tó sǎmràp sǎwng khon khâ/khráp** โต๊ะสำหรับสองคนค่ะ/ครับ
We've reserved.	**rao jawng wái** เราจองไว้
We haven't reserved.	**rao mâi dâi jawng** เราไม่ได้จอง

คุณจองไว้หรือเปล่า **khun cawng wái rǔeh-plào**	Do you have a reservation?
ชื่ออะไรคะ/ครับ **chûeh arai khá/khráp**	What name, please?
ทางนี้ค่ะ/ครับ **thaang níi khâ/khráp**	This way, please.

โต๊ะนี้จองแล้ว	This table is reserved.
tó níi jawng láehw	
อีกสิบห้านาทีจะมีโต๊ะว่างค่ะ/ครับ	We'll have a table free in
ìik sìp-hâa naa-thi jà mii tó wâang khâ/khráp	fifteen minutes.
คอยได้ไหมคะ/ครับ	Would you mind waiting?
khoi dâi măi khá/khráp	

Is the restaurant open yet?	*ráan aahăan pòeht rŭe yang* ร้านอาหารเปิดหรือยัง
What time does the restaurant open?	*ráan aahăan pòeht kìi mohng* ร้านอาหารเปิดกี่โมง
What time does the restaurant close?	*ráan aahăan pìt kìi mohng* ร้านอาหารปิดกี่โมง
Can we wait for a table?	*rao raw tó wâang dâi măi* เรารอโต๊ะว่างได้ไหม
Do we have to wait long?	*rao tâwng raw naan măi* เราต้องรอนานไหม
Is this seat taken?	*thîi nîi mii khon nâng rŭeh yang* ที่นี่มีคนนั่งหรือยัง
Could we sit here?	*rao nâng thîi nîi dâi măi* เรานั่งที่นี่ได้ไหม
Are there any tables outside?	*mii tó khâng nâwk măi* มีโต๊ะข้างนอกไหม
Do you have another chair for us?	*khăw kâo-îi ìik tua nueng khâ/khráp* ขอเก้าอี้อีกตัวหนึ่งค่ะ/ครับ
Do you have a high chair?	*mii kâo-îi dèk măi khâ/khráp* มีเก้าอี้เด็กไหมคะ/ครับ

4.2　Ordering

Where are the restrooms?	*hâwng náam yùu thîi năi khá/khráp* ห้องน้ำอยู่ที่ไหนคะ/ครับ
We'd like something to eat.	*rao yàak hăa àrai thaan nòi* เราอยากหาอะไรทานหน่อย

We'd like something to drink.	*rao yàak hǎa arai dùehm nòi* เราอยากหาอะไรดื่มหน่อย
We'd like to have a drink first.	*rao khǎw khrûeang dùehm kàwn* เราขอเครื่องดื่มก่อน
Could we see the menu, please?	[FEMALE] *khǎw duu mehnuu aahǎan dâi mǎi khá* ขอดูเมนูอาหารได้ไหมคะ [MALE] *khǎw duu mehnuu aahǎan dâi mǎi khráp* ขอดูเมนูอาหารได้ไหมครับ
Could we see the wine list, please?	[FEMALE] *khǎw duu mehnuu waai dâi mǎi khá* ขอดูเมนูไวน์ได้ไหมคะ [MALE] *khǎw duu mehnuu waai dâi mǎi khráp* ขอดูเมนูไวน์ได้ไหมครับ
Do you have a menu in English?	*khun mii mehnuu pen phaasǎa angkrît mǎi* คุณมีเมนูเป็นภาษาอังกฤษไหม
Do you have a dish of the day?	*khun mii aahǎan phísèht wan nîi mǎi* คุณมีอาหารพิเศษวันนี้ไหม
We haven't made a choice yet.	*rao yang mâi dâi lûeak* เรายังไม่ได้เลือก
What do you recommend?	*khun náe-nam àrai bâang* คุณแนะนำอะไรบ้าง
What are the local specialties?	*mii aahǎan phúehn mueang àrai bâang* มีอาหารพื้นเมืองอะไรบ้าง
What are your specialties?	*mii aahǎan náenam àrai bâang* มีอาหารแนะนำอะไรบ้าง
I like strawberries.	*chǎn châwp sàtrawboehrîi* ฉันชอบสตรอเบอรี่
I like olives.	*chǎn châwp mákàwk* ฉันชอบมะกอก
I don't like meat.	[FEMALE] *chǎn mâi châwp núea* ฉันไม่ชอบเนื้อ [MALE] *phǒm mâi châwp núea* ผมไม่ชอบเนื้อ

I don't like fish.	[FEMALE] *chăn mâi châwp plaa* ฉันไม่ชอบปลา [MALE] *phŏm mâi châwp plaa* ผมไม่ชอบปลา
What's this?	*nîi arai* นี่อะไร
Does it have…in it?	*sài…rǔe plào* ใส่…หรือเปล่า
Is it stuffed with…?	*yát sâi dûai…châi măi* ยัดไส้ด้วย…ใช่ไหม
What does it taste like?	*rót châat mǔean àrai* รสชาติเหมือนอะไร
Is this a hot or a cold dish?	*jaan níi ráwn rǔeh yen* จานนี้ร้อนหรือเย็น
Is this sweet?	*níi wăan măi* นี่หวานไหม
Is this hot/spicy?	*níi phèt măi* นี่เผ็ดไหม
I'm on a salt-free diet.	*chăn mâi thaan kluea* ฉันไม่ทานเกลือ
I can't eat pork.	*chăn thaan mǔu mâi dâi* ฉันทานหมูไม่ได้
I can't have sugar.	*chăn thaan námtaan mâi dâi* ฉันทานน้ำตาลไม่ได้
I'm on a fat-free diet.	*chăn mâi thaan khăi man* ฉันไม่ทานไขมัน
I can't have spicy food.	*chăn thaan aahăan phèt mâi dâi* ฉันทานอาหารเผ็ดไม่ได้
We'll have what those people are having.	*rao khăw bàehp thîi phûak kháo kamlang thaan kan* เราขอแบบที่พวกเขากำลังทานกัน
I'd like…	*khăw…* ขอ …

คุณจะทานอะไร *khun jà thaan arai*	What would you like (to eat)?
คุณตัดสินใจหรือยัง *khun tàt-sǐn-jai rǔeh-yang*	Have you decided?

คุณอยากดื่มก่อนไหม *khun yàak dùehm kàwn mái*	Would you like a drink first?
คุณอยากดื่มอะไร *khun yàak dùehm àrai*	What would you like to drink?
…หมดแล้ว *(beer)…mòt láehw*	We've run out of…(e.g. beer).
ทานให้อร่อยนะคะ/ครับ *than hâi àròi ná khá/khráp*	Enjoy your meal/Bon appétit!
ทุกอย่างเรียบร้อยไหม *thúk yang rîap rói mǎi*	Is everything all right?
ขอเก็บโต๊ะนะคะ/ครับ *khǎw kèp tó ná khá/khráp*	May I clear the table?

Could I have some more bread, please?	[FEMALE] *khǎw khànǒm pang ìik dâi mǎi khá* ขอขนมปังอีกได้ไหมคะ [MALE] *khǎw khànǒm pang ìik dâi mǎi khráp* ขอขนมปังอีกได้ไหมครับ
Could I have some more rice, please?	[FEMALE] *khǎw khâo ìik dâi mǎi khá* ขอข้าวอีกได้ไหมคะ [MALE] *khǎw khâo ìik dâi mǎi khráp* ขอข้าวอีกได้ไหมครับ
Could I have another bottle of water, please?	[FEMALE] *khǎw náam ìik khùat dâi mǎi khá* ขอน้ำอีกขวดได้ไหมคะ [MALE] *khǎw náam ìik khùat dâi mǎi khráp* ขอน้ำอีกขวดได้ไหมครับ
Could I have another bottle of wine, please?	[FEMALE] *khǎw wai ìik khùat dâi mǎi khá* ขอไวน์อีกขวดได้ไหมคะ [MALE] *khǎw wai/bia ìik khùat dâi mǎi khráp* ขอไวน์อีกขวดได้ไหมครับ
Could I have another bottle of beer, please?	[FEMALE] *khǎw bia ìik khùat dâi mǎi khá* ขอเบียร์อีกขวดได้ไหมคะ [MALE] *khǎw bia ìik khùat dâi mǎi khráp* ขอเบียร์อีกขวดได้ไหมครับ
Could I have another portion of…, please?	*khǎw…ìik nòi dâi mǎi khá/khráp* ขอ…อีกหน่อยได้ไหมคะ/ครับ

Could I have the salt and pepper, please? *khǎw kluea kàp phrík thai nòi dâi mǎi khá/khráp* ขอเกลือกับพริกไทยหน่อยได้ไหมคะ/ครับ

Could I have a napkin, please? *khǎw kradàat chét mueh nòi dâi mǎi khá/khráp* ขอกระดาษเช็ดมือหน่อยได้ไหมคะ/ครับ

Could I have some toothpicks, please? *khǎw mái jîm fan nòi dâi mǎi khá/khráp* ขอไม้จิ้มฟันหน่อยได้ไหมคะ/ครับ

Could I have a glass of water, please? *khǎw náam kâeo nùeng dâi mǎi khá/khráp* ขอน้ำแก้วหนึ่งได้ไหมคะ/ครับ

Could I have a straw please? *khǎw làwt dâi mǎi khá/khráp* ขอหลอดได้ไหมคะ/ครับ

The next round's on me. *râwp nâa chǎn líang* รอบหน้าฉันเลี้ยง

Could we have a "doggy bag," please? *khǎw hǎw klàp bâan dâi mǎi khá/khráp* ขอห่อกลับบ้านได้ไหมคะ/ครับ

The bill

See also 8.2 Settling the bill

How much is this dish? *jaan níi thâorài* จานนี้เท่าไร

Could I have the bill, please? *kid tang dûai khâ/khráp* คิดตังค์ด้วยค่ะ/ครับ

All together. *thángmòt* ทั้งหมด

Everyone pays separately. *yâehk kan jàai* แยกกันจ่าย

Let's go Dutch. *hǎan kan* หารกัน

Could we have the menu again, please? *khǎw mehnuu ìik dâi mǎi khá/khráp* ขอเมนูอีกได้ไหมคะ/ครับ

The...is not on the bill. *mâi dâi yùu nai bin* …ไม่ได้อยู่ในบิล…

It's on me today (my treat). *wan níi chǎn/phǒm pen jâo múe khâ/khráp* วันนี้ฉัน/ผม เป็นเจ้ามือเองค่ะ/ครับ

Thank you for the meal. *khàwp khun sǎmràp aahǎan múe níi khâ/khráp* ขอบคุณสำหรับอาหารมื้อนี้ค่ะ/ครับ

4.4 Complaints

Westerners tend to make a complaint or complain in order to improve the food or service, at least for the next person or, perhaps, for their next visit. Thais, on the other hand, rarely complain in this manner. You might see Thai body language expressed when someone is dissatisfied, but they will often accept what is done/given to them without comment. Instead of causing a fuss or showing distaste, Thais are unlikely to revisit a place that has displeased them. The following phrases are for those who feel the need to complain…

It's taking a very long time.	*chái wehlaa naan mâak* ใช้เวลานานมาก
We've been here an hour already.	*rao raw naan láehw* เรารอนานแล้ว
This is not what I ordered.	*nîi mâi châi thîi sàng* นี่ไม่ใช่ที่สั่ง
I ordered…	*chăn sàng…* ฉันสั่ง…
There's a dish missing.	*hăi pai jaan nueng* หายไปจานหนึ่ง
This is not clean.	*nîi mâi sa-àat* นี่ไม่สะอาด
The food's cold.	*aahăan yen chûeht* อาหารเย็นชืด
The food's not fresh.	*aahăan mâi sòt* อาหารไม่สด
The food's too salty.	*aahăan khem pai* อาหารเค็มไป
The food's too sweet.	*aahăan wăan pai* อาหารหวานไป
The food's too spicy.	*aahăan phèt pai* อาหารเผ็ดไป
The meat's too rare.	*núea dìp pai* เนื้อดิบไป
The meat's overdone.	*núea sùk pai* เนื้อสุกไป
The meat's tough.	*núea nĭao* เนื้อเหนียว
The meat is off.	*núea sĭa* เนื้อเสีย
The meat has gone bad.	*núea mii klìn* เนื้อมีกลิ่น
Could I have something else instead of this?	*khăw arai yàang ùehn thîi mâi châi nîi dâi măi* ขออะไรอย่างอื่นที่ไม่ใช่นี้ได้ไหม

The bill is not right.	*bin níi mâi thùuk* บิลนี้ไม่ถูก	
This amount is not right.	*yâwt níi mâi thùuk* ยอดนี้ไม่ถูก	
There's no toilet paper in the restroom.	*mâi mii kradàat chamrá nai hâwng náam* ไม่มีกระดาษชำระในห้องน้ำ	
Will you call the manager, please?	*chûai rîak phûu jàt kaan hâi nòi khâ/ khráp* ช่วยเรียกผู้จัดการให้หน่อยค่ะ/ครับ	

4.5 Paying a compliment

That was a wonderful meal.	*aahǎan àròi mâak* อาหารอร่อยมาก
The...in particular was delicious.	*dohy chàpháw...àròi mâak* โดยเฉพาะ...อร่อยมาก

4.6 The menu

ขนมปัง
khanǒm-pang
bread

ซอสพริก
sàwt phrík
chili sauce

เครื่องดื่ม
khrûeng–dùehm
drinks

น้ำปลา *náam plaa*
fish sauce

ค่าบริการ
khâa borikaan
service charge/
  cover charge

ภาษี/แว็ท *phasǐi*
VAT (tax)

อาหารว่าง
aahǎan wâang
entrée/starter/
  hors d'oeuvres

เมนูหลัก
mehnuu lâhk
main course

สลัด *salàt* salad

ซุป *súp* soup

ขนมเค้ก
khanǒm kéhk
cakes

ของหวาน
khǎwng wǎan
dessert

ปลา *plaa* fish

ข้าว *khâao* rice

แกง *kaehng*
curry

ผลไม้ *phǒnlamái*
fruit

เนื้อ *néua*
meat (red meat,
  not pork)

อาหารจานเคียง
aahǎan jaan khiang
side dishes

อาหารพิเศษ
aahǎan phísèt
specialties

ไอศครีม *ai-sà-khriim*
ice-cream

ผัก *phàk*
vegetables

4.7 Drinks and dishes

Soups and entrées

กะหรี่ปั๊บ
karìi páp
Curry puffs

ไก่สะเต๊ะ
kài saté
Chicken satay

ลาบเนื้อ
lâap núea
Spicy minced meat

เนื้อหวาน
núea wǎan
Sweet crisp beef

ปูจ๋า *puu jǎa*
Fried stuffed crab

ส้มตำ *sôm tam*
Green papaya salad

ยำมะเขือเผา
yam mákhǔea phǎo
Eggplant salad

ยำเนื้อ
yam núea
Thai beef salad

ทอดมันปลา
thâwt man plaa
Spicy fish cakes

ยำปลาหมึก
yam plaa mùek
Squid salad

ยำกุ้ง
yam kûng
Prawn salad with
  mint and lemon
  grass

ไก่ห่อใบเตย
kài hàw bai toei
Chicken in pandanus
  leaves

ขนมปังหน้าหมู
khanǒm pang nâa mǔu
Pork (and often
  prawn) toasts

ต้มยำกุ้ง
tôm yam kûng
Hot and sour prawn
  soup

ต้มข่าไก่
tôm khàa kài
Mildly spicy coconut
  and galangal soup
  with chicken

Main meals

หมูกรอบ
mǔu kràwp
Crisp pork

หมูหวาน
mǔu wǎan
Sweet pork

โป๊ะแตก *pó tàehk*
Hot seafood soup

ยำเต้าหู้
yam tâo hûu
Spicy tofu salad

ผัดไทย
phàt thai
Thai fried noodles

ข้าวผัดกุ้ง
khâo phàt kûng
Fried rice with prawns

ข้าวต้มกุ้ง
khâo tôm kûng
Rice soup with
  prawns

ข้าวต้มโป๊ะแตก
khâo tôm pó tàehk
Seafood and rice
  soup

หมี่กรอบ
mìi kràwp
Sweet crispy fried
  noodles

แกงจืดข้าวโพดอ่อน
*kaehng jùeht khâo
  phôht àwn*
Corn and prawn soup

ข้าวมันไก่
khâo man kài
Rice with steamed
  chicken

ผัดเผ็ดเนื้อ
phàt phèt núea
Chili beef

ผัดซีอิ๊ว
phàt sii-íu
Stir-fried noodles
  with soy sauce

ไก่ย่าง
kài yâang
Thai barbecued
(BBQ) chicken

แกงกะหรี่กุ้ง
kaehng karìi kûng
Yellow prawn curry

แกงเขียวหวานไก่
kaehng khĭao wăan kài
Chicken green curry

แกงเลียงฟักทอง
*kaehng liang fák
thawng*
Pumpkin spicy soup

แกงมัสมั่นเนื้อ
kaehng Mátsamàn núea
Masuman beef curry

แกงป่าเนื้อ
kaehng pàa núea
Jungle curry beef

ปูผัดพริก
puu phàt phrík
Chili crab

ข้าวหมูแดง
khâo mŭu daehng
Rice with red pork

ปลากรอบราดพริก
plaa kràwp râat phrík
Crispy deep-fried fish
with chili

ไก่ผัดเม็ดมะ
ม่วงหิมพานต์
*kài phàt mét mámûang
hĭ mmáphaan*
Stir-fried chicken
with cashew nuts

หมูผัดเปรี้ยวหวาน
mŭu phàt prîao wăan
Thai sweet and sour
pork

ก๋วยเตี๋ยวราดหน้า
kŭai tĭao râat nâa
Fried noodles with
gravy-like sauce

เนื้อผัดน้ำมันหอย
núea phàt námman hŏi
Stir-fried beef with
oyster sauce

แพนงไก่
phanaehng kài
Mild chicken curry
with coconut milk

ไก่ผัดใบกะเพรา
kài phàt bai kapraw
Stir-fried chicken
with chili and basil

ไก่ผัดขิง
kài phàt khĭng
Stir-fried chicken
with ginger

ไข่ยัดไส้อาหารทะเล
*khài yát sâi aahăan
thaleh*
Stuffed seafood
omelette

ห่อหมกปลา
hàw mòk plaa
Steamed fish curry
served in a small
banana leaf
container

ทะเลผัดฉ่า
thàleh phàt chàa
Stir-fried seafood
with basil

ผัดถั่วงอก
phàt thùa ngâwk
Stir-fried bean
sprouts

ทอดมันข้าวโพด
thâwt man khâo phôht
Fried corn cakes

ต้มข่าไก่
tôm khàa kài
Chicken and coconut
soup

ผัดผักรวมมิตร
phàt phàk ruam mít
Stir-fried mixed
vegetables

ไข่ยัดไส้ *khài yát sâi*
Stuffed omelette,
generally served with
minced pork

ผัดผักบุ้งใส่กระเทียม
*phàt phàk bûng sài
kràthiam*
Stir-fried Morning
Glory (*phàk bûng*)
with garlic

ปลาหมึกกระ
เทียมพริกไทย
*plaa mùek krathiam
phrík thai*
Squid with garlic and
black pepper

ปลาผัดเปรี้ยวหวาน
plaa phàt prîao wăan
Sweet and sour
stir-fried fish

ข้าวผัดสับปะรด
khâo phàt sapparót
Pineapple fried rice

Desserts

วุ้นกะทิ
wún kathí
Coconut jelly

กล้วยทอด
klûai thâwt
Fried bananas

สังขยา
săngkhayaa
Thai custard

ขนมกล้วย
khanŏm klûai
Banana pancakes

กล้วยเชื่อม
klûai chûeam
Bananas in syrup

ไอศครีมกะทิ
ais(a)khriim kathí
Coconut ice-cream

ข้าวเหนียวมะม่วง
khâo nĭao mámûang
Mangoes with
sticky rice

ข้าวเหนียวสังขยา
*khâo nĭao
săngkhayaa*
Sticky rice with
Thai custard

ขนมตะโก้
khanŏm tàkôh
Coconut and agar
agar cake

ขนมถ้วย
khanŏm thûai
Steamed coconut
pudding

กล้วยบวดชี
klûai bùat chii
Bananas in coconut
cream

สังขยาฟักทอง
*săngkhayaa fák
thawng*
Thai custard served
in a hollowed out
piece of pumpkin

Drinks

กาแฟ
kaafaeh
Coffee

น้ำชา
náam chaa
Tea

ใส่ครีม
sài khriim
– with cream

ใส่น้ำตาล
sài náamtaan
– with sugar

กาแฟดำร้อน
kaafaeh dam ráwn
Hot black coffee

ใส่นม
sài nom
– with milk

น้ำขิง
náam khĭng
Ginger drink

น้ำลำไย
náam lamyai
Longan juice

น้ำมะนาว
náam manao
Lime juice drink

น้ำมะพร้าว
náam máphráo
coconut juice

น้ำส้มคั้น
náam sôm khán
Orange juice

น้ำอ้อย
náam ôi
Sugarcane juice

โอเลี้ยง
ohlíang black coffee
Iced sweet
Thai-style

Snacks

มันฝรั่งทอด
man faràng thâwt
french fries/chips

เต้าหู้ทอด
tăo hûu thâwt
Fried tofu/beancurd

สาคูไส้หมู
săakhuu sâi mŭu
Tapioca with pork
filling

5. Getting Around

5.1 Asking directions

ที่นี่ *thîi nîi* here

ผ่าน *phàan* via

ใน *nai* in

ไป *pai* to

บน *bon* on

ใต้ *tâi* under

ที่นั่น *thîi nân* there

ตรงนี้ *trong níi* over here

ตรงนั้น *trong nán* over there

ไกล *klai* far away

ใกล้ *klâi* nearby

ขวา *khwǎa* right

ซ้าย *sáai* left

ติดกับ *tìt kàp* next to

ลง *long* down

ขึ้น *khûen* up

ตรงข้าม *trong khâam* opposite

บางที่ *baang thîi* somewhere

ด้านหน้า *dân nâa* in front of

ตรงกลาง *trong klaang* in the center

ข้างใน *khâang nai* inside

ข้างนอก *khâang nâwk* outside

ข้างหลัง *khâang lǎng* behind

ด้านหน้า *nâa* at the front

ไม่มีที่ไหน *mâi mii thîi nǎi* nowhere

ทุกที่ *thúk thîi* everywhere

ทางซ้าย *thaang sáai* on the left

ทางใต้ *thaang tâi* to the south

ทางขวา *thaang khwǎa* on the right

อยู่ทางขวาของ *yùu thaang khwǎa khǎwng* to the right of

อยู่ข้างซ้ายของ *yùu thaang sáai khǎwng* to the left of

ตรงข้ามกับ *trong khâam kàp* facing

ไปข้างหน้า *pai khâng nâa* forward

ข้างหลัง
khâng lǎng
at the back

ทางเหนือ
thaang nǔea
in the north

จากทางตะวันตก
jàak thaang ta-wan tòk
from the west

จากทางตะวันออก
jàak thaang ta-wan àwk
from the east

อยู่ทาง...ของ
yùu thaang...khǎwng...
to the...of

Excuse me, could I ask you something?	*khǎw thôht, khǎw thǎam arai nòi dâi mǎi khá/khráp* ขอโทษ ขอถามอะไรหน่อยได้ไหมคะ/ครับ
I've lost my way.	*chǎn lǒng thaang* ฉันหลงทาง
Is there a...around here?	*thǎeo níi mii...bâang mǎi* แถวนี้มี...บ้างไหม
Is this the way to...?	*nîi thaang pai...châi mǎi* นี่ทางไป...ใช่ไหม
Could you tell me how to get to...?	*chûai bàwk thaang pai...nòi dâi mǎi khá/khráp* ช่วยบอกทางไป...หน่อยได้ไหมคะ/ครับ
What's the quickest way to...?	*pai...thaang nǎi reo thîi sùt* ไป...ทางไหนเร็วที่สุด
How many kilometers is it to...?	*pai...kìi kilo* ไป...กี่กิโล
Could you point it out on the map?	*chûai chíi nai phǎehn thîi hâi nòi dâi mǎi* ช่วยชี้ในแผนที่ให้หน่อยได้ไหม

Key Vocabulary

ตึก
tùek
building

ตรงไป
trong pai
go straight ahead

เลี้ยวซ้าย
líao sái
turn left

ไฟจราจร
fai jà-raa-jawn
traffic lights

อุโมงค์
u-mohng
the tunnel

ป้ายหยุด
pâi yùt
"stop" sign

สะพาน
saphaan
bridge

ลูกศร
lûuk sǎwn
an arrow (symbol)

สะพานลอย
sàphaan loi
overpass

เลี้ยวขวา
líao khwǎa
turn right

แม่น้ำ
mâeh-náam
river

ที่มุมถนน
thîi mum thanǒn
at/on the corner

ตามไป
taam pai
follow

ถนน *thanǒn*
road/street

สี่แยก/ถนนตัดกัน
sìi yâek
(four-way) intersection/ crossroads

ป้ายชี้ไปที่...
pâi chíi pai thîi
(a) sign pointing to (a place/destination)

ทางข้าม
thaang khâam
crossing (ie. over the road/railway track)

ข้าม
khâam
cross (a road)

ฉันไม่ทราบ ฉันไม่รู้จักทางแถวนี้
chǎn mâi sâap/chǎn mâi rúu-jàk thaang thǎeo níi

I don't know/I don't know my way around here.

คุณกำลังไปผิดทาง
khun kamlang pai phìt thaang

You're going the wrong way.

คุณต้องกลับไปที่...
khun tâwng klàp pai thîi...

You have to go back to...

จากที่นั่นตามป้ายไป
jàak thîi nân taam pâai pai

From there on just follow the signs.

พอถึงที่นั่น ถามอีก
phaw thǔeng thîi nân thǎam ìik

When you get there, ask again.

5.2 Traffic signs

ระวัง
ráwang
beware/danger

ทางรถในบ้าน
thaang rót nai bâan
driveway

ที่จอดรถจำกัดเวลา
thîi jàwt rót jam-kàt wehlaa
parking for a limited period

เปลี่ยนเลน
plìan len
change lanes

ทางออก
thaang àwk
exit

มีสิทธิ์ไปก่อนที่สุดถนน
mii sìt pai kàwn thîi sùt thanǒn
right of way at end of road

อันตราย
antarai
danger(ous)

ห้ามโบกรถ
hâam bòok rót
no hitchhiking

ช่องทางฉุกเฉิน
châwng thaang chùk-chǒehn
emergency lane

ถนนปิด
thanǒn pìt
road closed

รถบรรทุกหนัก
rót banthúk nàk
heavy trucks

ทางแคบ
thaang khâep
narrow section of road/
  road narrows

ทางโค้ง
thaang khóhng
curves

ทางข้ามรถไฟ
thaang khâam rót-fai
rail crossing

ไหล่ถนนที่แซงไม่ได้
lài thanǒn thîi saeng mâi dâi
impassable shoulder

ชิดขวา/ซ้าย
chit khwǎa/sáai
keep right/left

ความเร็วสูงสุด
khwaam reo sǔung sùt
maximum speed

ห้ามเข้า/ห้ามคนเดินเท้า
*hâam khâw/hâam khon
  doehn tháo*
no entry/no pedestrian
  access

ห้ามเข้า
hâam khâo
no access

ทางม้าลาย
thaang máa-lai
pedestrian crossing

เขตควบคุม
khèt khûap-khum
control zone

บัตรจอดรถ
bàt jàwt rót
parking sticker

ป้ายแสดงสิทธิ์จอดรถ
  (ติดกระจกหน้ารถ)
*pâi sadaeng sìt jàwt rót
  (tìt krajòk nâa rót)*
parking permit (on front
  windscreen)

ทางเบี่ยง
thaang bìang
detour

ห้ามเลี้ยวขวา/ซ้าย
hâam líao khwǎa/sái
no right/left turn

งานซ่อมถนน
ngaan sâwm thanǒn
road works

หยุด
yùt
stop

รถเดินทางเดียว
rót doehn thaang diao
one way

ฝนหรือน้ำแข็ง…กิโลเมตร
*fǒn rǔeh náam-khǎeng…
  kiloh-mét*
rain or ice for (number
  of)…km

เกาะกลางถนน
*kòh klaang
  thanǒn*
traffic island

อย่าขวางทาง
yàa khwǎang thaang
do not obstruct

หน่วยช่วยเหลือข้างถนน
  (บริการรถเสีย)
*nùai chûai-lǔea khâang
  thanǒn (borikaan rót sǐa)*
road assistance
  (breakdown service)

ปั๊มน้ำมัน
pâm náam-man
service station/
  gas station

เขตห้ามจอดรถ
  (สองข้างถนน)
*khèt hâam jàwt rót
  (sǎwng khâang
  thanǒn)*
tow-away area (both
  sides of the road)

เปิดไฟหน้า
pòeht fai nâa
turn on the
  headlights

สี่แยก
sìi yâek
intersection/
crossroads

ถนนที่ถูกกั้น
*thanŏn thîi
thùuk kân*
road blocked

ระวัง หินตก
rawang hĭn tòk
beware, falling
rocks

จอดชั่วคราว
jàwt chûa khraaw
temporary
parking

จ่ายค่าผ่านทาง
*jàai khâa phàan
thaang*
toll payment

ขับช้าๆ
khàp cháa-cháa
slow down
(drive slowly)

ทางที่มีสิทธิ์ไปก่อน
*thaang thîi mii sìt pai
kàwn*
right of way

ความสูงที่รถลอดได้
*khwaam sŭung thîi
rót lâwt dâi*
maximum headroom

ที่จอดรถเสียเงิน/
ที่จอดรถสำรองเพื่อ
*thîi jàwt rót sĭa ngoehn/thîi
jàwt rót sămrong phêua*
paid car park/reserved
parking for

ห้ามผ่าน/ห้ามจอด
hâam phàan/hâam jàwt
no thoroughfare/
no parking

อู่ซ่อมรถ/ที่จอดรถมีคนเฝ้า
*ùu sâwm rót/thîi jàwt rót
mii khon fâo*
garage (for car/vehicle
repairs)/supervised
parking lot

พื้นผิวขรุขระ/ไม่เรียบ
phúen-phĭu khrù-khrà/mâi rîap
broken/uneven surface

5.3 Renting a car

Particular traffic regulations: Thais drive on the left as in the UK, Ireland, Hong Kong, Singapore, and Australia.

For **car and motorbike**: you'll need your own driving license as well as an international one, issued outside Thailand, valid for the type of vehicle you are going to drive.

Trailer: these are rare in Thailand. It's best to hire a small truck (*rót kabà lék*) and driver (*khon khàp*) to carry large items. For smaller items, a utility (*rót săwng thăeo*) will do.

Emergency equipment is not compulsory by any means, but you'd be wise to take a bulb kit, fire extinguisher and first-aid kit.

Roads upcountry are generally sealed, but you'll need to be wary of ten-wheeled trucks (*rót sìp láw*) that tend to hog the highway.

If your hired car should break down, phone the number displayed on, or near the dashboard, or refer to the car hire company's documentation. Broken down or parked vehicles must be parked on the side, or shoulder, of the road and display a warning sign. Your car's rear lights must be used to provide a warning for other road users after nightfall.

Speed limits: on super highways are up to 110 km/h, on major highways the limit is 100 km/h, reducing to 80 km/h where sign-posted. The limit is 60 km/h in urban areas.

The parts of a car

ล้อ
láw
wheel

พัดลม
phátlom
fan

แบตเตอรี่
bàettoehrîi
battery

ไฟท้าย
fai tháai
rear light

กระจกส่องหลัง
kracòk sàwng lăng
rear-view mirror

ถังน้ำมัน
thăng náamman
gas tank

หัวเทียน
hŭa thian
spark plugs

กระจกส่องข้าง
krajòk sàwng khâang
side mirror

กันชน
kan chon
bumper

ไฟเครื่องยนต์
fai khrûeang yon
ignition

สัญญาณเตือน
sănyaan tuean
warning light

คันเร่ง
khan rêng
accelerator

เบรคมือ
brèhk mueh
handbrake

หม้อพักไอเสีย
máw phák ai sĭa
muffler

กระโปรงหลัง
kraprohng lăng
trunk

ไฟหน้า
fai nâa
headlight

ไฟตัดหมอก
fai tàt màwk
fog lamp

คันเหยียบ
khanyuehb
pedal

ยางอะไหล่
yaang alài
spare wheel

ที่ปัดน้ำฝน
thîi pàt nám fŏn
windshield wiper

หน้าต่างหลังคารถ
nâatàang lăngkhaa rót
sunroof

ท่อไอเสีย
thâw ai sĭa
exhaust pipe

เข็มขัดนิรภัย
khĕm khàt niráphai
seat belt

คันเกียร์
khan kia
gear shift

กระจกหน้ารถ
krajòk nâa jót
windshield

I'd like to rent a…	*chăn yàak châo…* ฉันอยากเช่า…
Do I need a (special) license for that?	*chăn tâwng mii bai anúyâat (phísèht) rŭeh plào* ฉันต้องมีใบอนุญาต(พิเศษ)หรือเปล่า
I'd like to rent the…for…	*chăn yàak châo…naan…* ฉันอยากเช่า…นาน…
a day	*nùeng wan* …หนึ่งวัน…
two days	*săwng wan* …สองวัน…
How much is that per week?	*aathít lá thâorài* อาทิตย์ละ เท่าไร
How much is that per day?	*wan lá thâorài* วันละ เท่าไร
How much is the deposit?	*khâa mátjam thâorài* ค่ามัดจำเท่าไร
Could I have a receipt for the deposit?	*khăw bai sèt khâa mátjam dûai dâi măi* ขอใบเสร็จค่ามัดจำด้วยได้ไหม
How much is the surcharge per kilometer?	*khâa pràp kilohmét lá thâorài* ค่าปรับกิโลเมตรละเท่าไร
Does that include petrol?	*ruam náamman dûai rŭe plào* รวมน้ำมันด้วยหรือเปล่า
Does that include insurance?	*ruam prakan dûai rŭe plào* รวมประกันด้วยหรือเปล่า
What time can I pick the…up?	*maa ráp…dâi mûearài* มารับ…ได้เมื่อไร
When does the…have to be back?	*tâwng sòng…khuehn mûearài* ต้องส่ง…คืนเมื่อไร
What sort of fuel does it take?	*chái náamman àrai* ใช้น้ำมันอะไร

5.4 The gas/petrol station

Major international oil companies operate gas stations throughout Thailand. These are open 24 hours on main highways, but if they are far from the major roads, stations open around 5 a.m. and close at about 8 p.m. Gas stations rarely have repair shops on their premises, but can perform simple servicing and change tires if required.

Key Vocabulary

จีพีเอส	รถยนต์ไฮบริด	รถยนต์ไฟฟ้า
GPS (cii phii es)	**rót-yon hai-brìd**	**rót-yon fai-fáa**
GPS	hybrid car	electric car

How many kilometers to the next gas station, please?	**ìik kìi kiloh thǔeng pám náamman khâng nâa** อีกกี่กิโลถึงปั๊มน้ำมันข้างหน้า
I would like…liters of	**chuâi toehm…lít** ช่วยเติม…ลิตร
– super	**suupôeh** ซูเปอร์
– leaded	**náamman sǎan takùa** น้ำมันสารตะกั่ว
– unleaded	**náamman rái sǎan takùa** น้ำมันไร้สารตะกั่ว
– diesel	**diesel** ดีเซล
…liter worth of gas	**gas…lít** แก๊ซ…ลิตร
Fill it up, please.	**tem thǎng khâ/khráp** เต็มถังค่ะ/ครับ
Could you check…?	**chûai trùat…hâi nòi khâ/khráp** ช่วยตรวจ…ให้หน่อยค่ะ/ครับ
– the oil level	**rádàp náamman khrûeang** ระดับน้ำมันเครื่อง
– the tire pressure	**lom láw** ลมล้อ
Could you change the oil, please?	**chûai plìan náamman khrûeang hâi nòi khâ/khráp** ช่วยเปลี่ยนน้ำมันเครื่องให้หน่อยค่ะ/ครับ

Could you clean the windshield, please?	*chûai chét kracòk nâa hâi nòi khâ/khráp* ช่วยเช็ดกระจกหน้าให้หน่อยค่ะ/ครับ
Could you wash the car, please?	*chûai láang rót hâi nòi khâ/khráp* ช่วยล้างรถให้หน่อยค่ะ/ครับ

5.5 Breakdowns and repairs

My car has broken down, could you give me a hand?	*rót sǐa, chûai nòi dâi mǎi khá/khráp* รถเสีย ช่วยหน่อยได้ไหมคะ/ครับ
I have run out of gas.	*ṇáamman mòt* น้ำมันหมด
I've locked the keys in the car.	*chǎn luehm kunjaeh wái nai rót* ฉันลืมกุญแจไว้ในรถ
The car/motorbike/moped won't start.	<u>*rót/mawtôehsai/jàkkràyaan yon satàat*</u> *mâi tìt* รถ/มอเตอร์ไซค์/จักรยานยนต์ สตาร์ตไม่ติด
Could you contact the breakdown service for me, please?	*chûai tìt tàw bawríkaan rót sǐa* *dâi mǎi khá/khráp* ช่วยติดต่อบริการรถเสียได้ไหมคะ/ครับ
Could you call a garage for me, please?	*chûai thoh hǎa ùu sâwm rót dâi mǎi* *khá/khráp* ช่วยโทร.หาอู่ซ่อมรถได้ไหมคะ/ครับ
Could you give me a lift to the nearest garage?	[FEMALE] *chûai pai sòng thîi ùu sâwm* *rót klâi thîi sùt dâi mái khá* ช่วยไปส่งที่อู่ซ่อมรถใกล้ที่สุดได้ไหมคะ [MALE] *chûai pai sòng thîi ùu sâwm* *rót klâi thîi sùt dâi mái khráp* ช่วยไปส่งที่อู่ซ่อมรถใกล้ที่สุดได้ไหมครับ
Could you give me a lift to the nearest town?	[FEMALE] *chûai pai sòng thîi mueang* *klâi thîi sùt dâi mái khâ* ช่วยไปส่งที่เมืองใกล้ที่สุดได้ไหมคะ [MALE] *chûai pai sòng thîi mueang* *klâi thîi sùt dâi mái khráp* ช่วยไปส่งที่เมืองใกล้ที่สุดได้ไหมครับ

Can we hire a moped around here?

rao châo mawtersai thǎeo níi dâi mǎi
เราเช่ามอเตอร์ไซค์แถวนี้ได้ไหม

Can we hire a car around here?

rao châo rót thǎeo níi dâi mǎi
เราเช่ารถแถวนี้ได้ไหม

Could you tow me to a garage?

chûai lâak rót pai thîi ùu dâi mǎi
ช่วยลากรถไปที่อู่ได้ไหม

There's probably something wrong with…

khong jà mii arai phìt pàkàti kàp…
คงจะมีอะไรผิดปกติกับ...

Can you fix it?

khun sâwm dâi mǎi คุณซ่อมได้ไหม

Could you fix my tire?

khun sâwm yaang rót dâi mǎi
คุณซ่อมยางรถได้ไหม

Can you fix it so it'll get me to…?

khun sâwm dâi mǎi, chǎn jà dâi pai thîi…
คุณซ่อมได้ไหม ฉันจะได้ไปที่…

Could you change this wheel?

khun plìan láw níi dâi mǎi
คุณเปลี่ยนล้อนี้ได้ไหม

Which garage can help me?

ùu nǎi sâwm dâi khá/khráp
อู่ไหนซ่อมได้คะ/ครับ

When will my car/bicycle be ready?

rót/jàkkràyaan khǎwng phǒm/chǎn jà sèt mûearài
รถ/จักรยาน ของผม/ฉัน จะเสร็จเมื่อไร

Have you finished?

khun tham sèt láehw rǔeh
คุณทำเสร็จแล้วหรือ

Can I wait for it here?

chǎn raw thîi nîi dâi mǎi
ฉันรอที่นี่ได้ไหม

How much will it cost?

thángmòt thâorài ทั้งหมดเท่าไร

Could you itemize the bill?

chûai câehng rai lá-ìat khǎwng bin dâi mǎi
ช่วยแจ้งรายละเอียดของบิลได้ไหม

Could you give me a receipt for insurance purposes?

khǎw bai sèt pai hâi pràkan dâi mǎi khá/khráp
ขอใบเสร็จไปให้ประกันได้ไหมคะ/ครับ

5.6 Motorcycles and bicycles

Bikes can be hired in most Thai towns. Don't expect much consideration for bikes on the roads, however. Motorcycles may be tuned to be slightly noisy and to emit a certain amount of exhaust. Be aware that there are new pollution laws, and associated crackdowns by Thai police are common. There are no special speed limits for motorcycles; the same limits as cars apply, but you have to wear a crash helmet. Two (and sometimes more) can ride the same bike along with considerable baggage/goods in some cases, although such behavior is not recommended for the tourist!

ผมไม่มีอะไหล่รถ/จักรยานของคุณ *phǒm mâi mii alài rót/jàkkràyaan khǎwng khun*	I don't have parts for your car/ bicycle.
ผมต้องสั่งอะไหล่มาจากที่อื่น *phǒm tâwng sàng alài maa jàak thîi èun*	I have to get the parts from somewhere else.
ผมต้องสั่งอะไหล่มา *phǒm tâwng sàng alài maa*	I have to order the parts.
จะใช้เวลาครึ่งวัน *jà chái wehlaa khrûeng wan*	That'll take half a day.
จะใช้เวลาหนึ่งวัน *jà chái wehlaa nùeng wan*	That'll take a day.
จะใช้เวลาสองสามวัน *jà chái wehlaa sǎwng sǎam wan*	That'll take a few days.
จะใช้เวลาหนึ่งอาทิตย์ *jà chái wehlaa nùeng aathít*	That'll take a week.
รถคุณพังจนไม่คุ้มที่จะซ่อม *rót khun phang jon mâi khúm thîi jà sâwm*	Your car is a write-off.

ช่อมไม่ได้
sâwm mâi dâi

It can't be repaired.

รถ/มอเตอร์ไซค์/จักรยานยนต์/
จักรยานจะเสร็จตอน...โมง
*rót/mo-tôeh-sai/jàkkràyaan jà sèt
tawn...mohng*

The car/motorbike/bicycle will
be ready at ...o'clock.

The parts of a bicycle

อาน *aan* seat	กระบังล้อ *krabang láw* wheel guard	ซี่ลวดล้อ *sîi lûat láw* spoke
โซ่ *sôh* chain	กระบังโซ่ *krabang sôh* chain guard	บังโคลนล้อหลัง *bang khlohn láw lăng* mudguard
ไฟหลัง *fai lăng* rear light	แฮนด์ *haen* handlebar	เฟืองล้อขับ *fueang láw khàp* chain wheel
ล้อหลัง *láw lăng* rear wheel	สายเบรค *săi brèhk* brake cable	ที่รัดเท้า *thîi rát tháo* toe clip
กระดิ่ง *kradìng* bell	มาตราวัดความเร็ว *mâattraa wát khwaam reo* speedometer	แกนข้อเหวี่ยง *kaehn khâw wìang* crank axle
ยาง *yaang* tire	อานนั่งสำหรับเด็ก *aan nâng sămràp dèk* child's seat	ระบบเบรกแบบดรัม *rabop brèhk bàehp dram* drum brake
คันถีบ *khan thìip* pedal crank	กระบอกสูบลม *krabàwk sùup lom* pump	ขอบล้อ *khàwp láw* rim
ที่เปลี่ยนเกียร์ *thîi plìan kia* gear change	แผ่นสะท้อนแสง *phàen satháwn săehng* reflector	จุกเติมลมยาง *jùk toehm lom yaang* valve tube
ซี่ลวด *sîi lûat* wire		

ไฟหน้า
fai nâa
headlight

หลอดไฟ
láwt fai
bulb

บันได
bandai
pedal

จานจ่ายไฟ
caan càai fai
generator

โครง
khrohng
frame

ส่วนห้ามล้อที่บีบกับล้อ
sùan hâam láw thîi biip kàp láw
brake shoe

เครื่องมือกันขโมย
khrûeang mueh kan khamoey
anti-theft device

สายเกียร์
sǎi kia
gear cable

โครง
khrohng
fork

ล้อหน้า
láw nâa
front wheel

6. Traveling in Thailand

6.1   Modes of transportation
6.2   Immigration & customs
6.3   Luggage
6.4   Buying a ticket
6.5   Getting travel information

Modes of transportation

Bus tickets are purchased on buses, whether private or public routes, from either the driver or the conductor who shouts out *pâai* or *pai* to the driver, depending upon whether the bus is to stop or to go. Buses, taxis and tuktuks (*túk túk*) (three-wheeled motorized taxis) are the preferred mode of travel around town, with bicycles, mopeds or motorcycles available for hire in the provinces.

Thai train tickets can be purchased from stations or online. If you purchase tickets at the train stations, be sure to state single or return, and try to travel first or second class. For online tickets, you buy the e-tickets at either www.railway.co.th or www.thairailwayticket.com. You can use credit cards (Visa, MasterCard, JCB) or debit cards and you can also purchase tickets up 60 days in advance and no less than two hours before the train is scheduled to leave. Only four tickets are available per booking. The booking fee is 40 baht for 1st Class tickets, 30 baht for 2nd Class tickets, and 20 baht for 3rd Class tickets. It is possible to cancel tickets online or at your local train station.

Many major *sois* (lanes) in Bangkok have motorcycles ready to take pillion passengers into the smaller *sois* for 15 to 40 baht (depending on the journey). If you'd prefer to travel on the river, you can hire a long-tailed boat (*ruea hăng yao*) for a fast ride, or take a ferry boat for a cheap and easy way to cross the Chaopraya river (*mâehnáam jâo phráyaa*).

In Bangkok, BTS or skytrain tickets are available from ticket vending machines at stations en route. Tickets must be purchased for the particular zone to zone travel, but can be bought for several trips, and on a weekly or monthly basis as well.

MRT (Metropolitan Rapid Transit) or underground trains can be one of the most convenient methods to travel around Bangkok. Tokens are used for a single trip and can be purchased at ticket vending machines (coins and notes) and all Bangkok MRT Ticket Offices. You can also purchase a smart card with stored value and which can be topped up for multiple rides.

On arrival at a **Thai airport** (*thâa aakàatsayaan*), you will find the following signs:

Key Vocabulary

เช็คอิน
chék in
check-in

ต่างประเทศ
tàang prathêht
international

ภายในประเทศ
phai nai prathêht
domestic (flight)

ขาเข้า
khǎa khâw
arrivals

ขาออก
khǎa àwk
departures

ศุลกากร
sula-kaa-kawn
Customs

โรงแรมสนามบิน
rohng-raehm sanǎam-bin
airport hotel

บัตรผ่านขึ้นเครื่องบิน
bàt phàan khûen khrûeng-bin
boarding pass

ที่รับกระเป๋าเดินทาง
thîi ráp krapǎo doehn thaang
baggage claim

เครื่องกระตุ้นกล้ามเนื้อหัวใจ
khrûeng-kra-tûn klâam-núea hǔa-jai
pacemaker

ห้องนั่งเล่นอินเทอร์เน็ต
hâwng nâng-lên in-toeh-net
Internet lounge

เครื่องตรวจสแกน
khrûeng trùat sa-kaen
scanner

การจองตั๋วผ่านอินเทอร์เน็ต
kaan jawng tǔa phàan in-toeh-net
eBooking/eReservation

จองตั๋วออนไลน์
jawng tǔa awnlaai
online booking/ reservation

เครื่องมือตรวจคลื่นแม่เหล็ก
khrûeng mueh trùat khlûen mâe-lèk
metal detector

หน่วยรักษาความปลอดภัยสนามบิน
nùai raksǎa khwaam plàwt-phai sanǎam-bin
airport security

In addition to flying or taking an **air-conditioned coach/bus** for longer journeys you may wish to travel **by train**. When you purchase a ticket state whether you want a one-way or return fare. The lines are built north to Chiang Mai via Phitsanulok; north-east to Nong Khai (and Laos); west to Kanchanaburi and Nam Tok; east to Aranyaprathet (and Cambodia); and south to Hat Yai (then on to Malaysia and Singapore if you like the Orient Express!) The sprinter service, e.g. to Chiang Mai, is quite comfortable, but other trains can be an experience to say the least—third class carriages are just "open," and some passengers ride wherever there's a handhold. Many Thais prefer air-conditioned coach travel to go upcountry but, like train travel, watch your belongings!

There are plenty of **taxis** in Bangkok, as well as in major towns. In Bangkok metered taxi fares are quite reasonable. There are taxi queues at both airports in Bangkok, Suwannaphum and Don Muang. They are also to be found at major train and bus stations. Otherwise hail a taxi from the roadside. Use the meter for every trip, unless you bargain on a day's hire to see the sights (expect over 2,000 baht, but less upcountry). There is a surcharge for taxis using expressways as there are entry tolls to the often above ground structures. The taxi might have to leave one expressway to go up onto another, costing an additional toll—to save time, believe me! Tolls vary from 20 to 100 baht each time.

Key Vocabulary

ให้เช่า	ไม่ว่าง	ป้ายจอดแท็กซี่
hâi châo	*mâi wâang*	*pâi jàwt tháeksîi*
for hire	occupied	taxi stand

Taxi!	*tháeksîi* แท็กซี่
Could you get me a taxi, please?	*chûai rîak tháeksîi hâi nòi dâi măi khá/khráp* ช่วยเรียกแท็กซี่ห้หน่อยได้ไหมคะ/ครับ
Where can I find a taxi around here?	*thăeo níi hăa tháeksîi dâi thîi năi khá/khráp* แถวนี้หาแท็กซี่ได้ที่ไหนคะ/ครับ
Could you take me to the Grand Palace, please?	[FEMALE] *chûai pai sòng thîi Phra Borom Maha Ratcha Wang dâi mái khá* ช่วยไปส่งที่พระบรมมหาราชวังได้ไหมคะ [MALE] *chûai pai sòng thîi Phra Borom Maha Ratcha Wang dâi mái khráp* ช่วยไปส่งที่พระบรมมหาราชวังได้ไหมครับ

Could you take me to the Baiyoke hotel, please?	[FEMALE] *chûai pai sòng thîi rohng raehm Baiyoke dâi mái khá* ช่วยไปส่งที่โรงแรมใบหยกได้ไหมคะ [MALE] *chûai pai sòng thîi rohng raehm Baiyoke dâi mái khráp* ช่วยไปส่งที่โรงแรมใบหยกได้ไหมครับ
Could you take me to the town, please?	[FEMALE] *chûai pai sòng nai mueang dâi mái khá* ช่วยไปส่งในเมืองได้ไหมคะ [MALE] *chûai pai sòng nai mueang dâi mái khráp* ช่วยไปส่งในเมืองได้ไหมครับ
Could you take me to the city center, please?	[FEMALE] *chûai pai sòng jai klaang mueang dâi mái khá* ช่วยไปส่งใจกลางเมืองได้ไหมคะ [MALE] *chûai pai sòng jai klaang mueang dâi mái khráp* ช่วยไปส่งใจกลางเมืองได้ไหมครับ
Could you take me to the station, please?	[FEMALE] *chûai pai sòng sàthǎanii dâi mái khá* ช่วยไปส่งสถานีได้ไหมคะ [MALE] *chûai pai sòng sàthǎanii dâi mái khráp* ช่วยไปส่งสถานีได้ไหมครับ
Could you take me to the airport, please?	[FEMALE] *chûai pai sòng sànǎam bin dâi mái khá* ช่วยไปส่งสนามบินได้ไหมคะ [MALE] *chûai pai sòng sànǎam bin dâi mái khráp* ช่วยไปส่งสนามบินได้ไหมครับ
How much is the trip to Khao San?	*pai Khao San thâorài* ไปข้าวสารเท่าไร
How far is it to the airport?	*sànǎam bin yòu klai khâe nǎi* สนามบินอยู่ใกล้แค่ไหน
Could you turn on the meter, please?	*pòeht mítôeh dûai ná khá/khráp* เปิดมิเตอร์ด้วยนะคะ/ครับ
I'm in a hurry.	*chǎn rîip* ฉันรีบ

Could you speed up a little?	[FEMALE] *khàp reo nòi dâi măi khá* ขับเร็วหน่อยได้ไหมคะ [MALE] *khàp reo nòi dâi măi khráp* ขับเร็วหน่อยได้ไหมครับ
Could you slow down a little?	[FEMALE] *khàp cháa long nòi dâi măi khá* ขับช้าลงหน่อยได้ไหมคะ [MALE] *khàp cháa long nòi dâi măi khráp* ขับช้าลงหน่อยได้ไหมครับ
Could you take a different route?	*pai thaang ùehn dâi măi* ไปทางอื่นได้ไหม
I'd like to get out here, please.	*khăw long thîi nîi* ขอลงที่นี่
Go…	*pai* ไป…
You have to go left here.	*tâwng líao sái thîi nîi* ต้องเลี้ยวซ้ายที่นี่
You have to go right here.	*tâwng líao khwăa thîi nîi* ต้องเลี้ยวขวาที่นี่
You have to go straight here.	*tâwng trong pai thîi nîi* ต้องตรงไปที่นี่
Go straight ahead	*trong pai* ตรงไป
Turn left.	*líao sái* เลี้ยวซ้าย
Turn right.	*líao khwăa* เลี้ยวขวา
This is it.	*trong nîi làe* ตรงนี้แหละ
We're here.	*thŭeng láehw* ถึงแล้ว
Could you wait a minute for me, please?	*raw sák khrûu dâi măi khá/khráp* รอสักครู่ได้ไหมคะ/ครับ
Where does this train go to?	*rót fai khábuan níi pai năi* รถไฟขบวนนี้ไปไหน
Where does this skytrain go to?	*rót fai fáa khábuan níi pai năi* รถไฟฟ้าขบวนนี้ไปไหน
Can I take this bus to Chiang Rai?	[FEMALE] *chăn khûen rót meh khan níi pai Chiang Rai dâi măi* ฉันขึ้นรถเมล์คันนี้ไปเชียงรายได้ไหม

	[MALE] *phŏm khûen rót meh khan níi pai Chiang Rai dâi măi* ผมขึ้นรถเมล์คันนี้ไปเชียงรายได้ไหม
Does this train stop at Surat Thani?	*rót fai khábuan níi jàwt thîi Surat Thani măi* รถไฟขบวนนี้จอดที่สุราษฎร์ธานีไหม
Does this bus stop at Pattaya?	*rót meh khan níi jàwt thîi Pattaya măi* รถเมล์คันนี้จอดที่พัทยาไหม
Is this seat taken/free/reserved?	*thîi níi mii khon <u>nâng</u>/<u>wâang</u>/<u>jawng</u> wái rŭe plào* ที่นี่มีคน นั่ง/ว่าง/จองไว้ หรือเปล่า
I've reserved…	*chăn jawng…* ฉันจอง…
Could you tell me where I have to get off for Pattaya?	[FEMALE] *chûai bàwk dûai ná khá wâa thŭehng Pattaya tâwng long thîi năi* ช่อยบอกด้วยนะคะว่าถึงพัทยาต้องลงที่ไหน [MALE] *chûai bàwk dûai ná khráp wâa thŭehng Pattaya tâwng long thîi năi* ช่อยบอกด้วยนะครับว่าถึงพัทยาต้องลงที่ไหน
Could you let me know when we get to Hat Yai?	[FEMALE] *thŭeng Hat Yai láehw chûai bàwk dûai ná khá* ถึงหาดใหญ่แล้วช่วยบอกด้วยนะคะ [MALE] *thŭeng Hat Yai láehw chûai bàwk dûai ná khráp* ถึงหาดใหญ่แล้วช่วยบอกด้วยนะครับ
Could you stop at the next stop, please?	*chûai jàwt pâi nâa dûai ná khá/khráp* ช่วยจอดป้ายหน้าด้วยนะคะ/ครับ
Where are we?	*rao thŭeng năi láehw* เราถึงไหนแล้ว
Do I have to get off here?	*chăn tâwng long thîi níi châi măi* ฉันต้องลงที่นี่ใช่ไหม
Have we already passed Chiang Mai?	*rao phàan Chiang Mai láehw rŭeh yang* เราผ่านเชียงใหม่แล้วหรือยัง

How long have I been asleep?	*chăn làp pai naan thâorài* ฉันหลับไปนานเท่าไร
How long does the train stop here?	*rót-fai jàwt thîi nîi naan thâorài* รถไฟจอดที่นี่นานเท่าไร
Can I come back on the same ticket?	*chăn chái tŭa kào klàp maa dâi măi* ฉันใช้ตั๋วเก่ากลับมาได้ไหม
Can I change on this ticket?	*chăn chái tŭa níi plìan rót dài măi* ฉันใช้ตั๋วนี้เปลี่ยนรถได้ไหม
How long is this ticket valid for?	*tŭa níi chái dâi naan thâorài* ตั๋วนี้ใช้ได้นานเท่าไร
How much is the extra fare for the high speed train?	*rót-fai dùan tâwng sĭa khâa dohysăan phôehm ìik thâorài* รถไฟด่วนต้องเสียค่าโดยสารเพิ่มอีกเท่าไหร่

Announcements

รถไฟไป…จะเสียเวลา(ราว)…นาที *rót-fai pai…jà sĭa wehlaa (raao)…naathii*	The train to…has been delayed by (about)…minutes.
รถไฟไป…กำลังเข้าชานชาลาที่… *rót-fai pai…kamlang khâo chaan-chaalaa thîi…*	The train to…is now arriving at platform…
รถไฟจาก…กำลังเข้าชานชาลาที่… *rót-fai jàak…kamlang khâo chaan-chaalaa thîi…*	The train from…is now arriving at platform…
รถไฟไป…จะออกจากชานชาลาที่… *rót-fai pai…jà àwk jàak chaan-chaalaa thîi…*	The train to…will leave from platform…
วันนี้รถไฟไป…จะออกจากชานชาลาที่… *wan-níi rót-fai pai…jà àwk jàak chaan-chaalaa thîi…*	Today the train to…will leave from platform…
สถานีต่อไป… *sathăa-nii tàw pai…*	The next station is…

6.2 Immigration and customs

Key Vocabulary

ศุลกากร
sǎn-lá-kaa-kawn
Customs

มีสิ่งของต้องสำแดง
mii sìng khǎwng
tâwng sǎm-daehng
Goods to declare

ไม่มีสิ่งของต้องสำแดง
mâi mii sìng khǎwng
tâwng sǎm-daehng
Nothing to declare

เครื่องสแกน
khrûeang sà-kaehn
Scanner

ยืนหลังเส้น
yuehn lǎng sêhn
Stand behind this
line

ห้ามถ่ายรูป
hâam thàai rûup
No photography

In Thailand, it is advisable to have your **passport** with you. You'll
need it for specific purposes, such as going out to the bars at night,
taking a flight, changing money, hiring some equipment, renting a
room, etc. They will ask to see your actual passport as identification or possibly as security. But in most cases a photocopy of your
passport would be acceptable.

Border documents: valid passport. No visa is required if staying
for 30 days or less. A straightforward way to "stay longer" in
Thailand is to leave the Thai kingdom, and re-enter it. You go to
the border, e.g. Hat Yai on the Thai-Malaysian or Nong Khai on the
Thai-Lao border, and have your passport stamped "out"; then you
re-enter with it stamped "in," and can stay for up to another
30 days. Longer periods (up to six months) require a visa that can
be stamped with a limited number of entries into Thailand. Such
visas must be obtained from the Thai embassy or consulate in your
city before leaving. Charges apply.

Import and export specifications

Foreign currency: there are no restrictions on the import of currency into Thailand (amounts over US$20,000 must be declared).
While cash is handy, travelers' cheques are recommended for safety
and security. The Customs Hall has red (*châwng sǐi daehng*) and
green (*châwng sǐi khǐao*) channels for "goods to declare" and
"nothing to declare" respectively. Thai Customs can be difficult if
you do not act responsibly, and fines of four times assessed value
are charged when restricted goods are found. Thai Customs allow
the import without duty on:

– Alcohol: 1 liter of spirits, liquor or wine
– Tobacco: 200 cigarettes or 250 grams of cigars or tobacco

You must be aged 18 or over to import alcohol and tobacco. The above restrictions apply to all alcohol and tobacco purchased in duty-free shops. Personal items of up to 10,000 baht in total value are not likely to attract duty.

On leaving the kingdom there are limits on the export of Thai currency. The amount of 50,000 baht or more in Thai currency must be reported on departure. For those traveling to the Lao PDR, Myanmar, Cambodia, Malaysia and Vietnam are permitted to take out Thai currency not exceeding 500,000 baht.

เพศ
phêht
sex

ชาย
chaai
male

หญิง
yǐng
female

โสด
sòht
single

นามสกุล
naam sàkun
surname

ชื่อจริง
chûeh jing
first name

ชื่อย่อ
chûeh yâw
initials

ที่อยู่
thîi yùu
address

ม่าย
mâai
widowed

ถนน
thà nǒn
street

บ้านเลขที่
bâan lêhk thîi
number

รหัสไปรษณีย์
ráhàt praisànii
postal (zip) code

เมือง
mueang
town

สัญชาติ
sǎn châat
nationality

เชื้อชาติ
chúea châat
citizenship

บัตรประชาชน
bàt pràchaa chon
identity card

ใบขับขี่
bai khàp khìi
driving license

ลายเซ็น
laai sen
signature

วันเดือนปีเกิด
wan duean pii kòeht
date of birth

สถานที่เกิด
sàthǎan thîi kòeht
place of birth

อาชีพ
aachîip
occupation

สถานภาพสมรส
sathǎanáphâap sǒmrót
marital status

แต่งงาน
tàeng-ngaan
married

สถานที่ออกบัตร
sàthǎn thîi àwk bàt
place of issue

วันที่ออกบัตร
wan thîi àwk bàt
date of issue

ลูก....คน
lûuk [number] khon
(number of) children

หนังสือเดินทาง
nǎngsǔeh dern thaang
passport

ขอพาสปอร์ต (หนังสือเดินทาง) ค่ะ/ครับ *khǎw passport (nǎngsǔeh doehn-thaang)* *khâ/khráp*	Your passport, please.
ขอใบขับขี่ค่ะ/ครับ *khǎw bai-khàp-khìi khâ/khráp*	Your driving license, please.
ขอดูวีซ่าค่ะ/ครับ *khǎw duu wii-sâa khâ/khráp*	May I see your visa, please.
คุณจะไปไหน *khun jà pai nǎi*	Where are you going?
คุณคิดจะอยู่นานเท่าไร *khun khít jà yùu naan thâorai*	How long are you planning to stay?
คุณมีอะไรจะแจ้งไหม *khun mii arai jà jâeng mǎi*	Do you have anything to declare?
เปิดนี่ด้วยค่ะ/ครับ *pòet nîi dûai khâ/khráp*	Open this, please.

My children are entered on this passport.	*lûuk lûuk chái nǎngsǔeh doehn thaang níi* ลูกๆ ใช้หนังสือเดินทางนี้
I'm traveling through.	*chǎn doehn thaang phàan* ฉันเดินทางผ่าน
I'm going on vacation to…	*chǎn pai thîao thîi…* ฉันไปเที่ยวที่…
I'm on a business trip.	*chǎn pai tham thurákìt* ฉันไปทำธุรกิจ
I don't know how long I'll be staying.	*chǎn mâi sâap jà yùu naan thâorài* ฉันไม่ทราบจะอยู่นานเท่าไร
I'll be staying here for a weekend.	*chǎn jà yùu thîi nîi sák sào aathít nueng* ฉันจะอยู่ที่นี่สักเสาร์อาทิตย์หนึ่ง
I'll be staying here for a few days.	*chǎn jà yùu thîi nîi sák sǎwng sǎam wan* ฉันจะอยู่ที่นี่สักสองสามวัน
I'll be staying here a week.	*chǎn jà yùu thîi nîi sák aathít nùeng* ฉันจะอยู่ที่นี่สักอาทิตย์หนึ่ง

I'll be staying here for two weeks.	*chǎn jà yùu thîi nîi sák sǎwng aathít* ฉันจะอยู่ที่นี่สักสองอาทิตย์
I've got nothing to declare.	*chǎn mâi mii arai jà jâehng* ฉันไม่มีอะไรจะแจ้ง
I have a carton of cigarettes.	[FEMALE] *chǎn mii burìi nùeng klòng* ฉันมีบุหรี่หนึ่งกล่อง [MALE] *phǒm mii burìi nùeng klòng* ผมมีบุหรี่หนึ่งกล่อง
I have a bottle of whiskey.	[FEMALE] *chǎn mii lâo nùeng khùat* ฉันมีเหล้าหนึ่งขวด [MALE] *phǒm mii lâo nùeng khùat* ผมมีเหล้าหนึ่งขวด
I have some souvenirs.	[FEMALE] *chǎn mii khǎwng thîi ralúek* ฉันมีของที่ระลึก [MALE] *phǒm mii khǎwng thîi ralúek* ผมมีของที่ระลึก
These are personal items.	*nîi khǎwng chái sùan tua* นี่ของใช้ส่วนตัว
These are not new.	*nîi mâi mài* นี่ไม่ใหม่
Here's the receipt.	*nîi bai sèt* นี่ใบเสร็จ
This is for private use.	*nîi sǎmràp chái sùan tua* นี่สำหรับใช้ส่วนตัว
How much import duty do I have to pay?	*chǎn tâwng sǐa phaasǐi khǎa khâo thâorài* ฉันต้องเสียภาษีขาเข้าเท่าไร
May I go now?	*chǎn pai dâi rǔeh yang* ฉันไปได้หรือยัง

6.3 Luggage

Could you take this luggage to…?	*chûai khǒn kràpǎo pai thîi… dâi mǎi* ช่วยขนกระเป๋าไปที่…ได้ไหม
How much do I owe you?	*tâwng jàai thâorài* ต้องจ่ายเท่าไร

Where can I find a cart?	*ao rót khěn dâi thîi năi* เอารถเข็นได้ที่ไหน
Could you store this luggage for me?	*khun chûai kèp kràpǎo níi hâi nòi dâi măi* คุณช่วยเก็บกระเป๋านี้ให้หน่อยได้ไหม
Where are the luggage lockers?	*láwkkôeh kèp kràpǎo yùu thîi năi* ล็อคเกอร์เก็บกระเป๋าอยู่ที่ไหน
I can't get the locker open.	*chǎn pòeht láwkkôeh mâi dâi* ฉันเปิดล็อคเกอร์ไม่ได้
How much is it per item per day?	*chín lá thâorài tàw wan* ชิ้นละเท่าไรต่อวัน
My suitcase is damaged.	*kràpǎo doehn thaang khǎwng chǎn chamrút* กระเป๋าเดินทางของฉันชำรุด
There's one item missing.	*mii khǎwng hǎai bai nueng* มีของหายใบหนึ่ง
There's one bag missing.	*mii kràpǎo hǎai bai nueng* มีกระเป๋าหายใบหนึ่ง
There's one suitcase missing.	*mii kràpǎo doehn thaang hǎai bai nueng* มีกระเป๋าเดินทางหายใบหนึ่ง
Can I get any compensation during this time as my belongings are all in the missing luggage?	[FEMALE] *chǎn khǎw ngoehn chótchoei dâi mái phráw mii khǎwng chái sùan tua thúk yàang yòu nai kràpǎo* ฉันขอเงินชดเชยได้ไหม เพราะมีของใช้ส่วนตัวทุกอย่างอยู่ในกระเป๋าเดินทาง [MALE] *phǒm khǎw ngoehn chótchoei dâi mái phráw mii khǎwng chái sùan tua thúk yàang yòu nai kràpǎo* ผมขอเงินชดเชยได้ไหม เพราะมีของใช้ส่วนตัวทุกอย่างอยู่ในกระเป๋าเดินทาง
This is not my bag.	*nîi mâi châi kràpǎo doehn. thaang khǎwng chǎn* นี่ไม่ใช่ กระเป๋า/กระเป๋าเดินทาง ของฉัน
This is not my suitcase.	*nîi mâi châi kràpǎo/kràpǎo doehn thaang khǎwng chǎn* นี่ไม่ใช่ กระเป๋า/กระเป๋าเดินทาง ของฉัน

This is the address of my hotel.	[FEMALE] *nîi pen thîi yòu rohngraem thîi chǎn phák*
	นี่เป็นที่อยู่โรงแรมที่ฉันพัก
	[MALE] *nîi pen thîi yòu rohngraem thîi phǒm phák*
	นี่เป็นที่อยู่โรงแรมที่ผมพัก
Please send the luggage to my hotel.	[FEMALE] *chûai sòng kràpǎo maa thîi rohngraem dûay khâ*
	ช่วยส่งกระเป๋ามาที่โรงแรมด้วยค่ะ
	[MALE] *chûai sòng kràpǎo maa thîi rohngraem dûay khráp*
	ช่วยส่งกระเป๋ามาที่โรงแรมด้วยครับ

6.4 Buying a ticket

Where can I buy a ticket?	[FEMALE] *chǎn jà súeh tǔa dâi thîi nǎi*
	ฉันจะซื้อตั๋วได้ที่ไหน
	[MALE] *phǒm jà súeh tǔa dâi thîi nǎi*
	ผมจะซื้อตั๋วได้ที่ไหน
Where can I reserve a seat?	[FEMALE] *chǎn jà jawng thîi nâng dâi thîi nǎi*
	ฉันจะจองที่นั่งได้ที่ไหน
	[MALE] *phǒm jà jawng thîi nâng dâi thîi nǎi*
	ผมจะจองที่นั่งได้ที่ไหน
Where can I reserve a flight?	[FEMALE] *chǎn jà jawng tǔa khrûeang bin dâi thîi nǎi*
	ฉันจะจองตั๋วเครื่องบินได้ที่ไหน
	[MALE] *phǒm jà jawng tǔa khrûeang bin dâi thîi nǎi*
	ผมจะจองตั๋วเครื่องบินได้ที่ไหน
Could I have a single to Pattaya, please?	[FEMALE] *khǎw súeh tǔa thîao diao pai Pattaya khá*
	ขอซื้อตั๋วเที่ยวเดียวไปพัทยาค่ะ
	[MALE] *khǎw súeh tǔa thîao diao pai Pattaya khráp*
	ขอซื้อตั๋วเที่ยวเดียวไปพัทยาครับ

Could I have a return ticket to Hat Yai, please?	[FEMALE] *khǎw súeh tǔa pai klàp pai Hat Yai khá* ขอซื้อตั๋วไปกลับหาดใหญ่ค่ะ [MALE] *khǎw súeh tǔa pai klàp pai Hat Yai khráp* ขอซื้อตั๋วไปกลับหาดใหญ่ครับ
Could I have a first class ticket to Chiang Mai, please?	[FEMALE] *khǎw súeh tǔa chán nùeng pai Chiang Mai khá* ขอซื้อตั๋วชั้นหนึ่งไปเชียงใหม่ค่ะ [MALE] *khǎw súeh tǔa chán nùeng pai Chiang Mai khráp* ขอซื้อตั๋วชั้นหนึ่งไปเชียงใหม่ครับ
Could I have a second class ticket to Chiang Rai, please?	[FEMALE] *khǎw súeh tǔa chán sǎwng pai Chiang Rai khá* ขอซื้อตั๋วชั้นสองไปเชียงรายค่ะ [MALE] *khǎw súeh tǔa chán sǎwng pai Chiang Rai khráp* ขอซื้อตั๋วชั้นสองไปเชียงรายครับ
Could I have an economy class ticket to Hua Hin, please?	[FEMALE] *khǎw súeh tǔa chán prayàt pai Hua Hin khá* ขอซื้อตั๋วชั้นประหยัดไปหัวหินค่ะ [MALE] *khǎw súeh tǔa chán prayàt pai Hua Hin khráp* ขอซื้อตั๋วชั้นประหยัดไปหัวหินครับ
I'd like to reserve a seat.	[FEMALE] *chǎn khǎw jawng thîi nâng khá* ฉันขอจองที่นั่งค่ะ [MALE] *phǒm khǎw jawng thîi nâng khráp* ผมขอจองที่นั่งครับ
I'd like to reserve a cabin.	[FEMALE] *chǎn khǎw jawng tûu nawn khá* ฉันขอจองตู้นอนค่ะ [MALE] *phǒm khǎw jawng tûu nawn khráp* ผมขอจองตู้นอนครับ
I'd like to reserve a top berth in the sleeping car.	[FEMALE] *chǎn khǎw jawng thîi nawn chán bon nai rót nawn khá* ฉันขอจองที่นอนชั้นบนในรถนอนค่ะ [MALE] *phǒm khǎw jawng thîi nawn chán bon nai rót nawn khráp* ผมขอจองที่นอนชั้นบนในรถนอนครับ

I'd like to reserve a bottom berth in the sleeping car.	[FEMALE] *chǎn khǎw jawng thîi nawn chán lâang nai rót nawn khá* ฉันขอจองที่นอนชั้นล่างในรถนอนค่ะ
	[MALE] *phǒm khǎw jawng thîi nawn chán lâang nai rót nawn khráp* ผมขอจองที่นอนชั้นล่างในรถนอนครับ
I'd like to reserve a seat at the front.	[FEMALE] *chǎn khǎw jawng thîi nawn khâng nâa khá* ฉันขอจองที่นั่งข้างหน้าค่ะ
	[MALE] *phǒm khǎw jawng thîi nawn khâng nâa khráp* ผมขอจองที่นั่งข้างหน้าครับ
I'd like to reserve a seat at the back.	[FEMALE] *chǎn khǎw jawng thîi nawn khâng lǎng khá* ฉันขอจองที่นั่งข้างหลังค่ะ
	[MALE] *phǒm khǎw jawng thîi nawn khâng lǎng khráp* ผมขอจองที่นั่งข้างหลังครับ
There are three of us.	*rao mii sǎam khon* เรามีสามคน
We have a car.	*rao mii rót khan nùeng* เรามีรถคันหนึ่ง
We have a trailer.	*rao mii rót phûang khan nùeng* เรามีรถพ่วงคันหนึ่ง
We have two bicycles.	*rao mii jàkkrayaan sǎwng khan* เรามีจักรยานสองคัน
Do you have a travel card for 10 trips?	[FEMALE] *mii tǔa doehn thaang sìp thîao mǎi khá* มีตั๋วเดินทางสิบเที่ยวไหมคะ
	[MALE] *mii tǔa doehn thaang sìp thîao mǎi khráp* มีตั๋วเดินทางสิบเที่ยวไหมครับ
Do you have a weekly travel card?	[FEMALE] *mii tǔa doehn thaang nùeng aathít mǎi khá* มีตั๋วเดินทางหนึ่งอาทิตย์ไหมคะ
	[MALE] *mii tǔa doehn thaang nùeng aathít mǎi khráp* มีตั๋วเดินทางหนึ่งอาทิตย์ไหมครับ

Do you have a monthly
  season ticket?

[FEMALE] *mii tǔa duean mǎi khá*
มีตั๋วเดือนไหมคะ
[MALE] *mii tǔa duean mǎi khráp*
มีตั๋วเดือนไหมครับ

 Ticket types

ตั๋วชั้นหนึ่งหรือชั้นสอง *tǔa chán nùeng rǔeh chán sǎwng*	First or second class?
เที่ยวเดียวหรือไปกลับ *thîao diao rǔeh pai klàp*	Single or return?
นั่งใกล้หน้าต่างไหม *nâng klâi nâa-tàang mái*	Window seat?
ข้างหน้าหรือข้างหลัง *khâang-nâa rǔeh khâang-lǎng*	Front or back (of the train)?
ที่นั่งหรือตู้นอน *thîi-nâng rǔeh tûu-nawn*	Seat or berth/cabin?
ชั้นบน/กลางหรือล่าง *chán-bon/klaang rǔeh lâang*	Top, middle or bottom?
ชั้นประหยัดหรือชั้นหนึ่ง *chán prayàt rǔeh chán nùeng*	Economy or First Class?
เดี่ยวหรือคู่ *dìao rǔeh khûu*	Single or double?
เดินทางกี่คน *doehn-thaang kìi khon*	How many people are traveling?

 Destination

คุณจะเดินทางไปไหน *khun jà doehn-thaang pai nǎi*	Where are you traveling?
คุณจะไปเมื่อไหร่ *khun jà pai mûea-rai*	When are you leaving?
...ออกตอน... *...àwk tawn...*	(Your train/bus)...leaves at... .

คุณต้องเปลี่ยนที่… *khun tâwng plìan thîi…*	You have to change at… .
คุณต้องลงที่… *khun tâwng long thîi…*	You have to get off at… .
คุณต้องไปทาง… *khun tâwng pai thaang…*	You have to go via… .
ออกเดินทางวันที่… *àwk doehn-thaang wan-thîi…*	The outward journey is on (day/date)… .
เดินทางกลับวันที่… *doehn-thaang klàp wan-thîi…*	The return journey is on (day/date)….
คุณต้องขึ้นเครื่องก่อน… *khun tâwng khûen khrûeng kàwn…*	You have to be on board (the plane) by…(time)

 Onboard

ขอดูตั๋วค่ะ/ครับ *khǎw duu tǔa khâ/khráp*	Tickets, please.
ขอดูตั๋วจองค่ะ/ครับ *khǎw duu tǔa jawng khâ/khráp*	Your reservation, please.
ขอดูพาสปอร์ต (หนังสือเดินทาง) ค่ะ/ครับ *khǎw duu passport (nǎngsǔeh doehn-thaang) khâ/khráp*	Your passport, please.
คุณนั่งผิดที่ *khun nâng phìt thîi*	You're in the wrong seat.
คุณทำผิดแล้ว คุณอยู่ผิด… *khun tham phìt láehw/khun yùu phìt*	You have made a mistake/ You are in the wrong… .
ที่นั่งนี้จองแล้ว *thîi nâng níi jawng láehw*	This seat is reserved.
คุณต้องจ่ายเพิ่ม *khun tâwng jàai phôem*	You'll have to pay extra.
…มาช้า…นาที *…maa cháa…naathii*	The (train/bus)…has been delayed by…minutes.

6.5 Getting travel information

Key Vocabulary

ประชาสัมพันธ์
prà chaa sǎm phan
Information desk

สายบีทีเอส
sǎi BTS
Skytrain routes

ตารางรถไฟ
taa raang rótfai
Train schedule

แผนที่เส้นทางรถไฟ
phǎehn thîi sêhn thaang rótfai
Train system map

จอง **jawng**
Reservations

สายรถเมล์
sǎai rótmeh
City bus routes

ทาง **thaang**
Directions

Where's the information desk?	**tó khâw muun nák thawng thiao yùu thîi nǎi** โต๊ะข้อมูลนักท่องเที่ยวอยู่ที่ไหน
Do you have a city map with the bus routes?	[FEMALE] **mii phaehn thîi nai mueang thîi bàwk sǎi rót meh dûai mái khá** มีแผนที่ในเมืองที่บอกสายรถเมล์ด้วยไหมคะ [MALE] **mii phaehn thîi nai mueang thîi bàwk sǎi rót meh dûai mái khráp** มีแผนที่ในเมืองที่บอกสายรถเมล์ด้วยไหมครับ
Do you have a city map with the skytrain routes?	[FEMALE] **mii phaehn thîi nai mueang thîi bàwk sǎi BTS dûai mái khá** มีแผนที่ในเมืองที่บอกสายบีทีเอสด้วยไหมคะ [MALE] **mii phaehn thîi nai mueang thîi bàwk BTS dûai mái khráp** มีแผนที่ในเมืองที่บอกสายบีทีเอสด้วยไหมครับ
Do you have a schedule?	**mii taaraang wehlaa mǎi khá/khráp** มีตารางเวลาไหมคะ/ครับ
Will I get my money back?	**chàn jà dâi ngoehn khuehn mǎi** ฉันจะได้เงินคืนไหม

I'd like to change my reservation for Pattaya.	[FEMALE] *chăn khăw plìan tŭa thîi jawng pai Pattaya khá*
	ฉันขอเปลี่ยนตั๋วที่จองไปพัทยาค่ะ
	[MALE] *phŏm khăw plìan tŭa thîi jawng pai Pattaya khráp*
	ผมขอเปลี่ยนตั๋วที่จองไปพัทยาครับ
I'd like to cancel my reservation for Chiang Rai.	[FEMALE] *chăn khăw yók lôehk tŭa thîi jawng pai Chiang Rai khá*
	ฉันขอยกเลิกตั๋วที่จองไปเชียงรายค่ะ
	[MALE] *phŏm khăw yók lôehk tŭa thîi jawng pai Chiang Rai khráp*
	ผมขอยกเลิกตั๋วที่จองไปเชียงรายครับ
I'd like to change my trip to Pattaya.	[FEMALE] *chăn khăw plìan kaan doehn thaang pai Pattaya khá*
	ฉันขอเปลี่ยนการเดินทางไปพัทยาค่ะ
	[MALE] *phŏm chăn khăw plìan kaan doehn thaang pai Pattaya khráp*
	ผมขอเปลี่ยนการเดินทางไปพัทยาครับ
I'd like to cancel my trip to Chiang Rai.	[FEMALE] *chăn khăw yók lôehk kaan doehn thaang pai Chiang Rai khá*
	ฉันขอยกเลิกการเดินทางไปเชียงรายค่ะ
	[MALE] *phŏm khăw yók lôehk kaan doehn thaang pai Chiang Rai khráp*
	ผมขอยกเลิกการเดินทางไปเชียงรายครับ
I'd like to go to…	*chăn yàak pai…* ฉันอยากไป…
What is the quickest way to get there?	*thaang năi jà pai thŭeng thîi nân reo thîisùt*
	ทางไหนจะไปถึงที่นั่นเร็วที่สุด
How much is a single ticket to Hat Yai?	*tŭa thîao diao pai Hat Yai thâorài*
	ตั๋วเที่ยวเดียวไปหาดใหญ่เท่าไร
How much is a return ticket to Hat Yai?	*tŭa pai klàp pai Hat Yai thâorài*
	ตั๋วไปกลับไปหาดใหญ่เท่าไร
Do I have to pay extra?	*chăn tâwng jàai phôehm mái*
	ฉันต้องจ่ายเพิ่มไหม
Can I break my journey with this ticket?	*tŭa níi chái wáe klaang thaang dâi măi*
	ตั๋วนี้ใช้แวะกลางทางได้ไหม

How much luggage am I allowed?	*chăn ao kràpǎo pai dâi thâorài* ฉันเอากระเป๋าไปได้เท่าไร
Does the boat stop at any ports on the way?	*ruea níi jàwt taam thaang ìik mǎi* เรือนี้จอดตามทางอีกไหม
Does the train stop at Hua Hin?	*rót fai jàwt thîi HuaHin mǎi* รถไฟจอดที่หัวหินไหม
Does the bus stop at Pattaya?	*rót meh jàwt thîi Pattaya mǎi* รถเมล์จอดที่พัทยาไหม
Where do I get off?	*chăn tâwng long thîi nǎi* ฉันต้องลงที่ไหน
Is there a connection to…?	*tâwng tàw rót arai pai…mǎi* มีอะไรต่อไป…ไหม
How long do I have to wait?	*chăn tâwng raw naan thâorài* ฉันต้องรอนานเท่าไร
When does…leave?	*…àwk kìi mohng* ออกกี่โมง
What time does the first flight leave?	[FEMALE] *thîao râehk àwk kìi mohng khá* เที่ยวแรกออกกี่โมงคะ [MALE] *thîao râehk àwk kìi mohng khráp* เที่ยวแรกออกกี่โมงครับ
What time does the next bus leave?	[FEMALE] *thîao tàw pai àwk kìi mohng khá* เที่ยวต่อไปออกกี่โมงคะ [MALE] *thîao tàw pai àwk kìi mohng khráp* เที่ยวต่อไปออกกี่โมงครับ
What time does the last train leave?	[FEMALE] *thîao sùt tháai àwk kìi mohng khá* เที่ยวสุดท้ายออกกี่โมงคะ [MALE] *thîao sùt tháai àwk kìi mohng khráp* เที่ยวสุดท้ายออกกี่โมงครับ
How long does the journey take?	*chái wehlaa doehnthaang thâorài* ใช้เวลาเดินทางเท่าไร
Where does the train to Surat Thani leave from?	*rótfai pai Surat Thani àwk jàak thîi nǎi* รถไฟไปสุราษฎร์ธานีออกจากที่ไหน

6

Is this the train from Bangkok to Hua Hin?	*nîi rót fai (jàak) Krungthêp pai Hua Hin châi măi*
	นี่รถไฟ (จาก) กรุงเทพ ไปหัวหินใช่ไหม
Is this the bus from Bangkok to Chiang Mai?	*nîi rót meh (jàak) Krungthêp pai Chiang Mai châi măi*
	นี่รถเมล์ (จาก) กรุงเทพ ไปเชียงใหม่ใช่ไหม

7. Finding a Place to Stay

Accommodations in Thailand

There is a great variety of overnight accommodation in Thailand, ranging from camping in national parks, to staying in a lush beach bungalow, or in a fancy luxurious hotel. Prices vary from best budget places to the very expensive.

In Bangkok, the budget for accommodation will probably depend on the area where you stay. Banglamphu and Khao San Road have many cheap hostels and guesthouses with prices from 150 to 500 Baht. This is great for travelers on a budget and for backpackers. A slight step up for budget accommodation can be found in the Siam Square, Pratunam, Silom, Sukhumvit area, where the hub of the city's shopping district is, and along the skytrain line. In these areas you can find choices from the stylish serviced apartments to a very large range of hotels, with rooms generally ranging from 700 baht up to about 2,000 baht. An increasing number of hotels now accept reservations via their own website or online booking websites where you can obtain lower rates, such as Agoda, Booking, Hotels, Expedia, Airbnb, etc. For guesthouse or hostel accommodation, there's no necessity to make reservations. The better accommodations usually require reservations.

Upcountry resorts and towns usually have both hotel-style and bungalow/guesthouse-style accommodation. Camping is not yet popular in the lowlands, but is becoming more accepted when doing mountain trekking. It is recommended to do camping or trekking in the national park areas where park rangers are available 24 hours a day. The rangers can point out the main tourist attractions in the area for visitors to explore. Many of the national parks in Thailand have everything one needs to camp properly, including cots, mats, sleeping bags, tents, and even kerosene lamps available for rent.

I've booked a hotel online on your website.

[FEMALE] *chăn jawng phàan wébsái khâwng rohng raem*
ฉันจองผ่านเว็บไซต์ของโรงแรม
[MALE] *phŏm jawng phàan wébsái khâwng rohng raem*
ผมจองผ่านเว็บไซต์ของโรงแรม

I've booked a hotel online through Agoda.com.

[FEMALE] *chăn jawng rohng raem phàan àgohdâa*
ฉันจองโรงแรมผ่านอะโกด้า
[MALE] *phŏm jawng rohng raem phàan àgohdâa*
ผมจองโรงแรมผ่านอะโกด้า

How much is it per night? *khuehn lá thâorài* คืนละเท่าไร

How much is it per week? *aathít lá thâorài* อาทิตย์ละเท่าไร

How much is it per month? *duean lá thâorài* เดือนละเท่าไร

We'll be staying for at least three nights.

rao jà phák yàang nói săam khuehn
เราจะพักอย่างน้อยสามคืน

We'll be staying for at least one week.

rao jà phák yàang nói nùeng aathít
เราจะพักอย่างน้อยหนึ่งอาทิตย์

คุณจะพักนานเท่าไหร่
khun jà phàk naan thâorai

How long will you be staying?

ช่วยกรอกฟอร์มนี้นะคะ/ครับ
chûai kràwk fawm níi ná khá/khráp

Fill out this form, please.

ขอดูพาสปอร์ต (หนังสือเดินทาง) หน่อย
khăw duu passport (năngsŭeh doehn-thaang) nòi

Could I see your passport?

คุณต้องวางมัดจำ
khun tâwng waang mát-jam

I'll need a deposit.

คุณต้องจ่ายล่วงหน้า
khun tâwng jàai lûang nâa

You'll have to pay in advance.

We don't know yet.	*rao yang mâi sâap* เรายังไม่ทราบ
Do you allow pets (cats/dogs)?	*mii sàt líang (maeo/sunák) dâi măi khá/khráp* มีสัตว์เลี้ยง(แมว/สุนัข)ได้ไหมคะ/ครับ
What time does the gate open?	*pràtuu yài pòeht kìi mohng* ประตูใหญ่เปิดกี่โมง
What time does the door close?	*pràtuu lék pìt kìi mohng* ประตูเล็กปิดกี่โมง
Could you get me a taxi, please?	*rîak tháeksîi hâi nòi dâi măi khá/khráp* เรียกแท็กซี่ให้หน่อยได้ไหมคะ/ครับ
Is there any mail for me?	*mii jòt măai thŭeng phŏm/chăn măi khá/khráp* มีจดหมายถึงผม/ฉันไหมคะ/ครับ

 7.2 **At the hotel**

Key Vocabulary

ต่อคน *tàw khon* per person ต่อห้อง *tàw hâwng* per room

Do you have a single room available?	*mii hâwng tiang dìao wâang mái* มีห้องเตียงเดี่ยวว่างไหม
Do you have a double room available?	*mii hâwng tiang khûu wâang mái* มีห้องเตียงคู่ว่างไหม
Does that include breakfast?	*ruam aahăan cháo dûai mái* รวมอาหารเช้าด้วยไหม
Does that include lunch?	*ruam aahăan thîang dûai mái* รวมอาหารเที่ยงด้วยไหม
Does that include dinner?	*ruam aahăan yen dûai mái* รวมอาหารเย็นด้วยไหม
Could we have two adjoining rooms?	*rao khăw hâwng tìt kan dâi măi* เราขอห้องติดกันได้ไหม
Could we have a room with a toilet?	*rao khăw hâwng thîi mii hâwng náam dâi măi* เราขอห้องที่มีห้องน้ำได้ไหม

Could we have a room without a bath/a shower?	*rao khǎw hâwng thîi mâi mii hâwng àap náam dâi mǎi* เราขอห้องที่ไม่มีห้องอาบน้ำได้ไหม
Could we have a room facing the street?	*rao khǎw hâwng thîi tìt thanǒn dâi mǎi* เราขอห้องที่ติดถนนได้ไหม
Could we have a room at the back?	*rao khǎw hâwng thîi yùu khâng lǎng dâi mǎi* เราขอห้องที่อยู่ข้างหลังได้ไหม
Could we have a room with a sea view?	*rao khǎw hâwng thîi mii wiu tháleh dâi mǎi* เราขอห้องที่มีวิวทะเลได้ไหม
Could we have a room without a sea view?	*rao khǎw hâwng thîi mâi mii wiu thaleh dâi mǎi* เราขอห้องที่ไม่มีวิวทะเลได้ไหม
Is there free Wifi in the hotel?	*mii waai faai frii mǎi* มีวายฟายฟรีไหม
Is there an elevator in the hotel?	*mii bandai lûean nai rohng raehm rǔe plào* มีบันไดเลื่อนในโรงแรมหรือเปล่า
Do you have room service?	*mii room service rǔe plào* มีรูมเซอร์วิซหรือเปล่า
Could I see the room?	*khǎw duu hâwng dâi mǎi* ขอดูห้องได้ไหม
There is a toilet and shower on the same floor.	*mii hâwng náam kap hâwng àap náam yòu chán diao kan* มีห้องน้ำกับห้องอาบน้ำอยู่ชั้นเดียวกัน
There is a toilet and shower in the room.	*mii hâwng náam kap hâwng àap náam nai tua* มีห้องน้ำกับห้องอาบน้ำในตัว
I'll take this room.	*phǒm/chǎn jà ao hâwng níi* ผม/ฉันจะเอาห้องนี้
We don't like this one.	*rao mâi châwp hâwng níi* เราไม่ชอบห้องนี้
Do you have a larger room?	*khun mii hâwng yài kwàa mǎi* คุณมีห้องใหญ่กว่าไหม

Do you have a less expensive room?	*khun mii hâwng thùuk kwàa măi* คุณมีห้องถูกกว่าไหม
Could you put in a cot?	*khăw tiang dèk nòi dâi măi* ขอเตียงเด็กหน่อยได้ไหม
What time's breakfast?	*aahăan cháo kìi mohng khá/khráp* อาหารเช้ากี่โมงคะ/ครับ
Where's the dining room?	*hâwng aahăan yùu thîi năi* ห้องอาหารอยู่ที่ไหน
Can I have breakfast in my room?	*thaan aahăan cháo thîi hâwng dâi măi* ทานอาหารเช้าที่ห้องได้ไหม
Where's the emergency exit?	*thaang àwk chùk chŏehn yùu thîi năi* ทางออกฉุกเฉินอยู่ที่ไหน
Where's the fire escape?	*thaang nĭi fai yùu thîi năi* ทางหนีไฟอยู่ที่ไหน
Where can I park my car (safely)?	*jàwt rót thîi năi (plàwt phai) dâi* จอดรถที่ไหน (ปลอดภัย) ได้
The key to room…, please.	*khăw kunjaeh hâwng…khâ/khráp* ขอกุญแจห้อง…ค่ะ/ครับ
Could you put this in the safe, please?	*chûai ao sài nai séhf dâi măi khá/khráp* ช่วยเอาใส่ในเซฟได้ไหมคะ/ครับ
Could you wake me at 9 a.m. tomorrow?	[FEMALE] *chûai plùk tawn kâo mohng cháo phrûng níi dâi măi khá* ช่วยปลุกตอนเก้าโมงเช้าพรุ่งนี้ได้ไหมคะ [MALE] *chûai plùk tawn kâo mohng cháo phrûng níi dâi măi khráp* ช่วยปลุกตอนเก้าโมงเช้าพรุ่งนี้ได้ไหมครับ
Could you find a babysitter for me?	*chûai hăa khon líang dèk dâi măi khá/khráp* ช่วยหาคนเลี้ยงเด็กได้ไหมคะ/ครับ
Could I have an extra blanket?	*khăw phâa hòm phôehm dâi măi khá/khráp* ขอผ้าห่มเพิ่มได้ไหมคะ/ครับ
What days do the cleaners come in?	*khon tham khwaam sà-àat maa wan năi* คนทำความสะอาดมาวันไหน
When are the sheets changed?	*plìan phâa puu thîi nawn mûearài* เปลี่ยนผ้าปูที่นอนเมื่อไร

| When are the towels changed? | *plìan phâa chét tua mûearài*
เปลี่ยนผ้าเช็ดตัวเมื่อไร |
| When are the dish towels changed? | *plìan phâa chét jaan mûearài*
เปลี่ยนผ้าเช็ดจานเมื่อไร |

มีห้องน้ำกับห้องอาบน้ำ อยู่ชั้นเดียวกัน *mii hâwng náam kap hâwng* *àap náam yòu chán diao kan*	There is a toilet and shower on the same floor.
มีห้องน้ำกับห้องอาบน้ำ ในตัว *mii hâwng náam kap hâwng* *àap náam nai tua*	There is a toilet and shower in the room.
ทางนี้ค่ะ/ครับ *thaang níi khâ/khráp*	This way, please.
ห้องคุณอยู่ชั้น...เบอร์... *hâwng khun yùu chán...boeh...*	Your room is on the...floor, number...

7.3 Complaints

While westerners (*faràng*) might complain over both large and small matters, Thais would rather say little or nothing at all. The point is partly one of face, but it is also Thai custom to praise the good and ignore the bad. Complain if you must, but try to be more accommodating than you might otherwise be at home. Such will not only help your relationship with Thais now, but will also assist those wishing to follow after you. The Thais will respect you as a *faràng*, and you will enjoy your stay even more.

| We can't sleep because it's too noisy. | *rao nawn mâi làp phráw sǐang dang mâak*
เรานอนไม่หลับเพราะเสียงดังมาก |
| Could you turn the radio down, please? | *chûai rìi wítthayú nòi dâi mǎi khá/khráp*
ช่วยหรี่วิทยุหน่อยได้ไหมคะ/ครับ |

We're out of toilet paper.	**kradàat chamrá mòt** กระดาษชำระหมด
There aren't any...	**mâi mii...** ...ไม่มี....
There's not enough...	**mii...mâi phaw** มี...ไม่พอ
The bed linen's dirty.	**phâa puu tiang sòkkàpròk** ผ้าปูเตียงสกปรก
The room hasn't been cleaned.	**hâwng yang mâi dâi tham khwaam sà-àat** ห้องยังไม่ได้ทำความสะอาด
The kitchen is not clean.	**khrua mâi sà-àat** ครัวไม่สะอาด
The kitchen utensils are dirty.	**khrûeang khrua sòkkàpròk** เครื่องครัวสกปรก
The heater's not working.	**khrûeang tham khwaam ráwn mâi tham ngaan** เครื่องทำความร้อนไม่ทำงาน
There's no hot water.	**mâi mii náam ráwn** ไม่มีน้ำร้อน
There's no electricity.	**mâi mii fai fáa** ไม่มีไฟฟ้า
...doesn't work.	**···. mâi tham ngaan/mâi tìt** .....ไม่ทำงาน/ไม่ติด
...is broken.	**···. sĭa** ...เสีย
Could you have that seen to?	**chûai hâi khrai duu dâi măi** ช่วยให้ใครดูได้ไหม
Could I have another room?	**khăw ìik hâwng dâi măi** ขออีกห้องได้ไหม
Could I have another site?	**khăw hâwng dâan ùehn dâi măi** ขอห้องด้านอื่นได้ไหม
The bed creaks terribly.	**tiang mii sĭang yâeh mâak** เตียงมีเสียงแย่มาก
The bed sags.	**thîi nawn yúp** ที่นอนยุบ
Could I have a board under the mattress?	**khăw mái kradaan waang tâi thîi nawn dâi măi** ขอไม้กระดานวางใต้ที่นอนได้ไหม

It's too noisy.	*sĭang dang mâak pai* เสียงดังมากไป
There are a lot of insects/ bugs.	*mii málaehng yóe yáe* มีแมลงเยอะแยะ
There are a lot of cockroaches here.	*mii málaehng sàap yóe yáe thîi nîi* มีแมลงสาบเยอะแยะที่นี่
This place is full of mosquitoes.	*thîi nîi yung chum mâak* ที่นี่ยุงชุมมาก

7.4 Departure

See also 8.2 Settling the bill

I'm leaving tomorrow.	*phŏm/chăn jà àwk phrûng níi* ผม/ฉัน จะออกพรุ่งนี้
Could I pay my bill, please?	*khăw jàai ngoehn nòi khâ/khráp* ขอจ่ายเงินหน่อยค่ะ/ครับ
What time should we check out?	*khuan check out tawn kìi mohng* ควรเช็คเอาท์ตอนกี่โมง
Could I have my room key deposit back, please?	[FEMALE] *khăw ngoehn mát jam kun jae hâwng khuehn dâi măi khá* ขอเงินมัดจำกุญแจห้องคืนได้ไหมคะ [MALE] *khăw ngoehn mát jam kun jae hâwng khuehn dâi măi khráp* ขอเงินมัดจำกุญแจห้องคืนได้ไหมครับ
Could I have my key card deposit back, please?	[FEMALE] *khăw ngoehn mát jam khii káat khuehn dâi măi khá* ขอเงินมัดจำคีย์การ์ดคืนได้ไหมคะ [MALE] *khăw ngoehn mát jam khii káat khuehn dâi măi khráp* ขอเงินมัดจำคีย์การ์ดคืนได้ไหมครับ
We're in a big hurry.	*rao kamlang rîip mâak* เรากำลังรีบมาก
Could you forward my mail to this address?	*khun chûai sòng jòt măai pai thîi thîi yùu níi dâi măi khá/khráp* คุณช่วยส่งจดหมายไปที่ที่อยู่นี้ได้ ไหมคะ/ครับ

Could we leave our luggage here until we leave?	*rao fàak kràpǎo wái thîi nîi jon kwàa rao jà pai dâi mǎi khá/khráp* เราฝากกระเป๋าไว้ที่นี่จนกว่าเราจะไปได้ไหมคะ/ครับ
Thanks for your hospitality.	*khàwp khun thîi chûai khâ/khráp* ขอบคุณที่ช่วยค่ะ/ครับ

7.5 Camping/backpacking

Where's the manager?	*phûu jàt kaan yùu thîi nǎi* ผู้จัดการอยู่ที่ไหน
Are we allowed to camp here?	*rao tâng kháehm thîi nîi dâi mǎi* เราตั้งแคมป์ที่นี่ได้ไหม
There are four of us and we have two tents.	*rao mii sìi khon láe mii sǎwng tén* เรามีสี่คนและเรามีสองเต็นท์
Can we pick our own site?	*rao lûeak thîi dâi mǎi* เราเลือกที่ได้ไหม
Do you have a quiet spot for us?	*mii thîi ngîap ngîap hâi mǎi* มีที่เงียบๆ ให้ไหม
Do you have any other sites available?	*mii thîi ùehn wâang ìik mǎi* มีที่อื่นว่างอีกไหม
It's too windy here.	*thîi nîi lom raehng mâak* ที่นี่ลมแรงมาก
It's too sunny here.	*thîi nîi dàeht ráwn mâak* ที่นี่แดดร้อนมาก
It's too shady here.	*thîi nîi rôm mâak* ที่นี่ร่มมาก
It's too crowded here.	*thîi nîi aeh àt koehn pai* ที่นี่แออัดเกินไป
The ground's too hard.	*din khǎeng pai* ดินแข็งไป
The ground's too uneven.	*din khrùkhrà pai* ดินขรุขระไป
Do you have a level spot for the camper?	*mii thîi jàwt rót rîap rîap sǎmràp rót kháehm mǎi* มีที่จอดเรียบๆสำหรับรถแคมป์ไหม
Do you have a level spot for the trailer?	*mii thîi jàwt rót rîap rîap sǎmràp rót lâak mǎi* มีที่จอดเรียบๆสำหรับรถลากไหม
Do you have a level spot for the folding trailer?	*mii thîi jàwt rót rîap rîap sǎmràp rót lâak pháp mǎi* มีที่จอดเรียบๆสำหรับรถลากพับไหม

Could we have adjoining sites?	*khăw rao yùu thîi tìt kan dâi măi* ขอเราอยู่ที่ติดกันได้ไหม
Can we park the car next to the tent?	*rao jàwt rót khâang tén dâi măi* เราจอดรถข้างเต็นท์ได้ไหม
How much is it per person?	*khon lá thâorài* คนละเท่าไร
How much is it per tent?	*tén lá thâorài* เต็นท์ละเท่าไร
How much is it per trailer?	*rót lâak khan lá thâorài* รถลากคันละเท่าไร
How much is it per car?	*rót khan lá thâorài* รถคันละเท่าไร
Do you have chalets for hire?	*mii bâan lék lék hâi châo măi* มีบ้านเล็กๆ ให้เช่าไหม
Are there any hot showers?	*mii thîi àap náam ráwn măi* มีที่อาบน้ำร้อนไหม
Are there any cold showers?	*mii thîi àap náam yen măi* มีที่อาบน้ำเย็นไหม
Are there any washing machines?	*mii khrûeang sák phâa măi* มีเครื่องซักผ้าไหม
Is there a...on the site?	*mii...thîi nân măi* มี...ที่นั่นไหม
Is there somewhere for children to play?	*mii thîi hâi dèk lên măi* มีที่ให้เด็กเล่นไหม
Are there covered cooking facilities on the site?	*mii thîi tham aahăan nai rôm thîi nân măi* มีที่ทำอาหารในร่มที่นั่นไหม
Are we allowed to barbecue here?	*rao tham baa bì khiu thîi nîi dâi măi* เราทำบาร์บีคิวที่นี่ได้ไหม
Are there any power outlets?	*mii plák fai măi* มีปลั๊กไฟไหม
Is there drinking water?	*mii náam dùehm măi* มีน้ำดื่มไหม
When's the garbage collected?	*kèp khayà mûearài* เก็บขยะเมื่อไหร่ไร
Do you sell butane gas bottles?	*khun khăai káeht buuthehn kràpăwng măi* คุณขายแก๊สบิวเทนกระป๋องไหม
Do you sell propane gas bottles?	*khun khăai káeht phrohphehn kràpăwng măi* คุณขายแก๊สโปรเพนกระป๋องไหม

คุณเลือกที่ของคุณได้
khun lûeak thîi khǎwng khun dâi

You can pick your own site.

จะจัดที่ไว้ให้
jà jàt thîi wái hâi

You'll be allocated a site.

นี่หมายเลขที่ของคุณ
nîi mǎai-lêhk thîi khǎwng khun

This is your site number.

ติดให้แน่นที่รถของคุณนะคะ/ครับ
tìt hâi nâen thîi rót khǎwng khun khá/khráp

Please stick this firmly to your car.

บัตรนี้ต้องไม่ทำหาย
bàt níi tâwng mâi tham hǎai

You must not lose this card.

Camping equipment

ที่เก็บกระเป๋า
thîi kèp kràpǎo
luggage space

ที่เปิดกระป๋อง
thîi pòeht kràpǎwng
can opener

ก๊าซบูเทน
káat/káas buuthehn
butane gas

ขวด *khùat* bottle

เตาแก๊ซ
tao káeht/káehs
gas cooker

ผ้าใบปูพื้น
phâa bai puu phúehn
groundsheet

เปล *pleh*
hammock

แคมป์ไฟ *kháehm fai*
campfire

ถังแก๊ซ
thǎng káeht/káehs
gas can

ห่อน้ำแข็ง
hàw nám khǎeng
ice pack

เข็มทิศ *khěm thít*
compass

ที่เปิดจุก
thîi pòeht jùk
corkscrew

ถุงนอน *thǔng nawn*
sleeping bag

เต็นท์ *tén* tent

ไฟฉาย *fai chǎai*
flashlight

มีดพก *mîit phók*
penknife

เตาแก๊ซใช้ถัง
tao káeht/káehs chái thǎng
primus/gas stove

ที่จุดบุหรี่, ไฟแช็ค
thîi jùt burìi, fai cháek
lighter

กระเป๋าสะพาย
kràpǎo saphai
backpack

ตะเกียงเจ้าพายุ
takiang câo phaayú
storm lantern

หมุดเต็นท์ *mùt tén*
tent peg

เสาเต็นท์ *sǎo tén*
tent pole

ขวดน้ำ *khùat náam*
water bottle

8. Money Matters

8.1 **Changing money**
8.2 **Settling the bill**

In general, a number **of banks** provide money exchange services, but the rates can vary so you will have to do your own comparisons when in Thailand. Most banks are open on Monday to Friday from 8:30 a.m. to 3:30 p.m., but it is possible to find banks in the shopping mall open from 10 a.m. to 7 p.m. You can also find an exchange office (*thîi lâek ngoehn*) open in the towns and tourist centers after these hours. Proof of identity such as a passport is usually required to exchange currency.

Credit cards are widely accepted in Thailand; however, smaller stores will sometimes add three to five per cent of the bill to cover transaction costs. All major credit and debit cards such as Visa, Mastercard, JCB and American Express, are accepted in large businesses, hotels and restaurants, and upscale merchants in Thailand. However, you might find that smaller stores and cafes don't take cards, so carry some cash on you at all times.

ATM machines can be found all over Thailand from major cities to small towns. If your bank is a member of banking networks like Cirrus or PLUS, you should not have a problem using your ATM card in Thailand. If you use an ATM abroad, you can assume that you'll be charged by both your home bank and the ATM operator. It is possible that the Thai bank may charge a small fee of around 150–180 Baht for using their machine for each withdrawal.

Traveler's Checks are still widely accepted in major banks in Thailand. However, it is best to issue American Express Traveler's Checks which can be exchanged in banks and currency exchange offices in Thailand. You might encounter some difficulties with other type of Traveler's Checks.

 Changing money

Each major credit card network manages their own global cash network. VISA's network is called PLUS, while MasterCard manages two networks: Maestro and Cirrus. Therefore, you must know the symbols on the front and back of your ATM/Debit card. Match these symbols with the symbols on an ATM machine in the foreign country, and you can be sure you are getting cash the safest and cheapest way.

Key Vocabulary

เอทีเอ็ม *eh-thii-em*
ATM

เงินสด *ngoehn sòt*
ready cash

น้อยที่สุด *nòi thîi sùt*
minimum amount

มากที่สุด
mâak thîi sùt
maximum amount

บัตรเครดิต
bàt khrehdìt
credit card

อัตราแลกเปลี่ยน
àttraa lâehk plìan
exchange rate

แบงค์เล็ก
báeng lék
small change

Where can I find an ATM machine around here?	[FEMALE] *thǎeo níi mii tûu eh-thii-em thîi nǎi khá* แถวนี้มีตู้เอทีเอ็มที่ไหนคะ [MALE] *thǎeo níi mii tûu eh-thii-em thîi nǎi khráp* แถวนี้มีตู้เอทีเอ็มที่ไหนครับ
Where can I find a money changer around here?	[FEMALE] *thǎeo níi lâehk ngoehn dâi thîi nǎi khá* แถวนี้แลกเงินได้ที่ไหนคะ [MALE] *thǎeo níi lâehk ngoehn dâi thîi nǎi khráp* แถวนี้แลกเงินได้ที่ไหนครับ
Can I cash this…here?	[FEMALE] *chǎn lâehk ngoehn… thîi nîi dâi mǎi* ฉันแลกเงิน…ที่นี่ได้ไหม [MALE] *phǒm lâehk ngoehn… thîi nîi dâi mǎi* ผมแลกเงิน…ที่นี่ได้ไหม
Can I withdraw money on my credit card here?	[FEMALE] *chǎn thǎwn ngoehn jàak bàt khrehdìt thîi nîi dâi mǎi* ฉันถอนเงินจากบัตรเครดิต ที่นี่ได้ไหม [MALE] *phǒm thǎwn ngoehn jàak bàt khrehdìt thîi nîi dâi mǎi* ผมถอนเงินจากบัตรเครดิต ที่นี่ได้ไหม
I'd like to withdraw cash.	[FEMALE] *chǎn yàak jà thǎwn ngoehn sòt* ฉันอยากจะถอนเงินสด [MALE] *phǒm yàak jà thǎwn ngoehn sòt* ผมอยากจะถอนเงินสด

What's the maximum amount?	*mâak thîi sùt thâorài* มากที่สุดเท่าไร
What's the minimum amount?	*nòi thîi sùt thâorài* น้อยที่สุดเท่าไร
Can I take out less than that?	*phǒm/chǎn ao àwk nòi kwàa nán dâi mái* ผม/ฉันเอาออกน้อยกว่านั้นได้ไหม
I had some money transferred here.	*phǒm/chǎn mii ngoehn ohn maa thîi nîi* ผม/ฉันมีเงินโอนมาที่นี่
Has it arrived yet?	*maa thǔeng rǔeh yang* มาถึงหรือยัง
These are the details of my bank in the U.S.	*nîi pen raai lá-ìat khǎwng thanaakhaan phǒm/chǎn nai amehríkaa* นี่เป็นรายละเอียดของธนาคารผม/ฉันในอเมริกา
This is the number of my bank.	*nîi lêhk thîi banchii thánaakhaan* นี่เลขบัญชีธนาคาร
I'd like to change 100 pounds into Thai baht.	*khǎw lâehk ngoehn nùeng rói pawn pen ngoehn Thai* ขอแลกเงินหนึ่งร้อยปอนด์เป็นเงินไทย
I'd like to change 100 dollars into Thai baht.	*khǎw lâehk ngoehn nùeng rói dawn lâa pen ngoehn Thai* ขอแลกเงินหนึ่งร้อยดอลลาร์เป็นเงินไทย
What's the exchange rate?	*àtraa lâehk plìan thâorài* อัตราแลกเปลี่ยนเท่าไร
Could you give me some small change with it?	*khǎw báeng lék lék dûai ná khá/khráp* ขอแบงค์เล็กๆ ด้วยนะคะ/ครับ
This is not right.	*nîi mâi thùuk* นี่ไม่ถูก

At the bank

เซ็นที่นี่ *sen thîi níi*	Sign here, please.
กรอกที่นี่หน่อย *kràwk thîi níi nòi*	Fill this out, please.
ขอดูหนังสือเดินทางหน่อย *khǎw duu nǎngsǔeh* *doehn-thaang nòi*	Could I see your passport, please?
ขอดูบัตรประจำตัวหน่อย *khǎw duu bàt pràjam tua nòi*	Could I see your identity card, please?
ขอดูบัตรเครดิตหน่อย *khǎw duu bàt khrehdit nòi*	Could I see your credit card, please?

8.2 Settling the bill

Could you put it on my bill?	*sài nai bin phǒm/chǎn dâi mǎi* ใส่ในบิลผม/ฉันได้ไหม
Is the tip(s) included?	*ruam thíp rǔe yang* รวมทิปหรือยัง
Can I pay by credit card?	*jàai dûai bàt khrehdìt dâi mǎi* จ่ายด้วยบัตรเครดิตได้ไหม
Can I pay by debit card?	*jàai dûai bàt dehbìt dâi mǎi* จ่ายด้วยบัตรเดบิตได้ไหม
Can I pay with foreign currency?	*jàai ngoehn tàang prathêht dâi mǎi* จ่ายเงินต่างประเทศได้ไหม
You've given me too much change.	*khun thawn ngoehn koehn* คุณทอนเงินเกิน
You haven't given me enough change.	*khun thawn ngoehn mâi khróp* คุณทอนเงินไมครบ
Could you check this again, please?	*chék ìik thii dâi mǎi* เช็คอีกทีได้ไหม
Could I have a receipt, please?	*khǎw bai sèt dûai* ขอใบเสร็จด้วย

I don't have enough money on me.	*phŏm/chăn mâi mii ngoehn tìt tua phaw* ผม/ฉันไม่มีเงินติดตัวพอ
This is for you.	*hâi khun* ให้คุณ
Keep the change.	*mâi tâwng thawn* ไม่ต้องทอน

 At the cashier

เราไม่รับบัตรเครดิต *rao mâi ráp bàt khredìt*	We don't accept credit cards.
เราไม่รับเช็คเดินทาง *rao mâi ráp chék doehn-thaang*	We don't accept traveler's checks.
เราไม่รับเงินต่างประเทศ *rao mâi ráp ngoehn tàang phrathêht*	We don't accept foreign currency.
ขอดูบัตรเอทีเอ็ม/บัตรเดบิต ของคุณได้ไหม *khăw duu bàt eh-thii-em/bàt debìt khăwng khun dâi mái*	Can I see your ATM/debit card?
กรุณากดรหัสส่วนตัว *karunaa kòt rahàt sùan tua*	Please enter your PIN number.

9. Mail, Phones and Internet

9.1 Mail
9.2 Phones
9.3 Internet access

 Mail

Bangkok's Central Post Office (***praisanii klaang***) is open Monday to Friday from 8.30 a.m. to 8 p.m. and on weekends, and public holidays, from 8.30 a.m. to 12 p.m. Other major post offices and upcountry branches keep similar hours. There are also post offices conveniently located in shopping malls all over the country. Each post office offers a wide range of services from simply posting an item to personal banking. These include the basic services such as ordinary mail, parcel delivery services and express mail service. Financial services, for instance, International Electronic Money Order and money transfers, are also offered at the post offices. The post offices also sell postage stamps, collectible stamps, envelopes, and parcel packing materials.

The cost of sending a letter and parcel depends on its size and weight and for an airmail letter, it also depends on the zone it is being sent to. The Thai postal service is quite efficient, deliveries in the city are usually twice a day, and at least once a day upcountry, including Sundays. You will find the parcel service (air, SAL [sea-air-land] or surface) to be an effective way of mailing items home when your baggage is overweight. The usual customs declaration applies.

Key Vocabulary		
แสตมป์	แฟกซ์	ตู้รับไปรษณีย์
sa–taehm	*fáek*	*tûu ráp praisanii*
stamp(s)	fax	post office box
พัสดุ	ตั๋วเงิน	ต่างประเทศ
phátsadù	*tǔa ngoehn*	*tàang prathêht*
parcel(s)	money orders	international

Where is the nearest post office?	*praisanii klâi thîisùt yùu thîi năi* ไปรษณีย์ใกล้ที่สุดอยู่ที่ไหน
Where is the main post office?	*praisanii klaang yùu thîi năi* ไปรษณีย์กลางอยู่ที่ไหน
Where is the nearest mail box?	*tûu praisanii klâi thîisùt yùu thîi năi* ตู้ไปรษณีย์กลางอยู่ที่ไหน
Which counter should I go to remit a money order?	*sòng ngoehn thánaanát khuan pai khaotôeh năi* ส่งเงินธนาณัติควรไปเคาน์เตอร์ไหน
Which counter should I go to send a parcel?	*sòng phátsàdù khuan pai khaotôeh năi* ส่งพัสดุควรไปเคาน์เตอร์ไหน
Which counter should I go to send a postcard?	*sòng póhtsàkáat khuan pai khaotôeh năi* ส่งโปสการ์ดควรไปเคาน์เตอร์ไหน
Is there any mail for me?	*mii jòt-măai thŭeng phŏm/chăn mái* มีจดหมายถึงผม/ฉันไหม
My name's…	*phŏm/chăn chûeh…* ผม/ฉันชื่อ...

Stamps

What's the postage for a parcel to the United States?	*sòng phátsàdù pai àmehríkaa khâa sòng thâorài* ส่งพัสดุไปอเมริกาค่าส่งเท่าไร
Are there enough stamps on it?	*tìt sataehm phaw mái* ติดแสตมป์พอไหม
I'd like [quantity] [value] stamps	*phŏm/chăn yàak súeh sataehm… duang* ผม/ฉันอยากซื้อแสตมป์...ดวง
I'd like to send this by express mail.	[FEMALE] *chăn khăw sòng dùan* ฉันขอส่งด่วน [MALE] *phŏm khăw sòng dùan* ผมขอส่งด่วน
I'd like to send this by air mail.	[FEMALE] *chăn khăw sòng aemehl* ฉันขอส่งแอร์เมล์ [MALE] *phŏm khăw sòng aemehl* ผมขอส่งแอร์เมล์

I'd like to send this by registered mail.	[FEMALE] *chăn khăw sòng long thabian* ฉันขอส่งลงทะเบียน
	[MALE] *phŏm khăw sòng long thabian* ผมขอส่งลงทะเบียน
Please give me a customs declaration sticker.	*khăw bai jâehng sămràp sŭnlakaakawn nòi* ขอใบแจ้งสำหรับศุลกากรหน่อย

Photocopying, Scanning, Fax

Shall I fill out the form myself?	*phŏm/chăn tâwng kràwk khâw khwaam ehng mái* ผม/ฉันต้องกรอกข้อความเองไหม
Can I make photocopies here?	[FEMALE] *chăn thàai èhkkàsăan thîi nîi dâi mái* ฉันถ่ายเอกสารที่นี่ได้ไหม
	[MALE] *phŏm thàai èhkkàsăan thîi nîi dâi mái* ผมถ่ายเอกสารที่นี่ได้ไหม
Can I send a fax here?	[FEMALE] *chăn sòng fáek thîi nîi dâi mái* ฉันส่งแฟกซ์ที่นี่ได้ไหม
	[MALE] *phŏm sòng fáek thîi nîi dâi mái* ผมส่งแฟกซ์ที่นี่ได้ไหม
Can I scan this picture here?	[FEMALE] *khăw sà-kaen rûup phâap thîi níi dâi măi khá* ขอสแกนรูปภาพที่นี่ได้ไหมคะ
	[MALE] *khăw sà-kaen rûup phâap thîi níi dâi măi khráp* ขอสแกนรูปภาพที่นี่ได้ไหมครับ
Can I scan this photo here?	[FEMALE] *khăw sà-kaen rûup thàai thîi níi dâi măi khá* ขอสแกนรูปถ่ายที่นี่ได้ไหมคะ
	[MALE] *khăw sà-kaen rûup thàai thîi níi dâi măi khráp* ขอสแกนรูปถ่ายที่นี่ได้ไหมครับ
How much is it per page?	*nâa lá thâorài* หน้าละเท่าไร

9.2 Phones

Direct international calls can be made from blue public telephones showing the international phone symbol. The booths use a phone card—one available from many stores and smaller shops, as well as newspaper stands, and vending machines in Thai Telecom offices. Phone cards have various values ranging from 20 to 100 baht. Dial 001 to get out of Thailand, then the relevant country code (USA: 1; UK: 44; Australia: 61), city code and number. If you call using a THAICARD, dial 1544 for international access. To make a collect call from a public telephone, dial 100 to access the operator. Many operators speak English, but speak slowly, clearly and politely for the best service. A 24-hour call center is available on 02 614 1000. When phoning someone in Thailand, you will hear single long tones, but if engaged shorter, quicker tones. Thailand also supports the 900 MHz Digital GSM and 1800 MHz Digital PCN mobile phone networks for international roaming.

Key Vocabulary

โทรศัพท์
thoh rá sàp
phone call

สมุดโทรศัพท์
sàmùt thoh rá sàp
phone directory

คิดนาทีละ
khít naathii lá
charge per minute

รหัสประเทศ
ráhàt prà thêht
country code

บัตรโทรศัพท์
bàt thoh rá sàp
phone card

สมาร์ทโฟน
sà-máat fohn
smartphone

รหัสพื้นที่
ráhàt phúehn-thîi
area code

โทรศัพท์มือถือ
thoh rá sàp mueh thǔeh
mobile phone

May I use your phone, please?

khǎw chái thohrasàp nòi dâi mǎi khá/khráp
ขอใช้โทรศัพท์หน่อยได้ไหมคะ/ครับ

Could you give me the number for international directory assistance?

[FEMALE] *chǎn khǎw boehthoh sàwp thǎam mǎai lêhk tàang prà thêt*
ฉันขอเบอร์โทรสอบถามหมายเลขต่าง
ประเทศ

	[MALE] *phǒm khǎw boehthoh sàwp thǎam mǎai lêhk tàang prà thêt* ผมขอเบอร์โทรสอบถามหมายเลขต่างประเทศ
Could you give me the number of room 617?	[FEMALE] *chǎn khǎw boehthoh hâwng hòk nùeng jèt* ฉันขอเบอร์โทรห้อง 617 [MALE] *phǒm khǎw boehthoh hâwng hòk nùeng jèt* ผมขอเบอร์โทรห้อง 617
Could you give me the international access code?	[FEMALE] *chǎn khǎw ráhàt thaangklai tàang prà thêt* ฉันขอรหัสทางไกลต่างประเทศ [MALE] *phǒm khǎw ráhàt thaangklai tàang prà thêt* ผมขอรหัสทางไกลต่างประเทศ
Could you give me the country code for the United Kingdom?	[FEMALE] *chǎn khǎw ráhàt prà thêt angkrìt* ฉันขอรหัสประเทศอังกฤษ [MALE] *phǒm khǎw ráhàt prà thêt angkrìt* ผมขอรหัสประเทศอังกฤษ
Could you give the area code for Phuket?	[FEMALE] *chǎn khǎw ráhàt phúehn-thîi Phuket* ฉันขอรหัสพื้นที่ภูเก็ต [MALE] *phǒm khǎw ráhàt phúehn-thîi Phuket* ผมขอรหัสพื้นที่ภูเก็ต
Could you check if this number's correct?	*chûai chék nòi dâi mǎai wâa mǎai lêhk níi thùuk mǎi* ช่วยเช็คหน่อยได้ไหมว่าหมายเลขนี้ถูกไหม
Can I dial international direct?	*phǒm/chǎn thoh àwk tàang prathêht dâi mǎi* ผม/ฉันโทรออกต่างประเทศ ได้ไหม
Do I have to dial '0' first?	*phǒm/chǎn tâwng kòt sǔun kàwn rǔeh plào* ผม/ฉันต้องกดศูนย์ก่อนหรือเปล่า

Do I have to reserve my calls?	*phǒm/chǎn tâwng jawng rǔeh plào* ผม/ฉันต้องจองหรือเปล่า
Could you dial this number for me, please?	*chûai thoh boeh níi hâi nòi dâi mǎi khá/khráp* ช่วยโทรเบอร์นี้ให้หน่อยได้ไหมคะ/ครับ
Could you put me through to extension 111, please?	[FEMALE] *chûai tàw nùeng nùeng nùeng khá* ช่วยต่อ 111 ค่ะ [MALE] *chûai tàw nùeng nùeng nùeng khráp* ช่วยต่อ 111 ครับ
I'd like to place a collect call to the United States.	[FEMALE] *chǎn khǎw thoh pai àmehríkaa kèp ngoehn plai thaang* ฉันขอโทรไปอเมริกาเก็บเงินปลายทาง [MALE] *phǒm khǎw thoh pai àmehríkaa kèp ngoehn plai thaang* ผมขอโทรไปอเมริกาเก็บเงินปลายทาง
What's the charge per minute?	*naathii lá thâorài* นาทีละเท่าไร
Can I use my cell (mobile) phone here?	*phǒm/chǎn chái thohrasàp mueh tǔeh thîi nîi dâi mǎi khráp/khá* ผม/ฉัน ใช้โทรศัพท์มือถือที่นี้ได้ไหมครับ/คะ
Have there been any calls for me?	*mii thohrasàp thǔeng phǒm/chǎn mǎi* มีโทรศัพท์ถึงผม/ฉันไหม
Do you have a smartphone?	*khun mii sa-mart fone mǎi khráp/khá* คุณมีสมาร์ทโฟนไหมครับ/คะ
I've lost my SIM card.	*phǒm/chǎn tham sim-káad hǎi khráp/khâ* ผม/ฉัน ทำซิมการ์ดหายครับ/ค่ะ
I'd like to buy a SIM card.	*phǒm/chǎn yàak jà súeh sim-káad mài khráp/khâ* ผม/ฉัน อยากจะซื้อซิมการ์ดใหม่ ครับ/ค่ะ
The (mobile) signal is weak.	*thǎeo níi mâi mii sǎnyaan* แถวนี้ไม่มีสัญญาณ

The conversation

Hello, this is…	***sawàt dii khâ/khráp, nîi…*** สวัสดีค่ะ/ครับ นี่…
Who is this, please?	***nân khrai khá/khráp*** นั่นใครคะ/ครับ
Is this…?	***nân…châi mǎi*** นั่น...ใช่ไหม
I'm sorry, I've dialed the wrong number.	***khǎw thôht khâ/khráp thoh phìt*** ขอโทษค่ะ/ครับโทรผิด
I can't hear you.	***phǒm/chǎn mâi dâi-yin khâ/khráp*** ผม/ฉันไม่ได้ยินค่ะ/ครับ
I'd like to speak to...	***khǎw phûut kàp…nòi khâ/khráp*** ขอพูดกับ...หน่อยค่ะ/ครับ
Is there anybody who speaks English?	***mii khrai phûut phaasǎa angkrìt bâang mǎi*** มีใครพูดภาษาอังกฤษบ้างไหม
Extension…, please.	***tàw…khâ/khráp*** ต่อ...ค่ะ/ครับ

 On the phone

มีโทรศัพท์ถึงคุณ *mii thohrasàp thǔeng khun*	There's a phone call for you.
คุณต้องกดศูนย์ก่อน *khun tâwng kòt sǔun kàwn*	You have to dial '0' first.
สักครู่ค่ะ/ครับ *sàk khrûu khâ/khráp*	One moment, please.
ไม่มีคนรับ *mâi mii khon ráp*	There's no answer.
สายไม่ว่าง *sǎai mâi wâang*	The line's busy.
จะถือสายรอไหม *jà thǔu sǎai raw mái*	Do you want to hold?
ต่อให้แล้ว *taw hâi láehw*	Connecting you.

Mail, Phones and Internet

9

127

คุณโทรผิด *khun thoh phìt*	You've got the wrong number.
ตอนนี้เขาไม่อยู่ *tawn níi kháo mâi yùu*	He's/she's not here right now.
เขาจะกลับตอน… *kháo jà klàp tawn…*	He'll/she'll be back (time/time of day).
นี่เป็นเครื่องรับฝากข้อความของ… *nîi pen khrûeng ráp fàak khâw khwaam khǎwng…*	This is the answering machine of…

Could you ask him/her to call me back?	*chûai bàwk kháo hâi thoh klàp dâi mái khá/khráp* ช่วยบอกเขาให้โทรกลับได้ไหมคะ/ครับ
My name's…	*phǒm/chǎn chûeh…* ผม/ฉันชื่อ
My number's…	*boeh phǒm/chǎn…* เบอร์ผม/ฉัน…
Could you tell him/her I called?	*chûai bàwk kháo wâa phǒm/chǎn thoh maa* ช่วยบอกเขาว่าผม/ฉันโทร.มา
I'll call him/her back tomorrow.	*phǒm/chǎn jà thoh maa mài phrûng níi* ผม/ดิฉันจะโทร.มาใหม่พรุ่งนี้

9.3 Internet access

Key Vocabulary

อินเทอร์เน็ต *in-toeh-net* Internet

ร้านอินเทอร์เน็ต *ráan in-toeh-net* cybercafe

แทบเล็ท พีซี *tháeb-lét phii sii* tablet PC

ซอฟท์แวร์ *sawf-waeh* software

อีเมล์ *ii-mei* email

เอสเอ็มเอส *SMS* texting/sms

แล็ปท็อป *laep-tawp* laptop

รหัส *rahàt* password

เว็บไซต์ *web-sai* website

128

เบราว์เซอร์
brao-sôeh
browser

เครื่องมือช่วยค้นหา
khrûeng-mueh chûai khón hǎa
search engine

แอป/แอปพลิเคชั่น
áep/áep-phli-kheh-chân
app/application

ตัวปรับต่อ
tua pràp tàw
adaptor

แฮ็กเกอร์ *hác-ker*
hacker

ชื่อผู้ใช้
chûe phûu chái
username

ดอท *dàwt*
dot

เครื่องชาร์ท
khrûeng cháat
charger

หน้าแรก *nâa râek*
log-in-page

ไวรัส *wai-rút*
virus

วายฟาย *waai-faai*
Wifi

อีบุ๊ค *ii-búk*
e-book

บล็อก *bláwk*
blog

เฟสบุ๊ค *Fehs-búk*
Facebook

ทวิทเตอร์
tha-wít-toeh
Twitter

ทวีท *tha-wîit*
tweet

Did you receive my (e)mail?	[MALE] *khun dâi ráp jòtmǎai khǎwng phǒm rǔeh plào khráp* คุณได้รับจดหมายของผมหรือเปล่าครับ
I'd like to send an email.	[MALE] *phǒm yàak jà sòng ii-mei khráp/khá* ผมอยากจะส่งอีเมล์ครับ [FEMALE] *chǎn yàak jà sòng ii-mei khá* ฉันอยากจะส่งอีเมล์ค่ะ
Is there a cybercafé (Internet café) around here?	*thǎeo níi mii ráan in-toeh-net rǔeh plào* แถวนี้มีร้านอินเทอร์เน็ตหรือเปล่า
Is there Wifi around here?	*thǎeo níi mii waai-faai rǔeh plào* แถวนี้มีวายฟายหรือเปล่า
Do you have a Wifi connection here?	*thîi nîi tàw waai-faai dâi rǔeh plào* ที่นี่ต่อวายฟายได้หรือเปล่า
Do you do Facebook?	*khun lên Fehs-búk mǎi* คุณเล่นเฟสบุ๊คไหม
Can we become friends on Facebook?	*rao pen phûen kan nai Fehs-búk dâi mǎi* เราเป็นเพื่อนกันในเฟสบุ๊คได้ไหม

What's your Facebook ID?	*Fehs-búk khun chûeh arai* เฟสบุ๊คคุณชื่ออะไร
Can you upload your photos to Facebook?	*khun sài rûup khǎwng khun thîi Fehs-búk dâi mái* คุณใส่รูปของคุณที่เฟสบุ๊คได้ไหม
Do you use Twitter?	*khun dâi chái tha-wít-toeh rǔeh plào* คุณได้ใช้ทวิทเตอร์หรือเปล่า
Do you tweet?	*khun lên tha-wîit mǎi* คุณเล่นทวีทไหม
What is your Twitter handle?	*khun chai chûeh tha-wít-toeh aria* คุณใช้ชื่อทวิตเตอร์อะไร
What is your blog address?	*thîi yùu bláwk khǎwng khun chûeh arai* ที่อยู่บล็อกของคุณชื่ออะไร
My smartphone/iPhone is not working.	*sa-mart fone/ai-fone khǎwng phǒm/ chǎn sǐa* สมาร์ทโฟน/ไอโฟนของผม/ฉัน เสีย
Please text me/send me an SMS.	*karunaa sòng khâw-khwaam/sòng es-em-es hǎa phǒm/chǎn* กรุณาส่งข้อความ/ส่งเอสเอ็มเอสหาผม /ฉัน
I'll send you a text message.	*phǒm/chǎn jà sòng khâw-khwaam hǎa khun* ผม/ฉัน จะส่งข้อความหาคุณ
The phone connection is not good, it keeps dropping out.	*thorasàp sanyaan mâi dii sǐang khàat-khàat hǎi-hǎi* โทรศัพท์สัญญาณไม่ดี เสียงขาดๆ หายๆ
I can't get on the Internet (Net).	*phǒm/chǎn tàw in-toeh-net mâi dâi* ผม/ฉันต่ออินเทอร์เน็ตไม่ได้
You can find it on Google.	*khun sǎamâat khón-hǎa nai kuu-koel* คุณสามารถค้นหาในกูเกิล
Do I need a password to get onto the Internet?	*phǒm/chǎn tâwng mii ráhàt mái thǔeng jà tàw in-toeh-net dâi* ผม/ฉันต้องมีรหัสไหมถึงจะ ต่ออินเทอร์เน็ตได้

Do you have an Instagram (account)?	*khun mii In-sà-taa-graem mái?* คุณมีอินสตาแกรมไหม
Do you have a LINE (account)?	*khun mii Laai mái?* คุณมีไลน์ไหม
Can I have your Instagram user ID?	*khǎw chûeh In-sà-taa-graem khǎwng khun dâi-mái?* ขอชื่ออินสตาแกรมของคุณได้ไหม
Can I have your Line user ID?	*khǎw ai-dii Laai khǎwng khun dâi-mái?* ขอไอดีไลน์ของคุณได้ไหม
Could you please add me on Instagram?	[FEMALE] *chûai áet chǎn nai In-sà-taa-graem dâi-mái* ช่วยแอดฉันในอินสตาแกรมได้ไหม [MALE] *chûai áet phǒm nai In-sà-taa-graem dâi-mái* ช่วยแอดผมในอินสตาแกรมได้ไหม
Could you please add. me on Line?	[FEMALE] *chûai áet chǎn nai Laai dâi-mái* ช่วยแอดฉันในไลน์ได้ไหม [MALE] *chûai áet phǒm nai Laai dâi-mái* ช่วยแอดผมในไลน์ได้ไหม

10. Shopping

Shopping is one of the greatest experiences in Thailand. No matter which destinations you visit you will find exciting shopping, whether in the big cities, in the small towns, on islands, or in the local communities. Throughout Thailand, particularly in Bangkok, you can find night markets, classy boutiques, little shops packed with antiques and handicrafts, and mega shopping malls with every brand name. Most malls open daily from 10:00 a.m. to 10:00 p.m. It is safe to say night markets are always open until midnight, and local fresh markets open around 4:00 to 9:00 a.m. You should not miss out on such shopping experiences in Thailand.

You can bargain for better prices when you shop in Thailand, as bargaining is part of the culture. It is acceptable to bargain in markets or small stores, but not acceptable or practiced in convenience stores or at upscale shopping malls. If you want to bargain, the general rule is to ask for a price 20% lower than the initially stated price.

Key Vocabulary

ร้านตัดผม *ráan tàt phǒm*
barber

ร้านขายรองเท้า
ráan khǎai ráwng-tháo
shoe/footwear shop

ร้านตัดรองเท้า
ráan tàt ráwng-tháo
shoe repair shop

ร้านเครื่องเขียน
ráan khrûeng khǐan
stationery shop

ร้านซักรีด *ráan sák rîit*
laundry shop

เครื่องซักผ้าหยอดเหรียญ
khrûeang sák phâa yàwt rǐan
coin-operated laundry machine

ร้านซักแห้ง *ráan sák hâeng*
dry cleaning shop

ร้านซ่อมมอเตอร์ไซค์และจักรยาน
ráan sâwm mo-toeh-sai láe jàkkràyaan
motorbike and bicycle repairs

ร้านขายไวน์ *ráan khǎai wai*
wine/bottle shop

ร้านขายของชำ
ráan khǎai khǎwng cham
grocery shop

ร้านขายยา *ráan khǎai yaa*
pharmacy, chemist

ร้านขายเนื้อ
ráan khǎai núea
butcher's shop

ร้านหนังสือ *ráan nǎngsǔeh*
bookshop

ร้านก๋วยเตี๋ยว
ráan kǔai tǐao
noodle shop

ร้านขายดอกไม้
ráan khǎai dàwk-mái
florist

ร้านเบเกอรี่ *ráan bakery*
bakery

ร้านขายผัก
ráan khǎai phàk
greengrocer

ร้านขายไอศครีม
ráan khǎai ais-khriim
ice cream shop

ร้านขายอัญมณี
ráan khǎai an-yamanii
jeweler

ห้างสรรพสินค้า
hâng sapha-sǐn-kháa
department store

ร้านเสริมสวย
ráan sǒem sǔai
beauty salon

ร้านขายผ้า
ráan khǎai phâa
haberdashery

ร้านขายของมือสอง
ráan khǎai khǎwng mueh sǎwng
second-hand shop

ร้านขายเสื้อผ้า *ráan khǎai sûea-phâa*
clothing shop

ร้านขายเครื่องอุปกรณ์แคมป์
ráan khǎai khrûeng ùp-pakawn khaemping
camping supplies shop

ร้านขายเครื่องใช้ในบ้าน
ráan khǎai khrûeng chai nai bâan
household goods store

ร้านผลไม้และผัก *ráan phǒnlamái láe phàk*
fruit and vegetable shop

ร้านขายขนมหวาน *ráan khǎai khanǒm wǎan*
confectioner's shop

ร้านเค้ก *ráan khék*
cake shop

ร้านขายสมุนไพร *ráan khǎai samǔn-phrai*
herbalist's shop/herbalist

ที่ขายหนังสือพิมพ์
thîi khǎai nǎngsǔeh-phim
newsstand

ร้านขายกล้องถ่ายรูป
ráan khǎai klâwng thàai rûup
camera shop

ร้านขายเครื่องกีฬา
ráan khǎai khrûeng kiilaa
sporting goods store

ร้านขายเครื่องนอน *ráan khǎai khrûeng nawn*
household linen shop

ร้านเพลง
ráan phleng (sii dii, dii wii dii, em-phi-sǎam)
music shop (CDs, DVDs, MP3s, etc)

ร้านขายเครื่องไฟฟ้า
ráan khǎai khrûeng fai-fáa
household appliances (white goods)

ร้านขายต้นไม้ *ráan khǎai tôn-mái*
nursery (plants)

ร้านหนังสือการ์ตูน
ráan nǎngsǔeh kaa-tun
comic/animé shop

ตลาด *talàat*
market

ร้านนาฬิกา *ráan naalikaa*
watches and clocks

ร้านขายทอง
ráan khǎai thawng
goldsmith/gold shop

ร้านขายแว่นตา
ráan khǎai wâen-taa
optician/optometrist

ร้านนวด *ráan nûat*
massage shop

สถานอาบอบนวด
àab àwp nûat
massage parlor

ร้านขายปลา *ráan khǎai plaa*
fishmonger

ร้านขายไก่ *ráan khǎai kài*
poultry shop

ซูเปอร์มาร์เก็ต
su-poeh-maa-kèt
supermarket

ร้านเครื่องไฟฟ้า
ráan khrûeng fai-fáa
electronics shop

ร้านขายน้ำหอม
ráan khǎai náam-hǎwm
perfumery

ร้านขายเครื่องดนตรี
ráan khǎai khrûeng don-trii
musical instrument shop

ร้านขายเครื่องหนัง
ráan khǎai khrûeng nǎng
leather goods shop

ร้านขายของเล่นเด็ก
ráan khǎai khǎwng lên dèk
toy shop

ร้านขายเครื่องดื่ม
ráan khǎai khrûeng-dùehm
shop selling refreshments

ร้านรับซักผ้า/ซักแห้ง
ráan ráp sák phâa/sák hâeng
laundry/dry cleaners

ร้านคอมพิวเตอร์ *ráan khawm-phiu-toeh*
computer (hardware) shop

ร้านขายซอฟแวร์คอมพิวเตอร์
ráan khǎai sawf-wae khawm-phiu-toeh
computer (software) shop

ร้านเฟอร์นิเจอร์ *ráan foe-ni-coe (fer-ni-jer)*
furniture shop

ร้านขายของขวัญ
ráan khǎai khǎwng khwǎn
gift shop

ร้านขายของที่ระลึก
ráan khǎai khǎwng thîi ra-luk
souvenir shop

คลีนิค *khliník*
clinic (in shopping mall)

ร้านเกมส์ *ráan kem*
game store

ร้านหนังสือมือสอง
ráan nǎngsǔeh mueh sǎwng
used bookstore

10.1 At a store

Where can I get…?	*phǒm/chǎn súeh…dâi thîi nǎi* ผม/ฉันซื้อ…ได้ที่ไหน
When does this shop open?	*ráan níi pòeht kìi mohng* ร้านนี้เปิดกี่โมง
Could you tell me where the…department is?	*sâap mái khráp/khá wâa phanàehk…yùu thîi nǎi* ทราบไหมครับ/คะว่าแผนก…อยู่ที่ไหน
Could you help me, please?	*chuâi nòi dâi mǎi khráp/khá* ช่วยหน่อยได้ไหมครับ/คะ
Do you sell English newspapers?	*khun mii nangsǔeh phim angkrìt khǎai mái* คุณมีหนังสือพิมพ์จากอังกฤษขายไหม
Do you sell American newspapers?	*khun mii nangsǔeh phim amehrikaa khǎai mái* คุณมีหนังสือพิมพ์จากอเมริกาขายไหม
I'm looking for…	*phǒm/chǎn kamlang hǎa…* ผม/ฉันกำลังหา…

มีอะไรให้ช่วยไหม *mii àrai hâi chûai mái*	How can I help you?

No, I'd like…	*mâi mii khráp/khâ, phǒm/chǎn yàak dâi…* ไม่มีครับ/ค่ะ ผม/ฉันอยากได้…
I'm just looking, if that's all right.	*phǒm/chǎn duu chǒei chǒei ná khráp/khá* ผม/ฉันดูเฉยๆนะครับ/คะ
I don't need a bag.	*phǒm/chǎn mâi tâwng kaan thǔng phlas-tìk khráp/khâ* ผม/ฉันไม่ต้องการถุงพลาสติกครับ/ค่ะ
Can I have a receipt?	*khǎw bai set dûai khráp/khâ* ขอใบเสร็จด้วยครับ/ค่ะ

(ต้องการ) อะไรอีกไหมครับ/คะ   (Would you like) anything else?
(tâwng-kaan) arai ìik mái khráp/khá

Yes, I'd also like…	*tâwngkaan…dûai* ต้องการ…ด้วย
No, thank you. That's all.	*mâi khráp/khâ, khàwp khuṇ; thâo nán la* ไม่ครับ/ค่ะ ขอบคุณ เท่านั้นละ
Could you show me…?	*khǎw duu…nòi khráp/khâ* ขอดู…หน่อยครับ/ค่ะ
I'd prefer…	*phǒm/chǎn châwp…mâak kwàa* ผม/ฉันชอบ…มากกว่า
This is not what I'm looking for.	*nîi mâi châi thîi phǒm/chǎn tâwngkaan* นี่ไม่ใช่ที่ผม/ฉันต้องการ
Thank you, I'll keep looking.	*khàwp khun khráp/khâ, phǒm/chǎn jà hǎa tàw pai* ขอบคุณครับ/ค่ะ ผม/ฉันจะหาต่อไป
Do you have something less expensive?	*khun mii thîi thùuk kwàa níi mǎi* คุณมีที่ถูกกว่านี้ไหม
Do you have something smaller?	*khun mii thîi lék kwàa níi mǎi* คุณมีที่เล็กกว่านี้ไหม
Do you have something larger?	*khun mii thîi yài kwàa níi mǎi* คุณเมีที่ใหญ่กว่านี้ไหม
I'll take this one.	*phǒm/chǎn jà ao an níi* ผม/ฉันจะเอาอันนี้
Does it come with instructions?	*mii wíthii chái yùu dûai rǔeh plào* มีวิธีใช้อยู่ด้วยหรือเปล่า
It's too expensive.	*phaehng pai* แพงไป
I'll give you…	*phǒm/chǎn hâi…* ผม/ฉันให้…
Could you keep this for me?	*kèp níi wái hâi phǒm/chǎn dâi mǎi* เก็บนี้ไว้ให้ผม/ฉันได้ไหม
I'll come back for it later.	*phǒm/chǎn jà klàp maa ao thii lǎng* ผม/ฉันจะกลับมาเอาทีหลัง

| Could you gift wrap it, please? | *chûai hàw khǎwng khwǎn hâi nòi dâi mǎi* ช่วยห่อของขวัญให้หน่อยได้ไหม |
| Do you have a bag for me, please? | *khun mii thǔng mǎi* คุณมีถุงไหม |

🤝 With the shop assistant

ขอโทษนะครับ/คะ เราไม่มี *khǎw thôht ná khráp/khá rao mâi mii*	I'm sorry, we don't have that.
ขอโทษนะครับ/คะ ขายหมดแล้ว *khǎw thôht ná khráp/khá khǎai mòt láehw*	I'm sorry, we're sold out.
ขอโทษนะครับ/คะ จะไม่มีของจนถึง… *khǎw thôht ná khráp/khá jà mâimii khǎwng jon thǎeng…*	I'm sorry, it won't come back in until… .
กรุณาจ่ายที่เคาน์เตอร์ *kàrúnaa jàai thîi khao-toeh*	Please pay at the cash register.

10.2 At a food market

I'd like a hundred grams of…, please.	*phǒm/chǎn ao nùeng khìit* ผม/ฉัน เอาหนึ่งขีด
I'd like half a kilo of… .	[FEMALE] *chǎn ao…khrûeng kiloh khâ* ฉันเอา……ครึ่งกิโลค่ะ [MALE] *phǒm ao…khrûeng kiloh khráp* ผมเอา……ครึ่งกิโลครับ
I'd like five hundred grams of… .	[FEMALE] *chǎn ao… hâa rói kram khâ* ฉันเอา……ห้าร้อยกรัมค่ะ [MALE] *phǒm ao… hâa rói kram khráp* ผมเอา……ห้าร้อยกรัมครับ
I'd like a kilo of… .	*phǒm/chǎn ao…nùeng kiloh khráp/khâ* ผม/ฉันเอา…หนึ่งกิโลครับ/ค่ะ

Could you slice it up for me please?	[FEMALE] *chûai hàn hâi nòi khâ* ช่วยหั่นให้หน่อยค่ะ [MALE] *chûai hàn hâi nòi khráp* ช่วยหั่นให้หน่อยครับ
Could you cut it up for me please?	[FEMALE] *chûai tàt hâi nòi khâ* ช่วยตัดให้หน่อยค่ะ [MALE] *chûai tàt hâi nòi khráp* ช่วยตัดให้หน่อยครับ
Could you grate it for me please?	[FEMALE] *chûai soi hâi nòi khâ* ช่วยซอยให้หน่อยค่ะ [MALE] *chûai soi hâi nòi khráp* ช่วยซอยให้หน่อยครับ
Can I order it?	*sàng maa dâi măi khráp/khá* สั่งมาได้ไหมครับ/คะ
I'll pick it up tomorrow at...	*phŏm/chăn jà pai ao phrûng níi thîi...* ผม/ฉันจะไปเอาพรุ่งนี้ที่...
Can you eat this?	*kin an níi dâi măi* กินอันนี้ได้ไหม
Can you drink this?	*dùehm an níi dâi măi* ดื่มอันนี้ได้ไหม
What's in it?	*arai yùu khâang nai* อะไรอยู่ข้างใน

10.3 Clothing and shoes

Key Vocabulary

ซักมือ *sák mueh* Hand wash	ซักแห้ง *sák hâehng* Dry clean	อย่ารีด *yàa rîit* Do not iron
ซักเครื่องได้ *sák khrûeng dâi* Machine washable	อย่าปั่นแห้ง *yàa pàn hâehng* Do not spin dry	วางราบ *waang râap* Lay flat

---

I saw something in the window.	*phŏm/chăn hĕn arai baang yàang nai nâatàang* ผม/ฉันเห็นอะไรบางอย่างในหน้าต่าง
Shall I point it out?	*jà hâi chíi hâi duu măi* จะให้ชี้ให้ดูไหม
I'd like something to go with this.	*yàak dâi àrai thîi khâo kàp níi* อยากได้อะไรที่เข้ากับนี่

Do you have shoes to match this?	*mii rawng tháo thîi khâo chút kàp níi mǎi* มีรองเท้าที่เข้าชุดกับนี้ไหม
I'm a size 2 in the U.S.	[FEMALE] *chǎn sài sái sǎwng khǎwng amehríkaa* ฉันใส่ไซส์สองของอเมริกา [MALE] *phǒm sài sái sǎwng khǎwng amehríkaa* ผมใส่ไซส์สองของอเมริกา
I'm a size 6 in Australia.	[FEMALE] *chǎn sài sái hòk khǎwng áwstrehlia* ฉันใส่ไซส์หกของออสเตรเลีย [MALE] *phǒm sài sái hòk khǎwng áwstrehlia* ผมใส่ไซส์หกของออสเตรเลีย
Can I try this on?	*khǎw lawng dâi mǎi* ขอลองได้ไหม
Where's the fitting room?	*hâwng lawng sûea yùu thîi nǎi* ห้องลองเสื้ออยู่ที่ไหน
It doesn't suit me.	*mâi màw kàp phǒm/chǎn* ไม่เหมาะกับผม/ฉัน
This is the right size.	*khanàat níi thùuk tâwng* ขนาดนี้ถูกต้อง
It doesn't look good on me.	*phǒm/chǎn sài láeo duu mâi dii* ผม/ฉันใส่แล้วดูไม่ดี
Do you have this in a medium size?	*khun mii bàeb níi khanàat klaang mǎi* คุณมีแบบนี้ขนาดกลางไหม
Do you have this in blue?	*khun mii bàeb níi sǐi fáa mǎi* คุณมีแบบนี้สีฟ้าไหม
The heel's too high.	*sôn sǔung pai* ส้นสูงไป
The heel's too low.	*sôn tîa pai* ส้นเตี้ยไป
Is this real leather/ genuine hide?	*nîi nǎng tháeh rǔeh plào* นี่หนังแท้หรือเปล่า
I'm looking for a dress for a four-year-old child.	[FEMALE] *chǎn kamlang hǎa chút sǎmràp dèk sìi khùap* ฉันกำลังหาชุดสำหรับเด็กสี่ขวบ

	[MALE] *phǒm kamlang hǎa chút sǎmràp dèk sìi khùap* ผมกำลังหาชุดสำหรับเด็กสี่ขวบ
I'd like a silk shirt.	[FEMALE] *chǎn yàak dâi sûea phâa mǎi* ฉันอยากได้เสื้อผ้าไหม [MALE] *phǒm yàak dâi sûea phâa mǎi* ผมอยากได้เสื้อผ้าไหม
I'd like a cotton blouse.	[FEMALE] *chǎn yàak dâi sûea phâa fâai* ฉันอยากได้เสื้อผ้าฝ้าย [MALE] *phǒm yàak dâi sûea phâa fâai* ผมอยากได้เสื้อผ้าฝ้าย
I'd like a pair of woolen pants.	[FEMALE] *chǎn yàak dâi kaangkehng phâa khǒn sàt* ฉันอยากได้กางเกงผ้าขนสัตว์ [MALE] *phǒm yàak dâi kaangkehng phâa khǒn sàt* ผมอยากได้กางเกงผ้าขนสัตว์
I'd like a linen dress.	[FEMALE] *chǎn yàak dâi chút phâa línin* ฉันอยากได้ชุดผ้าลินิน [MALE] *phǒm yàak dâi chút phâa línin* ผมอยากได้ชุดผ้าลินิน
What temperature can I wash it at?	*khuan sák nai unhàphuum thâorài* ควรซักในอุณหภูมิเท่าไร
Will it shrink in the wash?	*sák láehw jà hòt mǎi* ซักแล้วจะหดไหม

At the shoe repair shop/stall

Could you mend these shoes?	*chûai sâwm rawng tháo níi dâi mǎi* ช่วยซ่อมรองเท้านี้ได้ไหม
Could you resole these shoes?	*chûai sài phúehn rawng tháo mài dâi mǎi* ช่วยใส่พื้นรองเท้าได้ไหม
Could you reheel these shoes?	*chûai sài sôn rawng tháo mài dâi mǎi* ช่วยใส่ส้นรองเท้าได้ไหม
When will they be ready?	*jà sèt mûearài* จะเสร็จเมื่อไร

I'd like a can of shoe polish, please.

[FEMALE] *chăn khăw yaa khàt rawng tháo nùeng krapăwng khâ*
ฉันขอยาขัดรองเท้าหนึ่งกระป๋องค่ะ

[MALE] *phŏm khăw yaa khàt rawng tháo nùeng krapăwng khráp*
ผมขอยาขัดรองเท้าหนึ่งกระป๋องครับ

I'd like a pair of shoelaces.

[FEMALE] *chăn khăw chûeak phùuk rawng tháo nùeng khûu khâ*
ฉันขอเชือกผูกรองเท้าหนึ่งคู่ค่ะ

[MALE] *phŏm khăw chûeak phùuk rawng tháo nùeng khûu khráp*

ผมขอเชือกผูกรองเท้าหนึ่งคู่ครับ

10.4 Cameras

Key Vocabulary

เอสแอลอาร์
es-ael-aa
single-lens-reflex camera (SLR)

วิดีโอ *widii-oh*
video

พิกเซล *piksehl*
pixel

กล้องดิจิตอล
klâwng dijitôn
digital camera

ออพติคอล ซูม
off-tik-khol suum
optical zoom

เอสดีการ์ด *es dii káat*
SD card

กล้องวงจรปิด
klâwng wongjawn pìt
face recognition camera

การตัดต่อ-รูปภาพ
kaan tàt-tàw rûup-phâap
photo-editing

Problems

Should I replace the batteries?

khuan plìan bàeht-toeh-rîi măi
ควรเปลี่ยนแบตเตอรี่ไหม

Could you have a look at my camera, please?

chûai duu klâwng hâi nòi dâi măi
ช่วยดูกล้องให้หน่อยได้ไหม

It's not working.

man mâi tham ngaan มันไม่ทำงาน

The…is broken.

sĭa … เสีย…

The flash isn't working.

fláet mâi tham ngaan แฟลชไม่ทำงาน

Processing and prints

I'd like to have these pictures printed, please.

phŏm/chăn yàak àt rûup nòi
ผม/ฉันอยากอัดรูปหน่อย

I'd like three prints from each negative.	[FEMALE] *chăn yàak dâi yàang lá săam chút* ฉันอยากได้อย่างละสามชุด
	[MALE] *phŏm yàak dâi yàang lá săam chút* ผมอยากได้อย่างละสามชุด
glossy	*man* มัน
matte	*dâan* ด้าน
6 x 9	*khà-nàat hòk khuun kâo* ขนาดหกคูณเก้า
I'd like to order reprints of these photos.	*phŏm/chăn yàak sàng àt rûup phûak níi ìik* ผม/ฉันอยากสั่งอัดรูปพวกนี้อีก
I'd like to have this photo enlarged.	*phŏm/chăn yàak khayăi rûup níi* ผม/ฉันอยากขยายรูปนี้
How much for printing?	*khâa àt thâorài* ค่าอัดเท่าไร
How much are the reprints?	*khâa àt phôehm thâorài* ค่าอัดเพิ่มเท่าไร
How much is it for enlargement?	*khâa khayăi rûup thâorài* ค่าขยายรูปเท่าไร
When will they be ready?	*jà sèt mûearài* จะเสร็จเมื่อไร
Can you process onto a CD?	*khun àt rûup khâo sii dii dâi măi* คุณอัดรูปเข้าซีดีได้ไหม
How much is it to process onto a CD?	*khâa àt rûup khâo sii dii thâorài* ค่าอัดรูปเข้าซีดีเท่าไร

10.5 At the hairdresser

Key Vocabulary

ตัดผม *tàt phŏm*
haircut

ทำสีผม *tham sĭi phŏm*
coloring

ดัดผม *dàt phŏm*
perm

สระผม *sà phŏm*
shampoo

ผมมัน *phŏm man*
oily scalp

รังแค *rangkhaeh*
dandruff

สเปรย์ *sà preh*
hairspray

โกนหนวดแบบใส่ครีม *kohn nùat bàehp sài khriim*
wet shave

Talking to the hairdresser

จะให้ตัดอย่างไร *jà hâi tàt yang-ngai*	How do you want it cut?
คุณอยากได้ทรงไหน *khun yàak dâi song nǎi*	What style did you have in mind?
คุณชอบสีไหน *khun châwp sǐi nǎi*	What color would you like?
อุณหภูมิพอดีไหม *un-haphuum phaw-dii mǎi*	Is the temperature all right for you?
คุณอยากอ่านอะไรไหม *khun yàak àan àrai mǎi*	Would you like something to read?
คุณอยากดื่มอะไรไหม *khun yàak dùehm àrai*	Would you like a drink?
คุณอยากได้อย่างนี้หรือ *khun yàak dâi yàang níi rǔeh*	Is this what you had in mind?

Do I have to make an appointment?	*phǒm/chǎn tâwng nát mǎi* ผม/ฉันต้องนัดไหม
Can I come in right now?	*phǒm/chǎn maa tawn níi dâi mǎi* ผม/ฉันมาตอนนี้ได้ไหม
How long will I have to wait?	*phǒm/chǎn tâwng raw naan thâorài* ผม/ฉันต้องรอนานเท่าไร
I'd like a shampoo.	[FEMALE] *chǎn yàak sà phǒm* ฉันอยากสระผม [MALE] *phǒm yàak sà phǒm* ผมอยากสระผม
I'd like a haircut.	[FEMALE] *chǎn yàak tàt phǒm* ฉันอยากตัดผม [MALE] *phǒm yàak tàt phǒm* ผมอยากตัดผม
I'd like a shampoo for oily hair, please.	[FEMALE] *chǎn yàak dâi chaehmphuu sǎmràp phǒm man khâ* ฉันอยากได้แชมพูสำหรับผมมันค่ะ

	[MALE] *phǒm yàak dâi chaehmphuu sǎmràp phǒm man khráp* ผมอยากได้แชมพูสำหรับผมมันครับ
I'd like a shampoo for dry hair, please.	[FEMALE] *chǎn yàak dâi chaehmphuu sǎmràp phǒm hâehng khâ* ฉันอยากได้แชมพูสำหรับผมแห้งค่ะ [MALE] *phǒm yàak dâi chaehmphuu sǎmràp phǒm hâehng khráp* ผมอยากได้แชมพูสำหรับผมแห้งรับ
I'd like an anti-dandruff shampoo.	*phǒm/chǎn yàak dâi chaehmphuu kan rangkhaeh* ผม/ฉันอยากได้แชมพูกันรังแค
I'd like a color-rinse shampoo, please.	*phǒm/chǎn yàak dâi chaehmphuu láang sǐi khráp/khâ* ผม/ฉันอยากได้แชมพูล้างสีครับ/ค่ะ
I'd like a shampoo with conditioner, please.	*phǒm/chǎn yàak dâi chaehmphuu thîi mii khriim nûat* ผม/ฉันอยากได้แชมพูที่มี ครีมนวด
I'd like highlights, please.	*phǒm/chǎn yàak dâi hailái(t) phǒm* ผม/ฉันอยากได้ไฮไลต์ผม
Do you have a color chart, please?	*khun mii phàen sǐi hâi lûeak mǎi* คุณมีแผ่นสีให้เลือกไหม
I'd like to keep the same color.	*phǒm/chǎn yàak kèp sǐi kào wai* ผม/ฉันอยากเก็บสีเก่าไว้
I'd like it darker.	[FEMALE] *chǎn yàak dâi sǐi khêm kwàa* ฉันอยากได้สีเข้มกว่า [MALE] *phǒm yàak dâi sǐi khêm kwàa* ผมอยากได้สีเข้มกว่า
I'd like it lighter.	[FEMALE] *chǎn yàak dâi sǐi àwn kwàa* ฉันอยากได้สีอ่อนกว่า [MALE] *phǒm yàak dâi sǐi àwn kwàa* ผมอยากได้สีอ่อนกว่า
I'd like hairspray.	[FEMALE] *chǎn yàak chìit sàpreh* ฉันอยากฉีดสเปรย์ [MALE] *phǒm yàak chìit sàpreh* ผมอยากฉีดสเปรย์

I don't want gel.	[FEMALE] *chăn mâi yàak sài jehl*
	ฉันไม่อยากใส่เจล
	[MALE] *phŏm mâi yàak sài jehl*
	ผมไม่อยากใส่เจล
I'd like lotion.	[FEMALE] *chăn yàak sài lohchân*
	ฉันอยากใส่โลชั่น
	[MALE] *phŏm yàak sài lohchân*
	ผมอยากใส่โลชั่น
I'd like short bangs (a short fringe).	*yàak dâi phŏm máa*
	อยากได้ผมม้า
Not too short at the back.	*khâng lăng mâi sân mâak*
	ข้างหลังไม่สั้นมาก
Not too long.	*mâi yao pai* ไม่ยาวไป
I'd like it curly.	[FEMALE] *chăn yàak hâi phŏm yìk*
	ฉันอยากให้ผมหยิก
	[MALE] *phŏm yàak hâi phŏm yìk*
	ผมอยากให้ผมหยิก
I'd like it not too curly.	[FEMALE] *chăn yàak hâi phŏm mâi yìk mâak*
	ฉันอยากให้ผมไม่หยิกมาก
	[MALE] *phŏm yàak hâi phŏm mâi yìk mâak*
	ผมอยากให้ผมไม่หยิกมาก
It needs a little taken off.	*tâwng ao àwk nít nòi*
	ต้องเอาออกนิดหน่อย
It needs a lot taken off.	*tâwng ao àwk yóe yóe*
	ต้องเอาออกเยอะๆ
I'd like a completely different style.	[FEMALE] *chăn yàak plìan song mài mòt*
	ฉันอยากเปลี่ยนทรงใหม่หมด
	[MALE] *phŏm yàak plìan song mài mòt*
	ผมอยากเปลี่ยนทรงใหม่หมด
I'd like it the same as that woman's.	[FEMALE] *chăn yàak hâi mŭean khăwng phûu yĭng khon nán*
	ฉันอยากให้เหมือนของผู้หญิงคนนั้น
	[MALE] *phŏm yàak hâi mŭean khăwng phûu chaai khon nán*
	ผมอยากให้เหมือนของผู้ชายคนนั้น

Could you turn the drier up a bit?	*chûai rêng dai pào phŏm ìik nòi dâi măi* ช่วยเร่งไดร์เป่าผมอีกหน่อยได้ไหม
Could you turn the drier down a bit?	*chûai lót dai pào phŏm ìik nòi dâi măi* ช่วยลดไดร์เป่าผมอีกหน่อยได้ไหม
I'd like to thin my hair a bit.	*phŏm/chăn yàak jà soi phŏm nít nùeng* ผม/ฉัน อยากจะซอยผมนิดหนึ่ง
I'd like a facial.	[FEMALE] *chăn yàak tham nâa* ฉันอยากทำหน้า [MALE] *phŏm yàak tham nâa* ผมอยากทำหน้า
I'd like a manicure.	[FEMALE] *chăn yàak tham lép* ฉันอยากทำเล็บ [MALE] *phŏm yàak tham lép* ผมอยากทำเล็บ
I'd like a massage.	[FEMALE] *chăn yàak nûat* ฉันอยากนวด [MALE] *phŏm yàak nûat* ผมอยากนวด
Could you trim my…, please?	*chûai lem…hâi nòi* ช่วยเล็ม…ให้หน่อย
– bangs (fringe)	*phŏm máa* ผมม้า
– beard	*khrao* เครา
– mustache?	*nùat* หนวด
I'd like a shave, please.	[MALE] *phŏm yàak kohn nùat/khrao* ผมอยากโกนหนวด/เครา
I'd like a wet shave, please.	[MALE] *phŏm yàak kohn nùat bàehp sài khriim* ผมอยากโกนหนวดแบบใส่ครีม

11. Tourist Activities

11.1 Places of interest
11.2 Going out
11.3 Booking tickets

11.1 Places of interest

Places of interest to tourists in Thailand are many and varied. At the renowned Lumpini Boxing Stadium (*sanǎam muai lumphínii*), for example, you can enjoy the excitement of Thai kick boxing (*muai thai*), and savor an authentic local experience in a colorful and often boisterous environment. The crocodile farm (*faam jawrákhêh*) at Samut Prakan (*samùt prakaan*) on the southeast fringe of Bangkok is most certainly worth the short trip, while the floating market (*talàat náam*) at Damnoen Saduak (*damnoehn sadùak*) in Ratchaburi* province, not far from the capital, will provide the visitor with a taste of another aspect of traditional Thai life.

Bangkok is famous for its frenetic, bustling nightlife, in particular the bars and discos of Patpong Road and its immediate environs; Soi 4 Sukhumvit Road, commonly known as "Soi Nana," and "Soi Cowboy" which runs between Soi 21 and Soi 23, parallel to Sukhumvit Road. The city is also well-known for its quiet, majestic temples: Wat Phra Kaeo—the Temple of the Emerald Buddha at the old Grand Palace; Wat Pho the Temple of the Reclining Buddha, and Wat Arun, the Temple of Dawn on the west bank of the Chaophraya River.

The best place to find out about what's on, and where, is the Tourism Authority of Thailand (TAT) whose web address is: http://www.tourismthailand.org/campaign/en/

In case you wish to make direct enquiries before your departure TAT have offices in many major cities around the world. Their head office is in the Le Concorde Building, 202 Ratchaphisek Road, Huai Khwang, Bangkok 10310, tel. (66)2 694 1222.

---

* Note: while generally written as Ratchaburi the word is actually pronounced *Rart-buri*. It can be pronounced both ways: *Rart-cha-buri*, or *Rart-buri*.

Of course, hotels, backpacker hostels and guesthouses all have information on places to visit, tours to take, and locations of shopping malls, souvenir shops, and supermarkets. Do be wary of touts, although they can be useful sources of information.

Key Vocabulary

เที่ยวหนึ่งวัน
thîao nùeng wan
day trips

ศาสนสถาน
sátsàná sàthăan
places of worship

ทัศนศึกษาชายทะเล
thátsaná sùeksǎa chaai thá-leh
seaside excursion

ห้างสรรพสินค้า
hâang sàp-phá-sǎn-khâa
shopping mall

ไกด์ *kái*
guided tour

เดินป่า *doehn pàa*
hiking

เวลาทำการ
weh laa tham kaan
hours of operation

รถบัสนั่ง ได้กี่คน
rót bát nâng dâi kìi khon
how many in a bus?

ค่าเข้า *khâa khâo*
admission fees

ราคาผู้สูงอายุ
raakhaa phûu sǔung aayú
senior discounts

ไกด์ที่พูดภาษาอังกฤษ
kái thîi phûut phaasǎa angkrit
English-speaking guide

การถ่ายรูป
kaan thàai rûup
photography

Where's the Tourist Information Center, please?	[FEMALE] *sǒun bawríkaan nák thâwng thîao yùu thîi nǎi khá* ศูนย์บริการนักท่องเที่ยวอยู่ที่ไหนคะ [MALE] *sǒun bawríkaan nák thâwng thîao yùu thîi nǎi khráp* ศูนย์บริการนักท่องเที่ยวอยู่ที่ไหนครับ
Do you have a city map?	*mii phǎehn thîi khǎwng mueang mǎi* มีแผนที่ของเมืองไหม
Where is the museum?	*phíphíthaphan yùu thîi nǎi* พิพิธภัณฑ์อยู่ที่ไหน
Where can I find a church?	*bòht yùu thîi nǎi* โบสถ์อยู่ที่ไหน
Could you give me some information about…?	*chûai bàwk phǒm/chǎn kìao kàp… nòi dâi mǎi* ช่วยบอกผม/ฉันเกี่ยวกับ… หน่อยได้ไหม

How much is that?	*nîi thâorài* นี่เท่าไร
What are the main places of interest?	*thîi nǎi nâa thîao bâang* ที่ไหนน่าเที่ยวบ้าง
Could you point them out on the map?	*chûai chíi nai phǎehn thîi hâi nòi dâi mǎi* ช่วยชี้ในแผนที่ให้หน่อยได้ไหม
What do you recommend?	*khun náe-nam arai dii* คุณแนะนำอะไรดี
We'll be here for a few hours.	*rao jà yùu thîi nîi sák sǎwng sǎam chûamohng* เราจะอยู่ที่นี่สักสองสามชั่วโมง
We'll be here for a day.	*rao jà yùu thîi nîi sák nùeng wan* เราจะอยู่ที่นี่สักหนึ่งวัน
We'll be here for a week.	*raà jà yùu thîi nîi sák nùeng aathít* เราจะอยู่ที่นี่สักหนึ่งอาทิตย์
We're interested in...	*rao sǒnjai...* เราสนใจ...
Are there any boat trips?	*mii nâng ruea thîao mǎi* มีนั่งเรือเที่ยวไหม
Where can we board?	*rao long ruea thîi nǎi dâi* เราลงเรือที่ไหนได้
Are there any bus tours?	*mii nâng rót thîao mǎi* มีนั่งรถเที่ยวไหม
Where do we get on?	*khûen rót dâi thîi nǎi* ขึ้นรถได้ที่ไหน
Is there a guide who speaks English?	*mii kái thîi phûut phaasǎa angkrìt mǎi* มีไกด์ที่พูดภาษาอังกฤษไหม
What trips can we take around the area?	*rao jà pai thîao râwp râwp bawríwehn dâi yàangrai* เราจะไปเที่ยวรอบๆบริเวณได้อย่างไร
Are there any excursions?	*mii thátsaná sùeksǎa mǎi* มีทัศนศึกษาไหม
Where do they go?	*phûak nán pai nǎi* พวกนั้นไปไหน
We'd like to go to...	*rao yâak pai...* เราอยากไป...
How long is the excursion?	*thátsaná sùeksǎa naan thâorài* ทัศนศึกษานานเท่าไร

How long do we stay in...?	*rao phák thîi...naan thâorài* เราพักที่...นานเท่าไร
Are there any guided tours?	*mii thua thîi mii kái măi* มีทัวร์ที่มีไกด์ไหม
How much free time will we have there?	*thîi nân rao mii wehlaa wâang thâorài* ที่นั่นเรามีเวลาว่างเท่าไร
We want to have a walk around.	*rao yàak pai doehn lên râwp râwp* เราอยากไปเดินเล่นรอบๆ
We want to go on foot.	*rao yàak doehn pai* เราอยากเดินไป
Can we hire a guide?	*rao câang kái dâi măi* เราจ้างไกด์ได้ไหม
Can we reserve a hillside hut?	*rao jawng krathâwn noehn khăo dâi măi* เราจองกระท่อมเนินเขาได้ไหม
What time does...open?	*...pòeht kìi mohng* ..เปิดกี่โมง
What time does...close?	*... pìt kìi mohng* ...ปิดกี่โมง
Which days is...open?	*...pòeht wan năi* ...เปิดวันไหน
Which days is...closed?	*... pìt wan năi* ..ปิดวันไหน
What's the admission price?	*khâa khâo thâorài* ค่าเข้าเท่าไร
Is there a group discount?	*pai pen klùm mii raakhaa phísèht măi* ไปเป็นกลุ่มมีราคาพิเศษไหม
Is there a child discount?	*mii raakhaa dèk măi* มีราคาเด็กไหม
Is there a discount for senior citizens?	*mii raakhaa phûu sŭung aayú măi* มีราคาผู้สูงอายุไหม
Can I take (flash) photos?	*thàai rûup (chái fláet) dâi măi* ถ่ายรูป (ใช้แฟลช) ได้ไหม
Can I film here?	*thàai widiioh dâi măi* ถ่ายวิดีโอได้ไหม
Do you have any postcards of...?	*mii pohtsakàat khăwng...măi* มีโปสการ์ดของ...ไหม
Do you have an English catalog?	*mii kháettaalàwk phaasăa angkrìt măi* มีแคตตาล็อกภาษาอังกฤษไหม

Do you have an English program?	*mii prohkraehm phaasǎa angkrìt mǎi* มีโปรแกรมภาษาอังกฤษไหม
Do you have an English brochure?	*mii phàehn pháp phaasǎa angkrìt mǎi* มีแผ่นพับภาษาอังกฤษไหม

 11.2 Going out

In Bangkok one can relax by having a traditional Thai-style massage (*nûat bàehp thai phàehn bohraan*). One can also enjoy a memorable evening at one of the many restaurants that combine a Thai-style meal with Thai classical music and dances, or patronize the numerous cabaret shows in town. For a spectacular cultural show watch Siam Niramita which showcases Thai art and heritage performances with special effects. Those who prefer hot music can head for the many discos found in hotels and other entertainment malls.

Other options: take a slow river cruise (with dinner included) down the Chaophraya and admire the beautiful night views of famous landmarks along the route. Or get a group of like-minded friends and have a roaring time at the karoake or go bowling—these are usually found in shopping malls. Feel like watching a movie? Thai and foreign movies are shown in cinemas—foreign films could be dubbed into Thai or left in the original language with Thai subtitles. English subtitles are usually provided for Thai films.

Key Vocabulary

คาบาเรต์โชว์
khaa baa rêh choh
cabaret shows

หนัง *nǎng*
movies

โรงละคร
rohng lakhawn
theater performances

ชิมอาหาร
chim aa-hǎan
food tasting

งานเทศกาล
ngaanthêht sà kaan
cultural events

การแสดงพื้นเมือง
kaan sà daehng phúehn mueang
traditional dances

เที่ยวกลางคืน
thîao klaang khuehn
night-life activities

แข่งฟุตบอล
khàehng fút-bawn
soccer matches

เที่ยวนอกเมือง
thîao nâwk mueang
countryside trips

Do you have this week's entertainment guide?	*khun mii raai kaan thiiwii khǎwng aathít níi mǎi* คุณมีรายการทีวีของอาทิตย์นี้ไหม
Do you have this month's entertainment guide?	*khun mii raai kaan thiiwii khǎwng duean níi mǎi* คุณมีรายการทีวีของเดือนนี้ไหม
What's on tonight?	*khuehn níi mii àrai* คืนนี้มีอะไร
We want to go to… .	*rao yàak pai thîi…* เราอยากไปที่…
What's playing at the cinema?	*mii nǎng àrai chǎai* มีหนังอะไรฉาย
What sort of film is that?	*nân pen nǎng praphêht nǎi* นั่นเป็นหนังประเภทไหน
It's not suitable for people under 12.	*mâi màw sǎmràp dèk aayú tàm kwàa sìp sǎwng* ไม่เหมาะสำหรับเด็กอายุต่ำกว่า 12
It's not suitable for people under 16.	*mâi màw sǎmràp dèk aayú tàm kwàa sìp hòk* ไม่เหมาะสำหรับเด็กอายุต่ำกว่า 16
It's suitable for everyone.	*màw sǎmràp thúk khon* เหมาะสำหรับทุกคน
It's the original version.	*nǎng tôn chàbàb* หนังต้นฉบับ
It's subtitled.	*nǎng thîi mii kham plae* หนังที่มีคำแปล
It's dubbed.	*nǎng phâak* หนังพากย์
Is it a continuous showing?	*chǎai tàw nûeang rǔeh plào* ฉายต่อเนื่องหรือเปล่า
What's on at the theater?	*mii àrai thîi rohng lákhawn* มีอะไรที่โรงละคร
What's on at the opera?	*mii àrai thîi rohng lákhawn ohpehrâa* มีอะไรที่โรงละครโอเปร่า
What's happening in the concert hall?	*mii àrai thîi khawnsòeht hawl* มีอะไรที่คอนเสิร์ตฮอลล์

Where can I find a good disco around here?	*thăeo níi mii dìtsakoh dii dii thîi năi* แถวนี้มีดิสโก้ดีๆที่ไหน
Is it members only?	*chàpháw samaachík thâo nán rŭeh* เฉพาะสมาชิกเท่านั้นหรือ
Where can I find a good nightclub around here?	*thăeo níi mii nái(t) khláp dii dii thîi năi* แถวนี้มีไนท์คลับดีๆที่ไหน
Is it evening wear only?	*sài dâi chapháw chút raatrii thâo nán rŭeh* ใส่ได้เฉพาะชุดราตรีเท่านั้นหรือ
Should I dress up?	[FEMALE] *chăn khuan tàehng tua dii rŭeh plào* ฉันควรแต่งตัวดีหรือเปล่า [MALE] *phŏm khuan tàehng tua dii rŭeh plào* ผมควรแต่งตัวดีหรือเปล่า
Should we dress up?	*rao khuan tàehng tua dii rŭeh plào* เราควรแต่งตัวดีหรือเปล่า
What time does the show start?	*ngaan rôehm kìi mohng* งานเริ่มกี่โมง
When's the next soccer match?	*fútbawn khûu tàw pai mûearai* ฟุตบอลคู่ต่อไปเมื่อไร
Who's playing?	*khrai lên* ใครเล่น

11.3 Booking tickets

Could you reserve some tickets for us?	*rao khăw jawng tŭa nòi dâi măi* เราขอจองตั๋วหน่อยได้ไหม
We'd like to book two seats.	*rao khăw jawng săwng thîi* เราขอจองสองที่
We'd like a table for three.	*rao khăw jawng tó sămràp săam khon* เราขอจองโต๊ะสำหรับสามคน
We'd like two seats in the orchestra in the main section.	*rao khăw jawng săwng thîi trong klaang nai awkhestrâa* เราขอจองสองที่ตรงกลางในออเคสตร้า
We'd like to book three seats in the circle.	*rao khăw jawng săam thîi nai wong klom* เราขอจองสามที่ในวงกลม

We'd like to book a box for two persons.	*rao khǎw jawng thîi nai báwk sǎmràp sǎwng khon* เราขอจองที่ในบ็อกซ์สำหรับสองคน
We'd like three front row seats.	*rao khǎw jawng sǎam thîi thǎeo nâa* เราขอจองสามที่แถวหน้า
We'd like a table for two at the front.	*rao khǎw jawng tó sǎmràp sǎwng khon thǎeo khâng nâa* เราขอจองโต๊ะสำหรับสองคนแถวข้างหน้า
We'd like three seats in the middle.	*rao khǎw jawng sǎam thîi trong klaang* เราขอจองสามที่ตรงกลาง
We'd like a table in the middle.	*rao khǎw jawng tó trong klaang* เราขอจองโต๊ะตรงกลาง
We'd like three back row seats.	*rao khǎw jawng sǎam thîi thǎeo lǎng* เราขอจองสามที่แถวหลัง
We'd like a table at the back.	*rao khǎw jawng tó thǎeo lǎng* เราขอจองโต๊ะแถวหลัง
Could I reserve four seats for the eight o'clock performance?	*khǎw jawng sìi thîi râwp sǎwng thûm* ขอจองสี่ที่รอบสองทุ่ม
Are there any seats left for tonight?	*mii thîi lǔea bâang mǎi sǎmràp khuehn níi* มีที่เหลือบ้างไหมสำหรับคืนนี้
How much is a ticket?	*tǔa bai lá thâorài* ตั๋วใบละเท่าไร
When can I pick up the tickets?	*ráp tǔa dâi mûearai* รับตั๋วได้เมื่อไร
I've got a reservation.	*phǒm/chǎn jawng tǔa wái láehw* ผม/ฉันจองตั๋วไว้แล้ว
My name's…	*phǒm/chǎn chûeh…* ผม/ฉันชื่อ…

At the performance

คุณอยากจองรอบไหน
khun yàak jawng râwp nǎi

Which performance/show do you want to make a reservation for?

คุณอยากนั่งที่ไหน
khun yàak nâng thîi nǎi

Where would you like to sit?

ตั๋วขายหมดแล้ว
tǔa khǎai mòt láehw

All the tickets are sold out.

มีแต่ที่ยืนเท่านั้น
mii tàe thîi yeun thâo-nán

It's standing room only.

เหลือแต่ที่แถวหน้า
lǔea tàe thîi thǎeo nâa

We've only got front row seats left.

เหลือแต่ที่แถวหลัง
lǔea tàe thîi thǎeo lǎng

We've only got seats left at the back.

คุณต้องการกี่ที่
khun tâwng-kaan kìi thîi

How many seats would you like?

คุณจะต้องมารับตั๋วก่อน…
khun jà tâwng maa ráp tǔa kàwn…

You'll have to pick up the tickets before…o'clock.

ขอตั๋วครับ/ค่ะ
khǎw tǔa khráp/khâ

Tickets, please.

นี่ที่ของคุณ
nîi thîi khǎwng khun

This is your seat.

คุณนั่งผิดที่
khun nâng phìt thîi

You're in the wrong seat.

12. Sports Activities

12.1 Sports facilities
12.2 At the beach
12.3 Taking a lesson

12.1 Sports facilities

Key Vocabulary

เดินป่า
doehn pàa
hiking

สปาน้ำแร่
sa-paa náam râeh
open-air bath

โยคะ
yoh-khá
yoga

เกณฑ์อายุ
kehn aa-yú
age limit

กีฬาทางน้ำ
kii-laa thaang náam
water sports

ค่าเรียนต่อครั้ง
khâa rian tàw khráng
cost per lesson

เรียนว่ายน้ำ
rian wâai náam
swimming lessons

เที่ยวไปเช้า-เย็นกลับ
*kaan thîao pai cháw-
yen klàp*
one-day trip

กลุ่มละกี่คน
klùm lá kìi khon
how many in a
group?

เรียนดำน้ำ
rian dam náam
diving/scuba diving
lessons

Where can we...around here?	*rao...dâi thîi năi thăeo níi* เรา...ได้ที่ไหนแถวนี้
Can I hire a kayak?	[FEMALE] *chăn châo ruea khàyák dâi măi* ฉันเช่าเรือคยักได้ไหม [MALE] *phŏm châo ruea khàyák dâi măi* ผมเช่าเรือคยักได้ไหม
Can I take swimming lessons?	[FEMALE] *chăn rian wâai náam dâi măi* ฉันเรียนว่ายน้ำได้ไหม [MALE] *phŏm rian wâai náam dâi măi* ผมเรียนว่ายน้ำได้ไหม
Can we take diving lessons?	*rao rian dam náam dâi măi* เราเรียนดำน้ำได้ไหม

Can I take water skiing lessons?	[FEMALE] *chǎn rian sàkii náam dâi mǎi* ฉันเรียนสกีน้ำได้ไหม [MALE] *phǒm rian sàkii náam dâi mǎi* ผมเรียนสกีน้ำได้ไหม
Can we take motor boating lessons?	*rao rian khàp ruea dâi mǎi* เราเรียนขับเรือได้ไหม
How much is that per hour?	*chûamohng lá thâorài* ชั่วโมงละเท่าไร
How much is that per day	*wan lá thâorài* วันละเท่าไร
How much is each one?	*an lá thâorài* อันละเท่าไร
Do you need a permit for that?	*tâwng mii bai anúyâat mǎi* ต้องมีใบอนุญาตไหม
Where can I get the permit?	*khǎw anúyâat dâi thîi nǎi* ขอใบอนุญาตได้ที่ไหน
Where's a good place to go hiking?	*thîi nǎi màw sǎmràp doehn pàa* ที่ไหนเหมาะสำหรับเดินป่า

12.2 At the beach

Key Vocabulary

เขตตกปลา
khèt tòk plaa
Fishing area

อันตราย
antàraai
Danger

งดว่ายน้ำ
ngót wâi-náam
No swimming

งดตกปลา
ngót tòk plaa
No fishing

อย่าเข้าใกล้บริเวณนี้
yàa khâo klâi baw-rí-wehn níi
Do not venture beyond this area

ระวังของมีคม
ráwang khǎwng mii khom
Watch out for sharp objects

ห้ามเล่นกระดานโต้คลื่น
hâam lêhn kradaan tôh khlûen
Surfboard riding prohibited

ระวังคลื่นสูงใกล้ฝั่ง
ráwang khlûen sûung klâi fang
Beware shore break

มีใบอนุญาตเท่านั้น
mii bai anu-yâat thâo nán
Permits only

งดเล่นกระดานโต้คลื่น
ngót lên kradaan tôh khlûen
No surfing

เส้นทางอพยพคลื่นสึนามิ
sêhn thaang òp-phá-yóp súe-naa-mí
Tsunami evacuation route

Is it far (to walk) to the sea?	*(doehn) pai tháleh klai mǎi* (เดิน) ไปทะเลไกลไหม
Is there a swimming pool around here?	*thǎeọ níi mii sà wâi náam mǎi* แถวนี้มีสระว่ายน้ำไหม
Is there a sandy beach around here?	*thǎeọ níi mii hàat saai mǎi* แถวนี้มีหาดทรายไหม
Is there a dock around here?	*thǎeọ níi mii thîi jàwt ruea mǎi* แถวนี้มีที่จอดเรือไหม
Are there any rocks here?	*thîi nîi mii khòht hǐn mǎi* ที่นี่มีโขดหินไหม
When's high tide?	*náam khûen mûea rài* น้ำขึ้นเมื่อไร
When's low tide?	*náam long mûea rài* น้ำลงเมื่อไร
What's the water temperature?	*unhàphuum náam thâorài* อุณหภูมิน้ำเท่าไหร่
Is it (very) deep here?	*thîi nîi náam lúek (mâak) mǎi* ที่นี่น้ำลึก(มาก)ไหม
Is it safe (for children) to swim here?	*plàwt phai (sǎmràp dèk) mǎi thîi jà wâai náam thîi nîi* ปลอดภัย(สำหรับเด็ก)ไหมที่จะว่ายน้ำที่นี่
Are there any currents?	*mii krasǎeh náam mǎi* มีกระแสน้ำไหม
Are there any rapids along this river?	*mâeh náam níi náam chîao mǎi* แม่น้ำนี้น้ำเชี่ยวไหม
Are there any waterfalls along this river?	*mâeh náam níi mii náam tòk mǎi* แม่น้ำนี้มีน้ำตกไหม

What does that flag mean?	*thong nán mǎai khwaam wâa àrai* ธงนั้นหมายความว่าอะไร
Is there a lifeguard on duty?	*mii nùai kûu phai prà-jam kaan rǔeh plào* มีหน่วยกู้ภัยประจำการหรือเปล่า
Are dogs allowed here?	*sùnák khâo dâi mǎi* สุนัขเข้าได้ไหม
Is camping on the beach allowed?	*tâng khaehm bon hàat dâi mǎi* ตั้งแคมป์บนหาดได้ไหม
Can we light a fire?	*jùt fai dâi mǎi* จุดไฟได้ไหม

12.3 Taking a lesson

Can I take intermediate jet skiing lessons here?	*rian jét sakii rádàp klaang thîi nîi dâi mǎi* เรียนเจ็ตสกีน้ำระดับกลางที่นี่ได้ไหม
How large are the groups?	*klùm yài khâeh nǎi* กลุ่มใหญ่แค่ไหน
What language are the classes in?	*chái phaasǎa àrai* ใช้ภาษาอะไร
I'd like to hire a water ski, please.	[FEMALE] *chǎn khǎw châo sàkii náam khâ* ฉันขอเช่าสกีน้ำค่ะ [MALE] *phǒm khǎw châo sàkii náam khráp* ผมขอเช่าสกีน้ำครับ
I'd like to hire a jet ski, please.	[FEMALE] *chǎn khǎw châo jét sàkii khâ* ฉันขอเช่าเจ็ตสกีค่ะ [MALE] *phǒm khǎw châo jét sàkii khráp* ผมขอเช่าเจ็ตสกีครับ
Are there any beaches safe to water ski around here?	*thǎeo níi mii hàat plàwt phai thîi lên sàkii náam dâi mǎi* แถวนี้มีหาดปลอดภัยที่เล่นสกีน้ำได้ไหม
Are there any beaches safe to jet ski around here?	*thǎeo níi mii hàat plàwt phai thîi lên jét sàkii dâi mǎi* แถวนี้มีหาดปลอดภัยที่เล่นเจ็ตสกีได้ไหม
Have the water-skiing areas been signposted?	*phúehn thîi lên sàkii náam mii pâai bàwk mǎi* พื้นที่เล่นสกีน้ำมีป้ายบอกไหม

Have the jet-skiing areas been signposted?	*phúehn thîi lên jét sàkii mii pâai bàwk mǎi*
	พื้นที่เล่นเจ็ตสกีมีป้ายบอกไหม
Is the water ski rental shop open?	*ráan châo sàkii náam pòeht mǎi*
	ร้านเช่าสกีน้ำเปิดไหม
Is the jet ski rental shop open?	*ráan châo jét sàkii pòeht mǎi*
	ร้านเช่าเจ็ตสกีเปิดไหม
Are the beach cafes open?	*ráan kaafaeh thîi hàat pòeht mǎi*
	ร้านกาแฟที่หาดเปิดไหม

13. Health Matters

13.1 Calling a doctor

If you become ill, there are hospitals in major towns and in shopping centers in Bangkok—most have a doctor on call. Clinics are used to treating such matters as diarrhea (*tháwng doehn*), STDs (*rôhk tìt tàw*) and tropical ailments. If you need emergency treatment, go to Casualty (*hâwng phûu pùai chùk chǒehn*) at the nearest hospital. Hospitals in Thailand are not free and can be quite expensive, so if you are insured at home, remember to have the desk clearly mark the sickness and treatment received on your receipt. A credit card may be needed as surety for any stay in hospital.

Key Vocabulary

นัด *nát*
appointment

ฉุกเฉิน *chùk chǒehn*
emergency

รถพยาบาล
rót pháyaabaan
ambulance

เบอร์โทรฉุกเฉิน
boeh thoh chùk chǒehn
emergency number

สายด่วนตำรวจ
sǎai dùan tam rùat
police hotline

หน่วยดับเพลิง
nùaidàp phloehng
fire department

ทางหนีไฟ
thaang nǐi fai
fire escape

Could you call (get) a doctor quickly, please?	*chûai rîak mǎw dùan* ช่วยเรียกหมอด่วน
When does the doctor have office hours?	*khliinìk mǎw pòeht kìi mohng* คลินิกหมอเปิดกี่โมง
When can the doctor come?	*mǎw maa kìi mohng* หมอมากี่โมง

Could I make an appointment to see the doctor?	*khǎw nát mǎw dâi mǎi* ขอนัดหมอได้ไหม
I've got an appointment to see the doctor at…o'clock.	*phǒm/chǎn nát mǎw wái tawn…* ผม/ฉันนัดหมอไว้ตอน…
Which doctor has night duty?	*ráan mǎw thîi nǎi pòeht tawn klaang khuehn* ร้านหมอที่ไหนเปิดตอนกลางคืน
Which pharmacy is open on weekends?	*ráan khǎai yaa thîi nǎi pòeht wan sǎo aathít* ร้านขายยาที่ไหนเปิดวันเสาร์อาทิตย์

13.2 What's wrong?

I don't feel well.	*phǒm/chǎn mâi khôi sàbaai* ผม/ฉันไม่ค่อยสบาย
I'm dizzy.	*phǒm/chǎn muen hǔa* ผม/ฉันมึนหัว
I'm ill.	[FEMALE] *chǎn pùai/mâi sàbaai* ฉันป่วย/ไม่สบาย [MALE] *phǒm pùai/mâi sàbaai* ผมป่วย/ไม่สบาย
I feel sick (nauseous).	*phǒm/chǎn khlûehn sâi* ผม/ฉันคลื่นไส้
I've got a cold.	*phǒm/chǎn pen wàt* ผม/ฉันเป็นหวัด
It hurts here.	*jèp thîi nîi* เจ็บที่นี่
I've been sick (vomited).	*phǒm/chǎn jà aa-jian* ผม/ฉันจะอาเจียน
I've got… .	*phǒm/chǎn pen…* ผม/ฉันเป็น…
I'm running a temperature of…degrees.	*phǒm/chǎn unhàphuum khûen… ongsǎa* ผม/ฉันอุณหภูมิขึ้น…องศา

I've been stung by a wasp.	[FEMALE] *chǎn dohn tàw tòi* ฉันโดนต่อต่อย [MALE] *phǒm dohn tàw tòi* ผมโดนต่อต่อย
I've been stung by a bee.	[FEMALE] *chǎn dohn phûeng tòi* ฉันโดนผึ้งต่อย [MALE] *phǒm dohn phûeng tòi* ผมโดนผึ้งต่อย
I've been stung by an insect.	[FEMALE] *chǎn dohn málaehng kàt* ฉันโดนแมลงกัด [MALE] *phǒm dohn málaehng kàt* ผมโดนแมลงกัด
I've been stung by a jellyfish.	[FEMALE] *chǎn dohn maehng kà phrun* ฉันโดนแมงกะพรุน [MALE] *phǒm dohn maehng kà phrun* ผมโดนแมงกะพรุน
I've been bitten by a dog.	[FEMALE] *chǎn dohn mǎa kàt* ฉันโดนหมากัด [MALE] *phǒm dohn mǎa kàt* ผมโดนหมากัด
I've been bitten by a snake.	[FEMALE] *chǎn dohn nguu kàt* ฉันโดนงูกัด [MALE] *phǒm dohn nguu kàt* ผมโดนงูกัด
I've been bitten by something.	[FEMALE] *chǎn dohn àrai baang yàang kàt* ฉันโดนอะไรบางอย่างกัด [MALE] *phǒm dohn àrai baang yàang kàt* ผมโดนอะไรบางอย่างกัด
I've cut myself.	*phǒm/chǎn dohn mîit bàat* ผม/ฉันโดนมีดบาด
I've burned myself.	*phǒm/chǎn thùuk lûak* ผม/ฉันถูกลวก
I've scratched myself.	*phǒm/chǎn khùan tua ehng* ผม/ฉันข่วนตัวเอง
I've had a fall.	*phǒm/chǎn hòk lóm* ผม/ฉันหกล้ม

I've grazed my knee.	[FEMALE] *chǎn tham khào thalàwk*
	ฉันทำเข่าถลอก
	[MALE] *phǒm tham khào thalàwk*
	ผมทำเข่าถลอก
I've grazed my elbow.	[FEMALE] *chǎn tham khâw sàwk thalàwk*
	ฉันทำข้อศอกถลอก
	[MALE] *phǒm tham khâw sàwk thalàwk*
	ผมทำข้อศอกถลอก
I've grazed my leg.	[FEMALE] *chǎn tham khǎa thalàwk*
	ฉันทำขาถลอก
	[MALE] *phǒm tham khǎa thalàwk*
	ผมทำขาถลอก
I've grazed my arm.	[FEMALE] *chǎn tham khǎehn thalàwk*
	ฉันทำแขนถลอก
	[MALE] *phǒm tham khǎehn thalàwk*
	ผมทำแขนถลอก
I've sprained my ankle.	*khâw tháo khlét* ข้อเท้าเคล็ด
I'd like the morning-after pill.	*yàak dâi yaa khum thîi thaan lǎng rûam pêht*
	อยากได้ยาคุมที่ทานหลังร่วมเพศ

13.3 The consultation

🖐 In the examining room

มีปัญหาอะไร *mii panhǎa àrai*	What seems to be the problem?
คุณเป็นมานานแล้วหรือยัง *khun pen maa naan láehw rǔeh-yang*	How long have you had these complaints?
เคยเป็นอย่างนี้มาก่อนหรือเปล่า *khoei pen yàang níi maa kàwn rǔeh-plào*	Have you had this trouble before?
ตัวร้อนไหม กี่องศา *tua ráwn mǎi kii ongsǎa*	Do you have a temperature? What is it?
ถอดเสื้อ *thâwt sûea*	Get undressed, please.

ถอดถึงเอว
thâwt thǔeng eo
Strip to the waist, please.

คุณไปถอดเสื้อที่นั่นได้
khun pai thâwt sûea thîi nân dâi
You can undress there.

เอาแขนเสื้อข้างซ้าย/ข้างขวาขึ้น
ao khǎen sûea khâang sáai/khâang khwǎa khûen
Roll up your left/right sleeve, please.

นอนที่นี่ *nawn thîi nîi*
Lie down here, please.

เจ็บไหม *jèp mǎi*
Does this hurt?

หายใจลึกๆ *hǎai-jai léuk-léuk*
Breathe deeply.

อ้าปาก *âa pàak*
Open your mouth.

 Past medical conditions

คุณแพ้อะไรหรือเปล่า
khun pháe àrai rǔeh-plào
Do you have any allergies?

คุณทานยาอะไรอยู่หรือเปล่า
khun thaan yaa àrai yùu rǔeh-plào
Are you on any medication?

คุณกำลังลดอาหารหรือเปล่า
khun kamlang lót aahǎan rǔeh-plào
Are you on a diet?

คุณท้องหรือเปล่า
khun tháwng rǔeh-plào
Are you pregnant?

คุณฉีดยากันบาดทะยักหรือเปล่า
khun chìit yaa kan bàat-tha-yák rǔeh-plào
Have you had a tetanus injection?

Patients' medical history

I'm a diabetic.
phǒm/chǎn pen bao wǎan
ผม/ฉันเป็นเบาหวาน

I have a heart condition.
phǒm/chǎn pen rôhk hǔa jai
ผม/ฉันเป็นโรคหัวใจ

I'm asthmatic.
phǒm/chǎn pen rôhk hàwp hùeht
ผม/ฉันเป็นโรคหอบหืด

I'm allergic to… .	*phǒm/chǎn pháeh…* ผม/ฉันแพ้…
I'm…months pregnant.	*chǎn tháwng…duean* ฉันท้อง…เดือน
I'm on a diet.	*phǒm/chǎn lót khwaam ûan* ผม/ฉันลดความอ้วน
I'm on medication.	[FEMALE] *chǎn kamlang ráksǎa yùu* ฉันกำลังรักษาอยู่ [MALE] *phǒm kamlang ráksǎa yùu* ผมกำลังรักษาอยู่
I'm on the pill.	[FEMALE] *chǎn kin yaa khum yùu* ฉันกินยาคุมอยู่
I've had a heart attack once before.	*phǒm/chǎn khoei hǔa jai waai maa láehw khráng nùeng* ผม/ฉันเคยหัวใจวายมาแล้วครั้งหนึ่ง
I've had a(n)…operation.	*phǒm/chǎn khoei phàa tàt…* ผม/ฉันเคยผ่าตัด…
I've been ill recently.	*mûea mâi naan maa níi phǒm/chǎn pùai* เมื่อไม่นานนี้ผม/ฉันป่วย
I've got a stomach ulcer.	*phǒm/chǎn pen rôhk krapháw* ผม/ฉันเป็นโรคกระเพาะ
I've got my period.	*chǎn mii prà-jam duean* ฉันมีประจำเดือน

🖐 The doctor's diagnosis

ไม่มีอะไรร้ายแรง *mâi mii arai ráai-raeng*	It's nothing serious.
…ของคุณหัก *…khǎwng khun hàk*	Your…is broken.
…ของคุณเคล็ด *…khǎwng khun khlét*	You've got a sprained… .
…ของคุณฉีกขาด *…khǎwng khun chìik khàat*	You've got (a) torn…

Thai	Transliteration	English

คุณติดเชื้อ *khun tìt chúea*   You've got an infection.

คุณมีอาการอักเสบ   You've got some inflammation.
khun mii aa kaan àk-sèp

คุณไส้ติ่งอักเสบ   You've got appendicitis.
khun sâi-tìng àk-sèp

คุณเป็นโรคหลอดลมอักเสบ   You've got bronchitis.
khun pen rôhk làwt-lom àk-sèp

คุณเป็นกามโรค   You've got venereal disease.
khun pen kaam má rôhk

คุณเป็นไข้หวัดใหญ่   You've got the flu.
khun pen khâi-wàt yài

คุณเป็นโรคหัวใจวาย   You've had a heart attack.
khun pen rôhk hǔa-jai waai

คุณติดเชื้อ ไวรัส/แบคทีเรีย   You've got an (viral/bacterial)
khun tìt chúea wai-rat/baektiirueh   infection.

คุณเป็นโรคปอดบวม   You've got pneumonia.
khun pen rôhk pàwt buam

คุณเป็นแผลในกระเพาะอาหาร   You've got gastritis/an ulcer.
khun pen phlǎe nai kra-phó aahǎan

คุณกล้ามเนื้อฉีก   You've pulled a muscle.
khun klâam núea chìik

อักเสบในช่องคลอด   (You've got) a vaginal infection.
àk-sèp nai châwng-khlâwt

อาหารเป็นพิษ *aahǎan pen phít*   (You've got) food poisoning.

คุณเป็นลมแดด   You've got sunstroke.
khun pen lom dàet

คุณแพ้… *khun pháeh…*   You're allergic to… .

คุณท้อง *khun tháwng*   You're pregnant.

…ขอตรวจเลือด   I'd like to have your blood tested.
…khǎw trùat lûeat

...ขอตรวจปัสสาวะ
...khǎw trùat pàtsǎawá

I'd like to have your urine tested.

...ขอตรวจอุจจาระ
...khǎw trùat ùtjaará

I'd like to have your stool tested.

ฉันจะส่งคุณไปหาหมอเฉพาะทาง
[FEMALE] *chǎn jà sòng khun pai hâa mǎw chà pháw thaang*

I'm referring you to a specialist.

ผมจะส่งคุณไปหาหมอเฉพาะทาง
[MALE] *phǒm jà sòng khun pai hâa mǎw chà pháw thaang*

ต้องเย็บ *tâwng yép*

It needs stitching.

ฉันจะส่งคุณไปโรงพยาบาล
[FEMALE] *chǎn jà sòng khun pai rohng pháyaabaan*

I'm sending you to hospital.

ผมจะส่งคุณไปโรงพยาบาล
[MALE] *phǒm jà sòng khun pai rohng pháyaabaan*

ต้องไปเอกซเรย์ *tâwng pai ex-ray*

You'll need some x-rays taken.

คุณจำเป็นต้องผ่าตัด
khun jam-pen tâwng phàa-tàt

You'll need an operation.

กรุณารอในห้องพักคนไข้
karunaa raw nai hâwng phák khon-khâi

Could you wait in the waiting room, please?

Is it contagious?	*rôhk níi tìt tàw rǔeh plào* โรคนี้ติดต่อหรือเปล่า
Do I have to go on a special diet?	*tâwng thaan aahǎan phísèht mǎi* ต้องทานอาหารพิเศษไหม
Am I allowed to travel?	*doehn thaang dâi mǎi* เดินทางได้ไหม
Can I make another appointment?	*khǎw nát mài ìik dâi mǎi* ขอนัดใหม่อีกได้ไหม
When do I have to come back?	*phǒm/chǎn tâwng klàp maa ìik mûearai* ผม/ฉันต้องกลับมาอีกเมื่อไร

I'll come back tomorrow.	*phǒm/chǎn jà klàp maa ìik phrûeng níi*
	ผม/ฉันจะกลับมาอีกพรุ่งนี้
How do I take this medicine?	*yaa níi thaan yang-ngai*
	ยานี้ทานอย่างไร

 The next appointment

พรุ่งนี้กลับมาใหม่นะคะ
[FEMALE] *phrûng-níi klàp maa mài ná khá*

พรุ่งนี้กลับมาใหม่นะครับ
[MALE] *phrûng-níi klàp maa mài ná khráp*

Come back tomorrow.

อีกสามวันกลับมาใหม่นะคะ
[FEMALE] *ìik sǎam wan klàp maa mài ná khá*

อีกสามวันกลับมาใหม่นะครับ
[MALE] *ìik sǎam wan klàp maa mài ná khráp*

Come back in three days' time.

 Medications and prescriptions

ยา *yaa*
medicine

ละลายในน้ำ
la-laai nai náam
dissolve in water

ก่อนอาหาร
kàwn aahǎan
before meals

ยาเม็ด *yaa-mét*
tablets/pills

หลังอาหาร
lǎng aahǎan
after meals

วันละ...ครั้ง
wan lá...khráng
...times a day

กลืน (ทั้งหมด)
kluen (tháng mòt)
swallow (whole)

ช้อนโต๊ะ *cháwn tó*
spoonful

ช้อนชา *cháwn chaa*
teaspoonful

ทุก...ชั่วโมง
thúk ... chûa-mohng
every (number of) ... hours

ยาทาภายนอก
yaa thaa phaai nâwk
external use only

ทานยาในใบสั่งให้หมด
thaan yaa nai bai sàng hâi mòt
finish the prescription

ฉีดยา
chìit yaa
injection

หยด *yòt*
drops

ยาทา *yaa thaa*
ointment

ทา *thaa*
rub on

...วัน *... wan*
for...days

กิน *kin*
take

How many pills/tablets each time?	**khráng lá kìi mét** ครั้งละกี่เม็ด
How many drops each time?	**khráng lá kìi yòt** ครั้งละกี่หยด
How many injections each time?	**khráng lá kìi khěm** ครั้งละกี่เข็ม
How many spoonfuls each time?	**khráng lá kìi cháwn** ครั้งละกี่ช้อน
How many times a day?	**wan lá kìi khráng** วันละกี่ครั้ง
I've forgotten my medication.	**phǒm/chǎn luehm ao yaa maa** ผม/ฉันลืมเอายามา
At home I take…	**thîi bâan, phǒm/chǎn thaan…** ที่บ้าน ผม/ฉันทาน…
Could you write a prescription for me?	**khǎw bai sàng dûai yaa** ขอใบสั่งยาด้วย

✋ The doctor's prescription

ฉันสั่งยาปฏิชีวนะ [FEMALE] *chǎn sàng yaa pàtichiiwaná* ผมสั่งยาปฏิชีวนะ [MALE] *phǒm sàng yaa pàtichiiwaná*	I'm prescribing antibiotics.
ฉันสั่งยานอนหลับ [FEMALE] *chǎn sàng yaa yaa nawn-làp* ผมสั่งยานอนหลับ [MALE] *phǒm sàng yaa yaa nawn-làp*	I'm prescribing a tranquilizer.
ยานี้ลดสมรรถภาพในการขับขี่ *yaa níi lót sà màt thà phâap nai kaan-kàp-khìi*	This medication impairs your driving.
ฉันสั่งยาแก้ปวด [FEMALE] *chǎn sàng yaa kâe-pùat* ผมสั่งยาแก้ปวด [MALE] *phǒm sàng yaa kâe-pùat*	I'm prescribing painkillers.
นอนพักมากๆ *nawn phák mâak-mâak*	Have lots of rest.
อยู่ในบ้าน *yùu nai bâan*	Stay indoors.
นอนพักบนเตียง *nawn phák bohn tiang*	Stay in bed .

13.5 At the dentist

Key Vocabulary

หมอฟัน *măw fan* dentist	อุดฟัน *ùt fan* filling	ยาแก้ปวด *yaa kâeh pùat* painkiller
ยาชา *yaa chaa* anesthetic	ซ่อมฟัน *sâwm fan* tooth repair	ปากเหม็น *pàak měn* bad breath
ที่ครอบฟันหัก *thîi khrâwp fan hàk* broken crown	ฟันปลอม *fan plawm* denture	ปวดฟัน *pùat fan* toothache

Do you know a good dentist?
khun rúujàk măw fan dii dii măi
คุณรู้จักหมอฟันดีๆ ไหม

Could you make a dentist's appointment for me?
chûai nát măw fan hâi nòi dâi măi
ช่วยนัดหมอฟันให้หน่อยได้ไหม

It's urgent.
dùan ด่วน

Can I come in today, please?
phŏm/chăn khâo maa wan níi dâi măi
ผม/ฉันเข้ามาวันนี้ได้ไหม

I have (terrible) toothache. *phŏm/chăn pùat fan (mâak)*
ผม/ฉันปวดฟัน (มาก)

I've got a broken tooth.
fan phŏm/chăn hàk ฟันผม/ฉันหัก

Could you prescribe me a painkiller?
[FEMALE] *chûai sàng yaa kâeh pùat hâi dâi măi khá*
ช่วยสั่งยาแก้ปวดให้ได้ไหมคะ
[MALE] *chûai sàng yaa kâeh pùat hâi dâi măi khráp*
ช่วยสั่งยาแก้ปวดให้ได้ไหมครับ

Could you give me a painkiller?
[FEMALE] *khăw yaa kâeh pùat dâi măi khá*
ขอยาแก้ปวดได้ไหมคะ
[MALE] *khăw yaa kâeh pùat dâi măi khráp*
ขอยาแก้ปวดได้ไหมครับ

My filling's come out.
thîi ùt fan lùt ที่อุดฟันหลุด

I've got a broken crown.	*thîi khrâwp fan hàk* ที่ครอบฟันหัก
I'd like a local anesthetic.	[FEMALE] *chǎn tâwngkaan yaa chaa chàpháw thîi* ฉันต้องการยาชาเฉพาะที่ [MALE] *phǒm tâwngkaan yaa chaa chàpháw thîi* ผมต้องการยาชาเฉพาะที่
I don't want a local anesthetic.	[FEMALE] *chǎn mâi tâwngkaan yaa chaa chàpháw thîi* ฉันไม่ต้องการยาชาเฉพาะที่ [MALE] *phǒm mâi tâwngkaan yaa chaa chàpháw thîi* ผมไม่ต้องการยาชาเฉพาะที่
Can you do a temporary repair?	*chûai sâwm chûa khrao dâi mǎi* ช่วยซ่อมชั่วคราวได้ไหม
I don't want this tooth pulled.	*phǒm/chǎn mâi tâwngkaan hâi thǎwn fan* ผม/ฉันไม่ต้องการให้ถอนฟัน
My denture is broken.	*fan plawm phǒm/chǎn hàk* ฟันปลอมผม/ฉันหัก
Can you fix it?	*khun sâwm dâi mǎi* คุณซ่อมได้ไหม

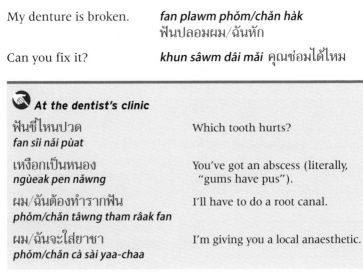

At the dentist's clinic

ฟันซี่ไหนปวด *fan sîi nǎi pùat*	Which tooth hurts?
เหงือกเป็นหนอง *ngùeak pen nǎwng*	You've got an abscess (literally, "gums have pus").
ผม/ฉันต้องทำรากฟัน *phǒm/chǎn tâwng tham râak fan*	I'll have to do a root canal.
ผม/ฉันจะใส่ยาชา *phǒm/chǎn cà sài yaa-chaa*	I'm giving you a local anaesthetic.

ฉันต้องถอนฟันซี่นี้
[FEMALE] *chăn tâwng thăwn fan sîi níi*
ผมต้องถอนฟันซี่นี้
[MALE] *phŏm tâwng thăwn fan sîi níi*

I'll have to pull this tooth.

ฉันต้องอุดฟันซี่นี้
[FEMALE] *chăn tâwng ùt fan sîi níi*

ผมต้องอุดฟันซี่นี้
[MALE] *phŏm tâwng ùt fan sîi níi*

I'll have to fill this tooth.

ฉันต้องขัดฟันซี่นี้
[FEMALE] *chăn tâwng khàt fan sîi níi*
ผมต้องขัดฟันซี่นี้
[MALE] *phŏm tâwng khàt fan sîi níi*

I'll have to file this tooth.

ผม/ฉันต้องกรอฟัน
phŏm/chăn tâwng kraw fan

I'll have to drill it.

อ้าปากครับ/คะ
âa pàak khráp/khá

Open wide, please.

ปิดปากครับ/คะ
pìt pàak khráp/khá

Close your mouth, please.

บ้วนปากครับ/คะ
bûan pàak khráp/khá

Rinse, please.

ยังเจ็บอยู่หรือเปล่า
yang jèp yùu rŭeh-plào

Does it still hurt?

14. Emergencies

14.1   Asking for help

Help!	*chûai dûai!* ช่วยด้วย
Fire!	*fai mâi!* ไฟไหม้
Police!	*tamrùat!* ตำรวจ
Quick/Hurry!	*reo reo!* เร็วๆ
Danger!	*antàraai* อันตราย
Watch out!	*ra-wang!* ระวัง
Stop!	*yùt!* หยุด
Be careful!	*rá-wang* ระวัง
You don't have to rush.	*mâi tâwng rip* ไม่ต้องรีบ
Get your hands off me!	*plòi phǒm/chǎn!* ปล่อยผม/ฉัน
Let go!	*plòi ná!* ปล่อยนะ
Stop thief!	*khàmohy* ขโมย
Could you help me, please?	*chûai phǒm/chǎn dâi mǎi* ช่วยผม/ฉันได้ไหม
Where's the police station?	*sathǎanii tamrùat yùu thîi nǎi* สถานีตำรวจอยู่ที่ไหน
Where's the emergency exit?	*thaang àwk chùk chǒehn yùu thîi nǎi* ทางออกฉุกเฉินอยู่ที่ไหน
Where's the fire escape?	*bandai nǐi fai yùu thîi nǎi* บันไดหนีไฟอยู่ที่ไหน
Where's the nearest fire extinguisher?	*thîi dàp fai klâi thîisùt yùu thîi nǎi* ที่ดับไฟใกล้ที่สุดอยู่ที่ไหน

Call the fire department!	*rîak nùai dàp phloehng!* เรียกหน่วยดับเพลิง
Call the police!	*rîak tamrùat!* เรียกตำรวจ
Call an ambulance!	*rîak rót phayaabaan!* เรียกรถพยาบาล
Where's the nearest phone?	*thohrasàp klâi thîisùt yùu thîi nǎi* โทรศัพท์ใกล้ที่สุดอยู่ที่ไหน
Could I use your phone?	*khǎw chái thohrasàp khun dâi mǎi* ขอใช้โทรศัพท์คุณได้ไหม
What's the emergency number?	*boeh jâehng hèht chùk chǒehn boeh arai* เบอร์แจ้งเหตุฉุกเฉินเบอร์อะไร
What's the number for the police?	*boeh tamrùat boeh àrai* เบอร์ตำรวจเบอร์อะไร

(14.2) Lost items

Key Vocabulary

แจ้งของหาย *jâehng khǎwng hǎai* reporting a loss	โทรศัพท์มือถือ *thoh-rá-sàp mueh-thǔeh* mobile phone	ของมีค่า *khǔwng mii khâa* valuables
หนังสือเดินทาง/ พาสปอร์ต *nǎng sǔeh doehn thaang/páat sà-pàwt* passport	สัตว์เลี้ยง *sàt líang* pet เด็ก *dèk* child	แผนกแจ้งของหาย *phà-nàehk jâehng khǎwng hǎai* Lost and Find Office

I've lost my (digital) camera.	*klâwng (di-jì-tâwn) khǎwng phǒm/chǎn hǎi* กล้อง(ดิจิตอล)ของผม/ฉันหาย
I've lost my wallet/purse.	*phǒm/chǎn tham krapǎo sataang hǎai* ผม/ฉันทำกระเป๋าสตางค์หาย
I lost my passport here yesterday.	[FEMALE] *chǎn tham nǎngsǔeh doehn thaang/páat sà pàwt hǎai thîi nîi mûeawaan níi* ฉันทำหนังสือเดินทาง/พาสปอร์ต หายที่นี่เมื่อวานนี้

[MALE] *phŏm tham năngsŭeh doehn thaang/páat sà-pàwt hăi thîi nîi mûeawaan nii*

ผมทำ หนังสือเดินทาง/พาสปอร์ต หาย ที่นี่เมื่อวานนี้

I left my mobile phone here.	[FEMALE] *chăn luehm thohrásàp muehthŭeh wái thîi nîi* ฉันลืมโทรศัพท์มือถือไว้ที่นี่ [MALE] *phŏm luehm thohrásàp muehthŭeh wái thîi nîi* ผมลืมโทรศัพท์มือถือไว้ที่นี่
Did you find my laptop?	[FEMALE] *khun hĕn nóht-búk/cawm-phíew-têr khăwng chăn măi* คุณเห็น โน้ตบุค/คอมพิวเตอร์ ของฉันไหม [MALE] *khun hĕn nóht-búk/cawm-phíew-têr khăwng phŏm măi* คุณเห็น โน้ตบุค/คอมพิวเตอร์ ของผมไหม
It was right here.	*yùu trong nîi* อยู่ตรงนี้
It's very valuable.	*mii khâa mâak* มีค่ามาก
Where's the lost and found office?	*phanàehk jâehng khăwng hăi yùu thîi năi* แผนกแจ้งของหายอยู่ที่ไหน

Accidents

Key Vocabulary

อุบัติเหตุ *ù-bat-tì-hèht* accident	จำนวนคนตาย *jam nuan khon taai* number of dead	ระเบิด *rá bòeht* explosion
จำนวนคนเจ็บ *jam nuan khon jèp* number of injured	ไฟไหม้ *fai mâi* fire	ควันพิษ *khwan phít* poisonous fumes

There's been an accident.	*kòeht ùbatìhèht* เกิดอุบัติเหตุ
Someone's fallen into the water.	*mii khon tòk náam* มีคนตกน้ำ
There's a fire.	*mii fai mâi* ไฟไหม้
Is anyone hurt?	*mii khrai bàat jèp măi* มีใครบาดเจ็บไหม

No one has been injured. *mâi mii khrai bàat jèp* ไม่มีใครบาดเจ็บ

Someone has been injured. *mii khon bàat jèp* มีคนบาดเจ็บ

Someone's still trapped inside the car. *yang mii khon tìt yùu nai rót* ยังมีคนติดอยู่ในรถ

Someone's still trapped. inside the train. *yang mii khon tìt yùu nai rót fai* ยังมีคนที่อยู่ในรถไฟ

It's not too bad/much hurt. *mâi yâeh mâak/jèp thâorai* ไม่ แย่มาก/เจ็บ เท่าไหร่

Don't worry. *mâi tâwng hùang* ไม่ต้องห่วง

Leave everything the way it is, please. *kàrúnaa plòi wái yàang nán* กรุณาปล่อยไว้อย่างนั้น

I want to talk to the police first. *phŏm/chăn yàak phûut kàp tamrùat kàwn* ผม/ฉันอยากพูดกับตำรวจก่อน

I want to take a photo first. *phŏm/chăn yàak thài rûup kàwn* ผม/ฉันอยากถ่ายรูปก่อน

Here's my name and address. *nîi chûeh kàp thîi yùu khăwng phŏm/chăn* นี่ชื่อกับที่อยู่ของผม/ฉัน

May I have your name and address? *khăw chûeh kàp thîi yùu khăwng khun nòi* ขอชื่อกับที่อยู่ของคุณหน่อย

Could I see your identity card? [FEMALE] *khăw duu bàt pràchaachon dâi măi khá* ขอดูบัตรประชาชนได้ไหมคะ
[MALE] *khăw duu bàt pràchaachon dâi măi khráp* ขอดูบัตรประชาชนได้ไหมครับ

Could I see your insurance papers? [FEMALE] *khăw duu pràkan khăwng khun dâi măi khá* ขอดูประกันของคุณได้ไหมคะ
[MALE] *khăw duu pràkan khăwng khun dâi măi khráp* ขอดูประกันของคุณได้ไหมครับ

Will you act as a witness? *khun jà pen phayaan măi* คุณจะเป็นพยานไหม

I need this information for insurance purposes.	*phǒm/chǎn tâwngkaan khâwmuun níi phûea prakan khǎwng phǒm/chǎn*
	ผม/ฉันต้องการข้อมูลนี้เพื่อประกันของผม/ฉัน
Are you insured?	*khun mii prakan rǔeh plào*
	คุณมีประกันหรือเปล่า
Third party or all inclusive?	*bukkhon thîi sǎam rǔeh ruam mòt*
	บุคคลที่สามหรือรวมหมด
Could you sign here, please?	*sen chûeh thîi nîi khráp/khâ*
	เซ็นชื่อที่นี่ครับ/ค่ะ

 Theft

I've been robbed.	*phǒm/chǎn thùuk plôn*
	ผม/ฉันถูกปล้น
My credit card has been stolen.	[FEMALE] *lûuk khǎwng chǎn hǎai*
	ลูกของฉันหาย
	[MALE] *lûuk khǎwng phǒm hǎai*
	ลูกของผมหาย
My car's been broken into.	*rót phǒm/chǎn thùuk ngát*
	รถผม/ฉันถูกงัด

14.5 Reporting a missing person

I've lost my child.	[FEMALE] *lûuk khǎwng chǎn hǎai*
	ลูกของฉันหาย
	[MALE] *lûuk khǎwng phǒm hǎai*
	ลูกของผมหาย
I've lost my grandmother.	[FEMALE] *yaai khǎwng chǎn hǎai*
	ยายของฉันหาย
	[MALE] *yaai khǎwng phǒm hǎai*
	ยายของผมหาย
Could you help me find him/her?	[FEMALE] *chûai hǎa dâi mǎi khá*
	ช่วยหาได้ไหมคะ
	[MALE] *chûai hǎa dâi mǎi khráp*
	ช่วยหาได้ไหมครับ

Have you seen a small child?	*khun hěn dèk lék lék mǎi* คุณเห็นเด็กเล็กๆ ไหม
He's six years old.	*dèk phûu chaai aayú hòk pii* เด็กผู้ชายอายุหกปี
She's four years old.	*dèk phûu yǐng aayú sìi pii* เด็กผู้หญิงอายุสี่ปี
He's got short brown hair.	*phûu chaai phǒm sân sǐi námtaan* ผู้ชายผมสั้นสีน้ำตาล
She's got long blond hair.	*phûu yǐng phǒm yaow sǐi thawng* ผู้หญิงผมยาวสีทอง
He's got curly red hair.	*phûu chaai phǒm pen lawn sǐi daehng* ผู้ชายผมเป็นลอนสีแดง
She's got straight black hair.	*phûu yǐng phǒm trong sǐi dam* ผู้หญิงผมตรงสีดำ
He's got frizzy gray hair.	*phûu chaai phǒm yìk sǐi thao* ผู้ชายผมหยิกสีเทา
Her hair is in a ponytail.	*phûu yǐng mát phǒm hǎang máa* ผู้หญิงมัดผมหางม้า
Her hair is in braids.	*phûu yǐng thàk pia* ผู้หญิงถักเปีย
Her hair is in a bun.	*phûu yǐng klâo muai* ผู้หญิงเกล้ามวย
He's got blue eyes.	*kháo taa sǐi fáa* เขาตาสีฟ้า
She's got brown eyes.	*kháo taa sǐi náam taan* เขาตาสีน้ำตาล
He's got green eyes.	*kháo taa sǐi khǐao* เขาตาสีเขียว
He's wearing swimming trunks.	*kháo sài chút wâai náam* เขาใส่ชุดว่ายน้ำ
She's wearing hiking boots.	*kháo sài rawng tháo búut* เขาใส่รองเท้าบู้ท
He's wearing glasses.	*kháo sài wâen taa* เขาใส่แว่นตา
She's not wearing glasses.	*kháo mâi sài wâen taa* เขาไม่ใส่แว่นตา
He's carrying a bag.	*kháo hîu thǔng* เขาหิ้วถุง
She's not carrying a bag.	*kháo mâi hîu thǔng* เขาไม่หิ้วถุง
She is tall.	*kháo sǔung* เขาสูง

He is short.	*kháo tîa* เขาเตี้ย
This is a photo of him/her.	*nîi rûup kháo* นี่รูปเขา
He/she must be lost.	*kháo khong lǒng thaang* เขาคงหลงทาง

14.6 At the police station

An arrest

 Talking to a policeman

ขอดูใบขับขี่ *khǎw duu bai khàp-khìi*	Your driver's license, please.
คุณขับเร็วเกินอัตรา *khun khàp reo koen àt-traa*	You were speeding.
คุณจอดที่นี่ไม่ได้ *khun jàwt thîi-nîi mâi dâi*	You're not allowed to park here.
ไฟรถคุณเสีย *fai rót khun sǐa*	Your lights aren't working.
ถูกปรับ … บาท *thùuk pràp … bàat*	That's a … baht fine.

I don't speak Thai.	*phǒm/chǎn phûut thai mâi dâi* ผม/ฉันพูดไทยไม่ได้
I didn't see the sign.	*phǒm/chǎn mâi hěn pâi (sǎnyaan)* ผม/ฉันไม่เห็นป้าย (สัญญาณ)
I don't understand what it says.	*phǒm/chǎn mâi khâo jai wâa bàwk àrai* ผม/ฉันไม่เข้าใจว่าบอกอะไร
I was only doing… kilometers an hour.	*phǒm/chǎn khàp khâeh…kiloh tàw chûamohng* ผม/ฉันขับแค่…กิโลต่อชั่วโมง
I'll have my car checked.	*phǒm/chǎn jà ao rót pai trùat* ผม/ฉันจะเอารถไปตรวจ

I was blinded by oncoming lights.

phǒm/chǎn mawng mâi hěn phráw fai rót sǔan maa jâa mâak

ผม/ฉันมองไม่เห็นเพราะ ไฟรถสวนมาจ้ามาก

👆 Making a police report

เหตุเกิดที่ไหน *hèht kòeht thîi nǎi* — Where did it happen?

อะไรหายบ้าง *àrai hǎi bâang* — What's missing?

เอาอะไรไปบ้าง *ao àrai pai bâang* — What's been taken?

ขอดูบัตรประจำตัว *khǎw duu bàt prà-jam tua* — Could I see your identity card/ some identification?

เหตุเกิดตอนไหน *hèht kòeht tawn nǎi* — What time did it happen?

มีพยานไหม *mii pháyaan mǎi* — Are there any witnesses?

เซ็นชื่อที่นี่ *sen chûeh thîi nîi* — Sign here, please.

ต้องการล่ามไหม *tâwng-kaan lâam mǎi* — Do you want an interpreter?

At the police station

I want to report a collision.

[FEMALE] *chǎn khǎw jâehng khwaam rót chon kan*
ฉันขอแจ้งความรถชนกัน
[MALE] *phǒm khǎw jâehng khwaam rót chon kan*
ผมขอแจ้งความรถชนกัน

I want to report a missing person.

[FEMALE] *chǎn khǎw jâehng khwaam khon hǎi*
ฉันขอแจ้งความคนหาย
[MALE] *phǒm khǎw jâehng khwaam khon hǎi*
ผมขอแจ้งความคนหาย

I want to report a rape.

[FEMALE] *chǎn khǎw jâehng khwaam khádii khòm khǔehn*
ฉันขอแจ้งความคดีข่มขืน
[MALE] *phǒm khǎw jâehng khwaam khádii khòm khǔehn*
ผมขอแจ้งความคดีข่มขืน

Could you make a statement, please?	*chûai hâi kaan dûai* ช่วยให้การด้วย
Could I have a copy for the insurance?	*khǎw sǎmnao nùeng chàbàp sǎmràp pràkan* ขอสำเนาหนึ่งฉบับสำหรับประกัน
I've lost everything.	*khǎwng khǎwng phǒm/chǎn hǎai mòt* ของของผม/ฉันหายหมด
I've no money left, I'm desperate.	*phǒm/chǎn mâi mii ngoehn lǔea loei, yâeh jing jing* ผม/ฉันไม่มีเงินเหลือเลย แย่จริงๆ
Could you lend me a little money?	*khǎw yuehm ngoehn nòi dâi mǎi* ขอยืมเงินหน่อยได้ไหม
I'd like an interpreter.	*phǒm/chǎn tâwngkaan lâam* ผม/ฉันต้องการล่าม
I'm innocent.	*phǒm/chǎn bawrísùt* ผม/ฉันบริสุทธิ์
I don't know anything about it.	*phǒm/chǎn mâi rúu rûeang àrai loei* ผม/ฉันไม่รู้เรื่องอะไรเลย
I want to speak to someone from the Australian embassy.	*phǒm/chǎn tâwngkaan tìt tàw sathǎan thûut áwstrehlia* ผม/ฉันต้องการติดต่อ สถานทูตออสเตรเลีย
I want a lawyer who speaks…	*phǒm/chǎn tâwngkaan thanaikhwaam thîi phûut phaasǎa…* ผม/ฉันต้องการทนายความที่พูดภาษา…

15. English-Thai Dictionary

A

about เกี่ยวกับ *kìao kàp*

about (approximately) ประมาณ *prà-maan*

absolutely/definitely/of course แน่นอน *nâe-nawn*

above เหนือ *nŭea*

abroad ต่างประเทศ *tàang prathêht*

accident อุบัติเหตุ *ubatìhèht*

accommodation ที่พัก *thîi-phák*

ache, to be in pain ปวด *pùat*

across ตรงข้าม *trong-khâam*

adaptor ตัวแปลงไฟฟ้า *tua plaehng fai fáa*

add ใส่ *sài*, เพิ่ม *phêrm*

address ที่อยู่ *thîi yùu*

admission การเข้าชม *kaan khâo chom*

admission price ค่าผ่านประตู *khâa phàan pratuu*

adorable (lovable) น่ารัก *nâa-rák*

adult ผู้ใหญ่ *phûu yài*

advice คำแนะนำ *kham náe-nam*

aeroplane เครื่องบิน *khrûeang bin*

afraid/scared กลัว *glua*

Africa แอฟริกา *Áp-frí-kaa*

after หลังจาก *lăng jàak*

afternoon ตอนบ่าย *tawn bàai*

again อีก *ìik*

against ต่อต้าน *tàw tâan*

age อายุ *aayú*

agree (with someone) เห็นด้วย *hěn-dûay*

AIDS โรคเอดส์ *rôhk ehd(s)*

air อากาศ *aa-kàat*

air conditioning ปรับอากาศ *pràp aakàat*

airmail จดหมายอากาศ *jòtmăai aakàat*

airplane เครื่องบิน *khrûeang bin*

airport สนามบิน, ท่าอากาศยาน *sanăam bin, thâa aakàatsayaan*

airport security หน่วยรักษาความปลอดภัยสนามบิน *nùai raksăa khwaam plàwt-phai sanăam-bin*

aisle seat ที่นั่งติดทางเดิน *thîi nâng tìt thaang doehn*

alarm เตือนภัย *tuean phai*

alarm clock นาฬิกาปลุก *naalíkaa plùk*

alcohol แอลกอฮอล์ *aehlkawhawn*

all day ทั้งวัน *tháng wan*, ตลอดวัน *talàwt wan*

all the time ตลอดเวลา *talàwt wehlaa*

allergy แพ้ *pháe*

alone เดียว *diao*

altogether ทั้งหมด *tháng mòt*

always เสมอ *samŏeh*

ambulance รถพยาบาล *rót phayaabaan*

America อเมริกา *amehríkaa*

American คนอเมริกัน *khon amehríkan*

amount จำนวน *jamnuan*

amusement park สวนสนุก *sŭan sanùk*

anaesthetic (local) ยาชา *yaa chaa*

anaesthetic (general) ยาสลบ *yaa salòp*

angry โกรธ *kròht*

animal สัตว์ *sàt*

ankle ข้อเท้า *khâw tháo*

answer คำตอบ *kham tàwp*

ant มด *mót*

antibiotics ยาปฏิชีวนะ *yaa patìchiiwaná*

antique โบราณ *bohraan*

antiseptic ยาฆ่าเชื้อ *yaa khâa chúea*

apartment อพาร์ตเม้นท์ *apaatmén*

apologies คำขอออภัย *kham khǎw aphai*

app แอป *áep*

appearance หน้าตา *nâa-taa*

apple แอปเปิ้ล *áeppôen*

apple juice น้ำแอปเปิ้ล *náam áeppôen*

application แอปพลิเคชัน *áep-phli-kheh-chân*

apply (for a job) สมัคร *sà-màk*

appointment นัด *nát*

April เมษายน *mehsǎayon*

appreciate/thanks ขอบคุณ *khàwp-khun*

appropriate/suitable เหมาะสม *màw-sǒm*

architecture สถาปัตยกรรม *sathǎapàtayákam*

area เขต พื้นที่ *khèht, phúehn thîi*

area code รหัสพื้นที่ *rahàt phúehn thîi*

arm แขน *khǎehn*

arrange จัดการ *jàtkaan*

arrive ถึง *thǔeng*

art ศิลปะ *sǐnlapà*

art gallery ห้องศิลป์ *hâwng sǐnlapà*

article บทความ *bòt khwaam*

artificial respiration การช่วยให้เขาหายใจทางปาก *kaan chûai hâi hǎi jai thaang pàak*

ask ถาม *thǎam*

ask for ขอ *khǎw*

aspirin ยาแอสไพริน *yaa aehsphairin*

assault ทำร้ายร่างกาย *tham rái râang kai*

assist ช่วย *chûuy*

at ที่ *thîi*

at home ที่บ้าน *thîi bâan*

at night กลางคืน *klaang khuehn*

at the back ข้างหลัง *khâng lǎng*

at the front ข้างหน้า *khâng nâa*

at the latest ล่าสุด *lâa sùt*

ATM เอทีเอ็ม *eh-thii-em*

August สิงหาคม *sǐnghǎakhom*

Australia ออสเตรเลีย *áws(a)trehlia*

Australian คนออสเตรเลีย *khon áws(a)trehlia*

automatic อัตโนมัติ *attànohmát*

autumn ฤดูใบไม้ร่วง *rúeduu bai mái rûang*

available, free (not busy) ว่าง *wâang*

awake ตื่น *tùehn*

B

baby ทารก *thaarók*

babysitter คนเลี้ยงเด็ก *khon líang dèk*

back (rear) ข้างหลัง *khâng lǎng*

back (part of body) หลัง *lǎng*

backpack กระเป๋าสะพายหลัง *krapǎo saphai lǎng*

bad (rotting) เสีย *sǐa*

bad (terrible) แย่ *yâeh*

bag ถุง, กระเป๋า *thǔng, krapǎo*

baggage claim ที่รับกระเป๋าเดินทาง *thîi ráp krapǎo doehn thaang*

baht (Thai currency) บาท *bàat*

bake (to be baked) อบ *òp*

balcony ระเบียง *rabiang*

ball ลูกบอล *lûuk bawn*

ballpoint pen ปากกาหมึกแห้ง *pàakkaa mùek hâehng*

banana กล้วย *glûai*

bandage ผ้าพันแผล *phâa phan phlǎeh*

bangs, fringes ผมม้า *phǒm mâa*

bank (finance) ธนาคาร *thanaakhaan*

bank (river) ฝั่ง *fang*

Bangkok กรุงเทพฯ *grung-thêp*

bar (café) บาร์ *baa*

barbecue บาร์บีคิว *baabìkhiu*

barber ช่างตัดผม *châang-tàt-phǒm*

basketball บาสเก็ตบอล *baasakèhtbawn*

bath อาบน้ำ *àap náam*

bathrobe ผ้าคลุมอาบน้ำ *phâa khlum àap náam*

bathroom ห้องน้ำ *hâwng náam*

bathtub อ่างอาบน้ำ *àang-àap-náam*

battery แบตเตอรี่ *baettoehrîi*, ถ่านไฟฉาย *thàan fai chǎai*

beach ชายหาด *chaai hàat hàat*, ทะเล *thá-leh*

beans ถั่ว *thùa*

beat (to strike) ตี *tii*

beautiful สวย *sǔai*

bed เตียง *tiang*

bedding เครื่องนอน *khrûeang nawn*

bedroom ห้องนอน *hâwng-nawn*

bedsheet ผ้าปูที่นอน *phâa-pou-thîi-nawn*

bee ผึ้ง *phûeng*

beef เนื้อวัว *núea wua*

beer เบียร์ *bia*

before ก่อน *gàwn*

begin เริ่ม *rôehm*

behind ข้างหลัง *khâng lǎng*

belt เข็มขัด *khěm khàt*

berth ที่นอน (บนเรือหรือรถไฟ) *thîi nawn (bon ruea rǔeh rót fai)*

best ดีที่สุด *dii-thîi-sùt*

better (to get) ดีขึ้น *dii khûen*

between ระหว่าง *rá-wàang*

bicycle รถจักรยาน *rót jàk-grà-yaan*

bikini ชุดว่ายน้ำ *chút wâi náam*

bill บิล *bin*

billiards บิลเลียด *billîat*

birthday วันเกิด *wan kòeht*

biscuit บิสกิต *biskìt*

bit นิดหน่อย *nít-nòi*

bite กัด *kàt*

bitter ขม *khǒm*

black ดำ *dam*

black and white ขาวดำ *khǎao dam*

bland (taste) จืด *cùeht*

blanket ผ้าห่ม *phâa hòm*

bleach ผ่าฝืน *fàa fǔehn*

bleed เลือดออก *lûeat àwk*

blind (on window) ที่กันแดด *thîi kan dàeht*

blister เม็ดพุพอง *mét phú phawng*

blog บล็อก *blàwk*

blond ผมทอง *phǒm thawng*

blood เลือด *lûeat*

blood pressure ความดันโลหิต *khwaam dan lohhìt*

blouse เสื้อ (ผู้หญิง) *sûea (phûu yǐng)*

blue สีฟ้า *sǐi fáa*

blue (dark) สีน้ำเงิน *sǐi-náam-ngoen*

boarding pass บัตรผ่านขึ้นเครื่องบิน *bàt phàan khûen khrûeang-bin*

boat เรือ *ruea*

body ตัว ร่างกาย *tua râang kai*

bone กระดูก *kradùuk*

book หนังสือ *nǎngsǔeh*

booked, reserved จองไว้ *jawng wái*

booking office ที่จองตั๋ว *thîi jawng tǔa*

bookshop ร้านหนังสือ *ráan nǎngsǔeh*

border ชายแดน *chaai daehn*

born เกิด *kòeht*

borrow ยืม *yuehm*

botanic gardens สวนพฤกษชาติ *sŭan phrúeksachâat*

both ทั้งคู่ *tháng khûu*

bottle ขวด *khùat*

bottle-warmer ที่อุ่นขวดนม *thîi ùn khùat nom*

bowl ชาม *chaam*

box กล่อง *glàwng*

box office ที่ขายตั๋ว *thîi khǎi tǔa*

boy เด็กชาย *dèk chaai*

boyfriend เพื่อนชาย *phûean chaai*

bra เสื้อชั้นใน *sûea chǎn nai*

bracelet สร้อยข้อมือ *sôi khâw mueh*

brake หยุด, เบรค *yùt, brèhk*

bread ขนมปัง *khanŏm pang*

break พัก *phák*

breakfast อาหารเช้า *aahǎan cháo*

breast หน้าอก *nâa òk*

breast milk นมแม่ *nom mâeh*

bride เจ้าสาว *jâo-sǎaw*

bridegroom เจ้าบ่าว *jâo-bàaw*

bridge สะพาน *saphaan*

briefs กางเกงใน *kaangkehng nai*

bring เอามา, นำมา *ao maa, nam maa*

bring up/raise (children) เลี้ยง *líang*

British (person) คนอังกฤษ *khon-àng-grìt*

British English ภาษาอังกฤษ *phaa-sǎa -àng-grìt*

brochure แผ่นพับ *phàen pháp*

broken พัง, แตก *phang, tàehk*

bronze ทองสัมฤทธิ์ *thawng sǎmrít*

broth น้ำซุป *námsup*

brother (elder) พี่ชาย *phîi chaai*

brother (younger) น้องชาย *náwng chaai*

brown สีน้ำตาล *sĭi nám taan*

browser เบราว์เซอร์ *brao-sôeh*

bruise รอยช้ำ *roi chám*

brush แปรง *praehng*

bucket ถัง *thǎng*

buddy (friend) เพื่อน *phûean*

bugs แมลง *malaehng*

building ตึก *tùek*

burglary การขโมย *gaan khamoey*

burn (injury) แผลไหม้ *phlǎeh mâi*

burn (v.) ไหม้ *mâi*

bus รถเมล์ *rót meh*

bus station ชุมสายรถเมล์ *chum sǎi rót meh*

bus stop ป้ายรถเมล์ *pâi rót meh*

business card นามบัตร *naam bàt*

business class ชั้นธุรกิจ *chán thurákìt*

business trip เดินทางไปธุรกิจ *doehn thaang pai thurákìt*

busy (schedule) ยุ่ง *yûng*

busy (traffic) ติดขัด *tit khàt*

but แต่ *tàeh*

butcher คนขายเนื้อ *khon khǎi núea*

butter เนย *noei*

button กระดุม *kradum*

buy ซื้อ *súe*

by airmail ทางอากาศ *thaang aakàat*

by phone ทางโทรศัพท์ *thaang thohrásàp*

C

cabbage กะหล่ำปลี *kalàmphlii*

cabin ห้อง *hâwng*

cabinet ตู้ *tôu*

cake ขนมเค้ก *khanŏm khéhk*

calculator เครื่องคิดเลข *khrûeang-khít-lêk*

call (phonecall) โทรศัพท์ *thohrásàp*

call (to phone) โทรศัพท์ *thohrásàp*, โทร *thoh*

camera กล้อง *glâwng*

camping ไปค่าย *pai khâi*

can *dâi* ได้

Can you....? ..*dâi mái?* ได้ไหม

Canada แคนาดา *khaeh-naa-daa*

cancel ยกเลิก *yók lôehk*

candle เทียน *thian*

candy ลูกกวาด *lûuk kwàat*, ท็อฟฟี่ *tháwffii*

cannot ไม่ได้ *mâi-dâi*

car รถ *rót*

car seat (child's) ที่นั่งเด็ก *thîi nâng dèk*

cardigan เสื้อหนาว *sûea nǎo*

careful ระวัง *ra-wang*

carpet พรม *phrom*

carriage ตู้รถไฟ *tûu rót fai*

carrot แครอท *khaehràwt*

carry (in the hands) หิ้ว, ถือ *hîw, thěu*

cartridge ตลับ *talàp*

cash เงินสด *ngoehn sòt*

casino บ่อนการพนัน *bàwn kaan phanan*

cat แมว *maeo*

cause สาเหตุ *sǎahèht*

cave ถ้ำ *thâm*

CD ซีดี *sii dii*

CD-ROM ซีดีรอม *sii dii rawm*

celebrate ฉลอง *chalǎwng*

cell (or mobile) phone โทรศัพท์มือถือ/ไมบาย *thorasàp mue-thǔe/moo-bai*

cemetery ที่ฝังศพ *thîi fǎng sòp*

center (middle) กลาง *glaang*

center (of city) ศูนย์กลาง *sǔun glaang*

centimeter เซนติเมตร *sentìméht*

central heating เครื่องทำความร้อนกลาง *khrûeang tham khwaam ráwn klaang*

certificate ประกาศนียบัตร *prakàatsaniiyábàt*

chair เก้าอี้ *kâo-îi*

champagne แชมเปญ *chaehmpehn*

change, swap เปลี่ยน *plìan*

change (money) เงินทอน *ngoehn thawn*

change (trains) ต่อรถไฟ *tàw rót fai*

charger เครื่องชาร์ท *khrûeng cháat*

charter flight เที่ยวบินพิเศษ *thîao bin phísèht*

chat คุย *khui*

cheap (in price) ถูก *thòuk*

cheat โกง *gohng*

checked luggage กระเป๋าที่ตรวจแล้ว *krapǎo thîi trùat láehw*

check, bill บิล *bin*

check (v.) ตรวจ *trùat*

check in เช็คอิน *chék in*

check out เช็คเอ้าท์ *chék ao(t)*

cheers! โชคดี *chôhk dii*

chef พ่อครัว *phâw khrua*

chess หมากรุก *màak rúk*

chewing gum หมากฝรั่ง *màak faràng*

chicken ไก่ *kài*

child เด็ก *dèk*

chili pepper พริก *phrík*

chilled (of body) เย็น *nǎo*

chilled (of foods) หนาว *yen*

chin คาง *khaang*

China จีน *jiin*

Chinese (language) ภาษาจีน *phaa-sǎa jiin*

Chinese (people) คนจีน *khon jiin*

chocolate ช็อกโกแลต *cháwkkohláet*

choose เลือก *lûeak*

chopsticks ตะเกียบ *tà-gìap*

church โบสถ์ *bòht*

cigar บุหรี่ซิการ์ *burìi siikaa*

cigarette บุหรี่ *burìi*

circle วงกลม *wong glom*

circus ละครสัตว์ *lá-khawn sàt*

citizen ประชาชน *pra-chaa-chon*

city เมือง *mueang*

class เรียน *rian*

clean สะอาด *sa-àat*

clean (v.) ทำความสะอาด *tham khwaam sa-àat*

clearance (sale) ขายเลหลัง *khǎi lehlǎng*

clever ฉลาด *chà-làat*

clock นาฬิกา *naalíkaa*

closed ปิด *pìt*

closed off (road) ปิดถนน *pìt thanǒn*

clothes เสื้อผ้า *sûea phâa*

clothes dryer ที่อบผ้า *thîi òp phâa*

clothing เสื้อผ้า *sûea phâa*

clutch (car) คลัช *khlát*

coat (jacket) เสื้อแจ็คเก็ต *sûea jáekkêt*

coat (overcoat) เสื้อนอก *sûea nâwk*

cockroach แมลงสาบ *malaehng sàap*

cocoa โกโก้ *kohkôh*

coconut มะพร้าว *má-práow*

coconut milk กะทิ *kà-thí*

coffee กาแฟ *gaa-faeh*

cold (not hot) เย็น *yen*

cold, flu หวัด *wàt*

collar ปกเสื้อ *pòk sûea*

collarbone ไหปลาร้า *haiplaaráa*

colleague เพื่อนทำงาน *phûean tham ngaan*

collision การชน *gaan chon*

color สี *sǐi*

comb หวี *wǐi*

come มา *maa*

come back กลับมา *glàp maa*

come from มาจาก *maa-jàak*

comfortable สบาย *sà-baai*

company บริษัท *baw-rí-sàt*

compartment ห้อง *hâwng*

compete (v.) แข่ง *khàeng*

complaint ร้องทุกข์ *ráwng thúk*

compliment คำชม *kham chom*

comprising ได้แก่ *dâi kàeh*

computer คอมพิวเตอร์ *khawm-phiu-toeh*

computer game เกมส์ คอมพิวเตอร์ *kem khawm-phiu-toeh*

concert คอนเสิร์ต *khawnsòeht*

concierge คนเฝ้าประตู *khon fâo pratuu*

concussion การถูกกระทบอย่างแรง *kaan thùuk grà-thóp yàang raehng*

condensed milk นมข้น *nom khôn*

condom ถุงยางอนามัย *thǔng yang à-naa-mai*

confectionery ขนมหวาน *khà-nǒm wǎan*

confident มั่นใจ *mân-jai*

confused งง *ngong*

congratulations! ขอแสดงความยินดีด้วย *khǎw sà-daehng khwaam yindii dûai*

connect ต่อ *tàw*

connection (transport) การต่อรถ *kaan tàw rót*

constipation ท้องผูก *tháwng phùuk*

consulate กงสุล *gong-sǔn*

consultation (by doctor) คำปรึกษา *kham prùeksǎa*

contact lens คอนแทคเลนซ์ *khawntháek len*

contagious ติดต่อ *tìt tàw*

contraceptive pill ยาคุมกำเนิด *yaa khum kamnòeht*

control (something) ควบคุม *khûap-khum*

convenient สะดวก *sà-dùak*

cook (male) กุ๊ก *kúk*, พ่อครัว *phâw khrua*

cook (female) กุ๊ก *kúk*, แม่ครัว *mâeh khrua*

cook (v.) ทำอาหาร *tham aahǎan*

cookie คุกกี้ *khúkkîi*

cool เย็น *yen*

copy ก็อปปี้ *káwp-pîi*

corkscrew จุกไม้ก๊อก *jùkmáikáwk*

corn ข้าวโพด *khâo-phôht*

corner มุม *mum*

correct ถูก *thùuk*

correspond เขียนจดหมาย *khǐan jòtmǎi*

corridor ทางเดินในตึก *thaang doehn nai tùek*

cosmetics เครื่องสำอาง *khrûeang sǎm-aang*

cost (price) ราคา *raa-khaa*

costume เครื่องแต่งตัว *khrûeang tàeng tua*

cot เตียงเด็ก *tiang dèk*

cotton ฝ้าย *fâai*

cotton wool สำลี *sǎmlii*

cough การไอ *kaan ai*

cough (v.) ไอ *ai*

cough syrup ยาแก้ไอ *yaa kâeh ai*

counter เคาน์เตอร์ *kháotôeh*

country (nation) ประเทศ *prà-thêht*

country (rural area) ชนบท, บ้านนอก *chonabòt, bâan nâwk*

country code รหัสประเทศ *rahàt prathêht*

course of treatment ระยะเวลารักษา *rayá wehlaa ráksǎa*

court (of law) ศาล *sǎan*

cousin ลูกพี่ลูกน้อง *lûuk phîi lûuk náwng*

crab ปู *puu*

cracker ขนมปังกรอบ *khanǒmpang kràwp*

crash ชน *chon*

crazy, mad บ้า *bâa*

cream ครีม *khriim*

create/build, to สร้าง *sâang*

credit card บัตรเครดิต *bàt khrehdìt*

crime อาชญากรรม *àatyaakam*

cross (road, river) ข้าม *khâam*

crossroad สี่แยก *sìi-yâehk*

crutch ไม้ยันรักแร้ *mái yan rák ráeh*

cry ร้องไห้ *ráwng hâi*

cubic meter ลูกบาศก์เมตร *lûukbàat méht*

cucumber แตงกวา *taehng gwaa*

cuff ข้อมือเสื้อ *khâw mueh sûea*

cufflinks กระดุมข้อมือ *grà-dum khâw mueh*

cup ถ้วย *thûai*

curly หยิก *yìk*

current (electric) กระแสไฟฟ้า *krasǎeh fai fáa*

cursor เคอร์เซอร์ *khoeh-sôeh*

curtains ม่าน *mâan*

cushion เบาะ *bàw*

custom ประเพณี *prà-pheh-nii*

customs ศุลกากร *sǔn-lá-gaa-gawn*

cut (injury) บาด *bàat*

cut (v.) ตัด *tàt*

cute น่ารัก *nâa-rák*

cutlery ช้อนส้อม *cháwn sâwm*

cybercafe ร้านอินเทอร์เน็ต *ráan in-toeh-net*

cycling ขี่จักรยาน *khìi jàk-grà-yaan*

D

dairy products ผลิตภัณฑ์นม *phalitaphan nom*

damage ความเสียหาย *khwaam sǐa hǎi*

dance เต้นรำ *tên ram*

danger อันตราย *antàraai*

dangerous น่าอันตราย *nâa antàraai*

dark (of color) เข้ม *khêm*

dark (complexion) คล้ำ *khlâm*

dark มืด *mûeht*

date วันที่ *wan thîi*

date of birth วันเกิด *wan gòeht*

daughter ลูกสาว *lûuk sǎo*

day วัน *wan*

day after tomorrow มะรืนนี้ *maruehn níi*

day before yesterday เมื่อวานซืน *mûea waansuehn*

day off วันหยุด *wan-yùt*

dead ตาย *taai*

dead zone ที่ไม่มีสัญญาณ *thîi mâi mii sǎnyaan*

deaf หูหนวก *hǔu nùak*

debt หนี้ *nîi*

decaffeinated กาแฟที่ไม่มีคาเฟอิน *gaa-faeh thîi mâi mii khaafeh-in*

December ธันวาคม *thanwaakhom*

declare (customs) แจ้ง (ศุลกากร) *jâeng (sǔnlakaakawn)*

deep ลึก *lúek*

deep-sea diving ดำน้ำทะเลลึก *dam náam thaleh lúek*

degrees องศา *ongsǎa*

delay ล่าช้า *lâa cháa*

delete ลบ *lóp*

delicious อร่อย *à-ròi*

dentist หมอฟัน *mǎw fan*

dentures ฟันปลอม *fan plawm*

deodorant ยาระงับกลิ่นตัว *yaa rangáp glìn tua*

depart ออกจาก *àwk-jàak*

department store ห้างสรรพสินค้า *hâang sapphasǐnkháa*

departure การออก *gaan àwk*

departure time เวลาออก *wehlaa àwk*

deposit (money in a bank) ฝาก (เงิน) *fàak (ngoehn)*

deposit (for safekeeping) ฝากของ *fàak khǎwng*

desert ทะเลทราย *thá-leh sai*

desk โต๊ะ *tóeh*

dessert ของหวาน *khǎwng wǎan*

destination จุดหมายปลายทาง *jùt mǎi plaai thaang*

detergent ผงซักฟอก *phǒng sák fâwk*

develop (photo) ล้างรูป *láang rûup*

diabetic เบาหวาน *bao-wǎan*

dial หมุน *mǔn*

diamond เพชร *phét*

diaper ผ้าอ้อม *phâa âwm*

diarrhoea ท้องเสีย *tháwng sǐa*

dictionary พจนานุกรม *phót-jà-naa-nú-grom*

die (become dead) ตาย *taai*

die (stop operation) เสีย *sǐa*

diesel oil น้ำมันดีเซล *náamman diisên*

diet จำกัดอาหาร *jamkàt aahǎan*

difficulty ความลำบาก *khwaam lambàak*

digital camera กล้องดิจิตอล *klâwng dì-jì-tâwn*

dining room ห้องอาหาร *hâwng aahǎan*

dinner อาหารเย็น *aahǎan yen*

direction ทิศทาง *thít thaang*

direct flight เที่ยวบินตรง *thîao bin trong*

dirty สกปรก *sòkkapròk*

disabled พิการ *phí-gaan*

disco ดิสโก้ *dís-gôh*

discount ลดราคา *lót raakhaa*

disease โรค *rôk*

dish จาน *jaan*

disinfectant ยาฆ่าเชื้อ *yaa khâa chúea*

dislike ไม่ชอบ *mâi-châwp*

distance ความไกล *khwaam klai*

distilled water น้ำกลั่น *náam glàn*

disturb รบกวน *róp-guan*

disturbance การรบกวน *gaan róp-guan*

dive ดำน้ำ *dam náam*

diving การดำน้ำ *gaan dam náam*

divorced หย่าแล้ว *yàa láehw*

dizzy งง *ngong*

do ทำ *tham*

doctor หมอ *măw*

document copy สำเนา *săm-nao*

dog หมา *măa*

do-it-yourself store ร้านของทำเอง *ráan khăwng tham ehng*

doll ตุ๊กตา *túk-gà-taa*

dollar ดอลลาร์ *dawn-lâa*

domestic ภายในครัวเรือน *phai nai khrua ruean*

done (cooked) สุก *sùk*

do not disturb อย่ารบกวน *yàa rópkuan*

door ประตู *prà-tuu*

double สองเท่า *săwng thâo*

down ลง *long*

download ดาวน์โหลด *daao-lòod*

downstairs ข้างล่าง *khâang-lâang*

draught ลม *lom*

dream (v.) ฝัน *făn*

dress แต่งตัว *tàeng tua*

drink (refreshment) เครื่องดื่ม *khrûeang dùehm*

drink (alcoholic) เครื่องดื่มเป็นเหล้า *khrûeang dùehm pen lâo*

drink (v.) ดื่ม *dùehm,* (informal) กินน้ำ *gin-náam*

drinking water น้ำดื่ม *náam dùehm*

drive ขับ *khàp*

driver คนขับ *khon khàp*

driver's licence ใบขับขี่ *bai khàp khìi*

drug ยา *yaa*

drugstore ร้านขายยา *ráan khăai yaa*

dry แห้ง *hâehng*

dry (v.) ตากให้แห้ง *tàak hâi hâehng*

drycleaners ร้านซักแห้ง *ráan sák hâehng*

duck เป็ด *pèt*

durian ทุเรียน *thú-rian*

during ระหว่าง *ra-wàang*

during the day ช่วงกลางวัน *chûang glaang wan*

duty (tax) ภาษี *phaasĭi*

duty-free shop ร้านสินค้าปลอดภาษี *ráan sĭnkháa plàwt phaasĭi*

DVD ดีวีดี *dii wii dii*

E

e-book อีบุ๊ค *ii-búk*

e-booking (reservation) จองตั๋วออนไลน์ *jawng tŭa awn-laai*

e-ticket ตั๋วอิเล็กทรอนิกส์ *tŭa ii-lék-tron-ník*

each other กัน *gan*

ear หู *hŭu*

earache ปวดหู *pùat hŭu*

earbud หูฟัง *hŭu fang*

ear drops ยาหยอดหู *yaa yàwt hŭu*

early แต่เนิ่นๆ *tàe nôehn nôehn*

earrings ตุ้มหู *tûm hǔu*

earth ดิน *din*

Earth โลก *lôhk*

earthenware เครื่องปั้นดินเผา *khruêang pân din phǎo*

east ตะวันออก *ta-wan àwk*

easy ง่าย *ngâi*

eat กิน *kin*

economy class ชั้นประหยัด *chán prayàt*

eel ปลาไหล *plaa lǎi*

egg ไข่ *khài*

eight แปด *pàet*

elbow ข้อศอก *khâw-sàwk*

electric ไฟฟ้า *fai fáa*

electricity ไฟฟ้า *fai fáa*

electronics อิเล็กทรอนิกส์ *ilék thrawník*

elephant ช้าง *cháang*

elevator ลิฟต์ *líf*

email อีเมล์ *iimeh(l)/email*

email address ที่อยู่อีเมล์ *thîi yùu ii-mei*

embassy สถานทูต *sathǎan thûut*

embrace/hug กอด *gàwt*

emergency ฉุกเฉิน *chùk-chǒehn*

emergency brake เบรคฉุกเฉิน *brèhk chùk chǒehn*

emergency exit ทางออกฉุกเฉิน *thaang àwk chùk chǒehn*

empty ว่างเปล่า *wâang plào*

end (ending) จบ *jòp*

engaged (on the phone) พูดโทรศัพท์ *phûut thohrasàp*

engaged (to be married) หมั้น *mân*

England ประเทศอังกฤษ *prathêht angkrit*

English ภาษาอังกฤษ *phaasǎa angrit*

enjoy สนุก *sà-nùk*

enough, sufficient พอ *phaw*

enquire สอบถาม *sàwp thǎam*

enter เข้า *khâo*

entrance ทางเข้า *thaang-khâo*

envelope ซอง *sawng*

errand ธุระ *thú-rá*

escalator บันไดเลื่อน *bandai lûean*

essential จำเป็น *jam-pen*

evening ตอนเย็น *tawn yen*

evening wear ชุดกลางคืน *chút glaang khuehn*

event เหตุการณ์ *hèht gaan*

every ทุก *thúk*

everyday ทุกวัน *thúk-wan*

everyone ทุกคน *thúk-khon*

everything ทุกอย่าง *thúk yàang*

everywhere ทุกแห่ง *thúk hàeng*

examine ตรวจสอบ *trùat sàwp*

excavation การขุดแจาะ *kaan khùt jàw*

excellent ยอดเยี่ยม *yâwt yîam*

exchange แลกเปลี่ยน *lâehk plìan*

exchange office ที่แลกเงิน *thîi lâehk ngoehn*

excursion ทัศนศึกษา *thátsanásùeksǎa*

exercise, to ออกกำลังกาย *àwk-gam-lang kaai*

exhibition นิทรรศการ *ní-thát-sa-gaan*

exit ทางออก *thaang àwk*

expenses ค่าใช้จ่าย *khâa chái cài*

expensive แพง *phaehng*

experience ประสบการณ์ *prà-sòp-gaan*

explain อธิบาย *athíbai*

express ด่วน *dùan*

external ภายนอก *pai nâwk*

extra พิเศษ *phí-sèt*

extremely ที่สุด *thîi-sùt*

eye ตา *taa*

eye drops ยาหยอดตา *yaa yàwt taa*

eye specialist หมอตา *mǎw taa*

F

fabric ผ้า *phâa*

face หน้า *nâa*

Facebook เฟสบุ๊ค *Fehs-búk*

factory โรงงาน *rohng ngaan*

faint เป็นลม *pen-lom*

fake (an imitation) ปลอม *plawm*

fall (season) ฤดูใบไม้ร่วง *rúeduu bai mái rûang*

fall (v.) ตก *tòk*

fall over ล้ม *lóm*

family ครอบครัว *khrâwp khrua*

famous ดัง *dang*

fan (admirer) แฟน *faehn*

fan พัดลม *phát-lom*

fancy หรู *rǔu*

far away ไกลโพ้น *klai phón*

farmer ชาวนา *chao naa*

fashion แฟชั่น *faehchân*

fast เร็ว *reo*

fat อ้วน *ûan*

father พ่อ *phâw*

father-in-law พ่อตา *phâw taa*

fault ความผิด *khwaam phìt*

fax แฟกซ์ *fáek(s)*

fear กลัว *glua*

February กุมภาพันธ์ *kumphaaphan*

fee ค่า *khâa*

feel รู้สึก *rúusùek*

feel like รู้สึกเหมือน *rúusùek mǔean*

fence รั้ว *rúa*

ferry เรือข้ามฟาก *ruea khâam fâak*

fever ไข้ *khâi*

fiancé, fiancée คู่หมั้น *khûu mân*

field, lawn สนาม *sà-nǎam*

field, paddy นา *naa*

fight สู้ *sôu*

fill เติม *toehm*

filling (in food) ทำให้อิ่ม *tham hâi ìm*

filling (dental) อุดฟัน *ùt fan*

fill out (form) กรอก *gràwk*

film (photo) ฟิล์ม *fiim*

film (cinema) หนัง *nǎng*

filter เครื่องกรอง *khrûeang krawng*

fine (good) ดี *dii*

fine (money) ค่าปรับ *khâa pràp*

finger นิ้ว *níu*

fire ไฟ *fai*

fire alarm สัญญาณไฟไหม้ *sǎnyaan fai mâi*

fire escape บันไดหนีไฟ *bandai nǐi fai*

fire extinguisher ที่ดับเพลิง *thîi dàp phloehng*

first แรก *râehk*

first aid ปฐมพยาบาล *pa-thǒm phayaa-baan*

first class ชั้นหนึ่ง *chán nùeng*

fish ปลา *plaa*

fish (v.) ตกปลา *tòk plaa*

fitness club สโมสรออกกำลังกาย *samohsǎwn àwk kamlang kaai*

fitting room ห้องลองเสื้อ *hâwng lawng sûea*

fix (puncture) แก้ *gâeh*

flag ธง *thong*

flash (camera) แฟลช *flâet*

flashdrive แฟลชไดร์ฟ *flàeht-dái*

flashlight ไฟฉาย *fai chǎai*

flavor รส *rót*

flavoring เครื่องปรุงรส *khrûeang prung rót*

flea market ตลาดขายของเก่า *talàat khǎi khǎwng kào*

flesh, meat เนื้อ *núea*

flight เที่ยวบิน *thîao bin*

flight number เที่ยวบินที่ *thîao bin thîi*

flirt จีบ *jìip*

float ลอย *loy*

flood น้ำท่วม *náam thûam*

floor พื้น *phúehn*

flour แป้ง *pâehng*

flower ดอกไม้ *dàwk-mái*

flu ไข้หวัดใหญ่ *khâi wàt yài*

flush เปล่งปลั่ง *plèng plàng*

fly (insect) แมลงวัน *malaehngwan*

fly (v.) บิน *bin*

fog หมอก *màwk*

folklore นิทานพื้นบ้าน *níthaan phúehn bâan*

follow ตาม *taam*

food (groceries) กับข้าว *kàp khâo*

food (meal) อาหาร *aahǎan*

food court ที่ขายอาหาร *thîi khǎi aahǎan*

food poisoning อาหารเป็นพิษ *aahǎan pen phít*

foot เท้า *tháo*

football (soccer) ฟุตบอล *fút-bawn*

foot brake ใช้เท้าเบรก *chái tháo brèhk*

foreign ต่างประเทศ *tàang prathêht*

forest ป่า *pàa*

forget ลืม *luehm*

fork ส้อม *sâwm*

form รูปแบบ *rûup bàehp*

forward (letter) ส่งจดหมาย *sòng còtmǎi*

fountain น้ำพุ *náam phú*

frame กรอบรูป *kràwp rûup*

France (country) ฝรั่งเศส *fà-ràng-sèt*

free (no charge) ฟรี *frii*

free (unoccupied) ว่าง *wâang*

free time เวลาว่าง *wehlaa wâang*

French (language) ภาษาฝรั่งเศส *phaa-sǎa-fà-ràng-sèt*

French (person) คนฝรั่งเศส *khon-fà-ràng-sèt*

french fries มันฝรั่งทอด *man faràng thâwt*

fresh สด *sòt*

Friday วันศุกร์ *wan sùk*

fried (in pieces) ทอด *thâwt*

friend เพื่อน *phûean*

friendly เป็นกันเอง *pen gan ehng*

frightened ตกใจ *tòk jai*

frozen แช่แข็ง *châeh khǎeng*

fruit ผลไม้ *phǒnlamái*

fruit juice น้ำผลไม้ *náam phǒnlamái*

fry ทอด *thâwt*

full เต็ม *tem*

fun สนุก *sanùk*

future อนาคต *à-naa-khót*

G

gallery ห้องแสดงภาพ *hâwng sadaehng phâap*

game เกม *gehm*

garage (car repair) อู่ซ่อมรถ *ùu sôm rót*

garbage ขยะ *khayà*

garlic กระเทียม *grà thiam*

garden สวน *sǔan*

garment เสื้อผ้า *sûea phâa*

gas (for heating) แก๊ซ *gáet*

gasoline น้ำมัน *náamman*

gas station ปั๊มน้ำมัน *pám náamman*

gate ประตู *prà-tuu*

gear (car) เกียร์ *gia*

gem เพชรพลอย *phét-phloi*

gender เพศ *phêht*

generous ใจดี *jai-dii*

German (language) ภาษาเยอรมัน *phaa-sǎa-yer-rá-man*

German (person) ภาษาเยอรมัน *khon-sǎa-yer-rá-man*

get (receive) ได้ *dâi*

get off ลง *long*

get on ขึ้น *khûen*

get up ตื่นนอน *tùen-nawn*

get หาย *well hǎay*

gift ของขวัญ *khǎwng khwǎn*

girl เด็กผู้หญิง *dèk phûu yǐng*

girlfriend เพื่อนหญิง, แฟน *phûean yǐng, faehn*

given name ชื่อ *chûeh*

glass (material) กระจก *grà-jòk*

glass (for drinking) แก้ว *gâew*

glasses, spectacles แว่นตา *wâen taa*

glossy (photo) เป็นมัน *pen man*

gloves ถุงมือ *thǔng mueh*

glue กาว *gaow*

go ไป *pai*

go back กลับไป *glàp pai*

go home กลับบ้าน *glàp-bâan*

go out ออกไป *àwk pai*

go straight ahead ตรงไป *trong-pai*

gold ทอง *thawng*

golf กอล์ฟ *káwf*

good afternoon สวัสดี *sawàt dii*

goodbye ลาก่อน *laa gàwn*

good evening สวัสดี *sawàt dii*

good morning สวัสดี *sawàt dii*

good night ราตรีสวัสดิ์ *raatrii sawàt*

GPS (Navigation) จีพีเอส *jii-phii-ehs*

gram กรัม *kram*

grandchild หลาน *lǎan sǎao*

granddaughter หลานสาว *lǎan sǎo*

grandfather (paternal) ปู่ *pùu*

grandfather (maternal) ตา *taa*

grandmother (paternal) ย่า *yâa*

grandmother (maternal) ยาย *yaai*

grandparents ปู่ย่าตายาย *pùu yâa taa yaai*

grandson หลานชาย *lǎan chaai*

grapes องุ่น *à-ngùn*

grass หญ้า *yâa*

grateful ขอบคุณ *khàwp-khun*

grave หลุมศพ *lǔm sòp*

gray, grey สีเทา *sǐi-thao*

guava ฝรั่ง *fà-ràng*

graze (injury) ถลอก *thalàwk*

greasy เปื้อนน้ำมัน *pûean náamman*

Great Britain อังกฤษ *ang-grìt*

green สีเขียว *sǐi khǐaw*

greengrocer ร้านขายผักผลไม้ *ráan khǎai phàk phǒnlamái*

greeting การทักทาย *gaan thák thai*

grey สีเทา *sǐi thao*

grilled ปิ้ง *pîng*

groceries ของชำ *khǎwng cham*

group กลุ่ม *klùm*

guava ฝรั่ง *fà-ràng*

guest (visitor) แขก *khàek*

guest house เรือนรับรอง *ruean ráp rawng*

guide (book) คู่มือ *khûu mueh*

guide (person) ไกด์, มัคคุเทศก์ *kái, mákkhúthêht*

guitar กีตาร์ *gii-tâa*

guilty ความผิด *khwaam phìt*

gym โรงยิม *rohng yim*

gynecologist สูตินแพทย์ *sǔutìphâeht*

H

hair ผม *phŏm*

hairbrush แปรง *praehng*

haircut ตัดผม *tàt phŏm*

hairdresser ช่างทำผม *châang tham phŏm*

hairdryer ที่เป่าผม *thîi pào phŏm*

half ครึ่ง *khrûeng*

half full ครึ่ง *khrûeng*

hand มือ *mueh*

handbag กระเป๋าถือ *krapǎo thǔeh*

hand brake เบรคมือ *brèhk mueh*

handkerchief ผ้าเช็ดหน้า *phâa chét nâa*

hand luggage กระเป๋าหิ้ว *grà-pǎo hîu*

handmade ทำด้วยมือ *tham dûai mueh*

happy มีความสุข *mii khwaam sùk*

harbor ท่าเรือ *thâa ruea*

hard (firm) แข็ง *khǎeng*

hard (difficult) ยาก *yâak*

hard (heavy, work) หนัก *nàk*

hardware ฮาร์ดแวร์ *háat-waeh*

hardworking, diligent ขยัน *khà-yǎn*

hat, cap หมวก *mùak*

hate เกลียด *glìat*

have, has มี *mii*

he, she เขา *khǎo*

head หัว *hǔa*

headache ปวดหัว *pùat hǔa*

headlights ไฟหน้า *fai nâa*

heal รักษา *rák-sǎa*

health food shop ร้านขายอาหารเพื่อสุขภาพ *ráan khǎi aahǎan phûea sùkhàphâap*

healthy สมบูรณ์, สุขภาพดี *sǒmbuun, sùkkhàphâap dii*

hear ได้ยิน *dâi-yin*

heart หัวใจ *hǔa jai*

heart attack หัวใจวาย *hǔa jai waai*

heat ความร้อน *khwaam ráwn*

heater เครื่องทำความร้อน *khrûeang tham khwaam ráwn*

heavy หนัก *nàk*

heel (of shoe) ส้นรองเท้า *sôn rawng tháo*

hello (greeting) สวัสดี *sà-wàt-dii*

hello ฮัลโหล *hal-lŏh*

help! ช่วยด้วย! *chûai dûai!*

help ช่วย *chûai*

helping (food) ปริมาณอาหารที่เสิร์ฟหนึ่งที่ *parimaan aahǎan thîi sòef nùeng thîi*

her ของเขา *khǎwng-khǎo*

herbal tea ชาสมุนไพร *chaa samǔn phrai*

here ที่นี่ *thîi nîi*

high สูง *sǔung*

high chair เก้าอี้เด็ก *kâo-îi dèk*

high tide น้ำขึ้นสุด *náam khûen sùt*

highway ทางหลวง *thaang lǔang*

hiking การเดินป่า *kaan doehn pàa*

him เขา *khǎo*

hip สะโพก *saphôok*

hire เช่า *châo*

his ของเขา *khǎwng-khǎo*

hit ตี *tii*

hitchhike โบกรถ *bòhk rót*

hobby งานอดิเรก *ngaan adirèhk*

holdup ปล้น, จี้ *plôn, cîi*

holiday (vacation) พักร้อน *phák ráwn*

holiday (festival) วันหยุดเทศกาล *wan yùt thêhtsakaan*

holiday (public) วันหยุดราชการ *wan yùt râatchakaan*

home บ้าน *bâan*, at home ที่บ้าน *thîi bâan*, to go home กลับบ้าน *klàp bâan*

homework การบ้าน *gaan-bâan*

homesick คิดถึงบ้าน *khít thǔeng bâan*

honest สุจริต, ซื่อสัตย์ *sùcarìt, sûehsàt*

honey น้ำผึ้ง *nám phûeng*

hope หวัง *wǎng*

horizontal แนวราบ *naew râap*

horrible น่าเกลียดมาก, แย่มาก *nâa klìat mâak, yâeh mâak*

horse ม้า *máa*

hospital โรงพยาบาล *rohng phayaabaan*

hospitality การรับรอง *gaan ráp rawng*

hot (warm) ร้อน *ráwn*

hot (sharp, spicy) เผ็ด *phèt*

hot spot จุดคลื่นสัญญาณถี่ *cùt khlûen sǎnyaan thìi*

hot spring น้ำพุร้อน *náam phú ráwn*

hot-water bottle กระเป๋าน้ำร้อน *krapǎo náam ráwn*

hotel โรงแรม *rohng raehm*

hour ชั่วโมง *chûamohng*

house บ้าน *bâan*

how? อย่างไร, ยังไง *yàangrai, yang-ngai*

how far? ไกลเท่าไร *klai thâorai*

how long (time)? นานเท่าไร *naan thâorai*

how many? เท่าไร, กี่อัน *thâorai, gìi an*

how much? เท่าไร *thâorai*

huge ใหญ่ *yài*

humid ชื้น *chúen*

humorous, funny ตลก *tà-lòk*

hundred grams ร้อยกรัม *ròi kram*

hungry หิว *hǐu*

hurry รีบ *rîip*

Hurry up! เร็วๆ *rew-rew!*

hurt (injured), sore เจ็บ *jèp*

husband สามี *sǎamii*

hut กระท่อม *krathâwm*

hybrid car รถยนต์ไฮบริด *rót yon hai-brid*

I

I (female) ฉัน *chǎn*, (male) ผม *phǒm*

ice น้ำแข็ง *nám-khoeng*

ice cream ไอศครีม *aiskhriim, aitiim*

ice cubes น้ำแข็งก้อน *nám khǎeng kâwn*

iced เย็น *yen*

ice-skating สเก็ตน้ำแข็ง *sakét nám khǎeng*

iced water น้ำเย็น *nám-yen*

idea ความคิด *khwaam khít*

identification (card) บัตรประจำตัว *bàt pracam tua*

identify ระบุ *rabù*

if ถ้า *thâa*

ill ป่วย *pùai*

illness ความเจ็บป่วย *khwaam cèp pùai*

image รูปภาพ *rôup-phâap*

imagine นึก, วาดภาพ *núek, wâat phâap*

immediately ทันที *than thii*

impatient ใจร้อน *jai-ráwn*

important สำคัญ *sǎmkhan*

import duty ภาษีนำเข้า *phaasǐi nam khâo*

impossible เป็นไปไม่ได้ *pen pai mâi dâi*

impressive ประทับใจ *prà-tháp-jai*

improve ปรับปรุง *pràp prung*

in ใน *nai*

in front ข้างหน้า *khâang-nâa*

in the evening ตอนเย็น *tawn yen*

in the morning ตอนเช้า *tawn cháo*

in-laws (female) สะใภ้ *sàphái*

in-laws (male) เขย *khǒei*

in order to เพื่อ *phûea*

incense stick ธูป *thôup*

including รวม *ruam*

inconvenient ไม่สะดวก *mâi-sà-dùak*

incorrect, wrong ผิด *phìt*

India อินเดีย *In-dia*

indicate บ่งชี้ *bòng chíi*

indigestion การไม่ย่อย *kaan mâi yôi*

inexpensive ไม่แพง *mâi phaehng*

infected ติดเชื้อ *tìt chéua*

infection การติดเชื้อ *kaan tìt chûea*

infectious ติดเชื้อ *tìt chûea*

inflammation ไวไฟ *wai fai*

inform แจ้ง *jâeng*

information ข้อมูล, ข่าวสาร
  khâwmuun, khào săan

information office สำนักงานข้อมูล
  sămnák ngaan khâwmuun

injection การฉีดยา *kaan chìit yaa*

injured บาดเจ็บ *bàat cèp*

inner tube ยางใน *yaang nai*

innocent บริสุทธิ์ *bawrísùt*

insect แมลง *malaehng*

insect repellant ยากันแมลง *yaa kan
  malaehng*

inside ข้างใน *khâng nai*

installments ผ่อนส่ง *phòn sòng*

instructions คำแนะนำ *kham náènam*

insurance การประกัน *kaan prakan*

interested, to be สนใจ *săn-jai*

interesting น่าสนใจ *nâa-sŏn-jai*

intermission พักครึ่งเวลา *phák
  khrûeng wehlaa*

internal ภายใน *phai nai*

international ต่างประเทศ *tàang
  prathêht*

Internet อินเทอร์เน็ต *in-toeh-net*

Internet café อินเทอร์เน็ตคาเฟ่
  in-toeh-net khaafêh

interpret/translate แปล *plae*

interpreter ล่าม *lâam*

intersection สี่แยก *sii yâehk*

interview สัมภาษณ์ *săm-phâat*

introduce oneself แนะนำตัวเอง
  náe-nam tua ehng

invite (formal) เชิญ *choehn*,
  (informal) ชวน *chuan*

iodine ไอโอดีน *ai-ohdiin*

iPhone ไอโฟน *ai-fone*

iPad ไอแพด *ai-pád*

iron (metal) เหล็ก *lèk*

iron (for clothes) เตารีด *tao rîit*

iron (v.) รีด *rîit*

island เกาะ *kàw*

Italy อิตาลี *i-taa-lĭi*

Italian (language) ภาษาอิตาลี
  phaa-săa-i-taa-lĭi

itch คัน *khan*

J

jack (for car) แม่แรง *mâe raehng*

jacket แจ็กเก็ต *cáekkêt*

jam แยม *yaehm*

January มกราคม *màkàraakhom*

Japan ญี่ปุ่น *yîi-pùn*

Japanese ภาษาญี่ปุ่น *phaa-săa-yîi-pùn*

jar (a large water jar) โอ่ง *òhng*

jaw กราม *kraam*

jeans กางเกงยีนส์ *kaangkehng yiin*

jellyfish แมงกะพรุน *maengkàphrun*

jewelery เพชรพลอย *phét phloi*

job งาน *ngaan*

jog วิ่งออกกำลัง *wîng áwk kamlang*

joke ตลก *talòk*

journalist นักข่าว *nák-khàaw*

journey การเดินทาง *kaan doehn
  thaang*

juice น้ำผลไม้ *nám phǒnlamái*

jump กระโดด *grà-dòht*

July กรกฎาคม *karákadaakhom*

June มิถุนายน *míthùnaayon*

jungle ป่า *pàa*

just now เพิ่ง *phôeng*

K

kale คะน้า *khá-náa*

keep เก็บ *gèp*

kerosene น้ำมันก๊าด *náamman káat*

kettle กาน้ำ *gaa-nám*

key กุญแจ *kunjaeh*

key (on keyboard) แป้นพิมพ์ (แผงแป้นพิมพ์) *pâen phim (phǎeng pâen phim)*

kick เตะ *tè*

kid (child) เด็ก *dèk*

kidney ไต *tai*

kill ฆ่า *khâa*

kilogram กิโลกรัม *kilohkram*

kilometer กิโลเมตร *gì-loh-mét*

king พระมหากษัตริย์ *phrá-mahǎa-kasàt*

kiss จูบ *jùup*

kiss (v.) จูบ *jùup*

kitchen ครัว *khrua*

knee เข่า *khào*

knife มีด *mîit*

knit ถักนิตติ้ง *thàk níttîng*

know รู้ *rúu*

know (familiar with someone) รู้จัก *rúu-jàk*

knowledge ความรู้ *khwaam rúu*

Korea เกาหลี *gao-lǐi*

Korean ภาษาเกาหลี *phaa-sǎa-gao-lǐi*

Korean drama ละคร(ทีวี)เกาหลี *lakawn (thii-wii) kao-lii*

K-pop ป๊อปเกาหลี *páwp kao-lǐi*

L

laces (for shoes) เชือกผูกรองเท้า *chûeak phùuk rawng tháo*

ladder บันได *bandai*

lake ทะเลสาบ *thaleh sàap*

lamb (mutton) เนื้อแกะ *núca kàe*

lamp ตะเกียง *takiang,* โคมไฟ *khom fai*

land (ground) พื้นดิน *phúehn din,* (property) ที่ดิน *thîi-din*

land (v.) ลง *long*

lane (of traffic) เลน *lehn*

language ภาษา *phaasǎa*

laptop computer คอมพิวเตอร์แล็ปท็อป *khawm-píu-toeh làep tháwp*

large ใหญ่ *yài*

last (final) สุดท้าย *sùt thái*

last (endure) อยู่ได้นาน *yùu dâi naan*

last night เมื่อคืนนี้ *mûea khuehn níi*

last week อาทิตย์ที่แล้ว *aathít thîi láehw*

late สาย *sǎi*

laugh หัวเราะ *hǔaráw*

launderette ร้านซักรีด *ráan sák rîit*

law กฎหมาย *kòtmǎi*

lawyer ทนายความ *thanai khwaam*

laxative ยาถ่าย *yaa thài*

leak รั่ว *rûa*

learn, study เรียน *rian*

leather หนัง *nǎng*

leave ออกจาก *àwk càak*

leave a message ฝากข้อความ *fàk-khâw-khwaam*

left (direction) ซ้าย *sái*

left behind ทิ้งไว้ *thíng wái*

leg ขา *khǎa*

leisure เวลาว่าง *wehlaa wâang*

lemon มะนาว *manao*

lemongrass ตะไคร้ *tà-khrái*

lend ให้ยืม *hâi yuehm*

lens (camera) เลนส์ *len*

less น้อยกว่า *nòi kwàa*

lesson บทเรียน *bòt rian*

letter จดหมาย *jòtmǎai*

lettuce ผักกาดแก้ว *phàkkàat kâeo*

level (floor) ชั้น *chǎn*

level crossing ทางข้าม *thaang khâam rótfai*

library ห้องสมุด *hâwng samùt*

license ใบอนุญาต *bai anúyâat*

lie (not tell the truth) พูดเท็จ *phûut thét*

lie (falsehood) โกหก *kohhòk*

lie down นอนลง *nawn long*

life ชีวิต *chii-wít*

lift (elevator) ลิฟต์ *líf*

light (lamp) ไฟ *fai*

light (not dark) สว่าง *sawàang*

light (not heavy) เบา *bao*

lighter ที่จุดบุหรี่ *thii cut burìi*

lightning ฟ้าผ่า *fáa phàa*

like (v.) ชอบ *châwp*

line เส้น *sên*

lip ริมฝีปาก *rim-fǐi-pàak*

liquor store ร้านเหล้า *ráan lâo*

liqueur เหล้า *lâo*

listen ฟัง *fang*

litre ลิตร *lít*

literature วรรณคดี *wannákhadii*

little (small) เล็ก *lék*

little (amount) น้อย *nói*

live (alive) มีชีวิต *mii chiiwít*

live (v.) อยู่ *yùu*

lobster กุ้งใหญ่ *kûng yài*

local ท้องถิ่น *tháwng thìn*

lock ล็อค *láwk*

log off ล็อกออฟ *láwk awf*

log on ล็อกออน *láwk awn*

long (in length) ยาว *yao*

long-distance call โทร.ทางไกล *thoh thaang klai*

look at ดู *duu*

look for หา *hǎa*

look up ชมเชย *chom choei*

lose หาย *hǎi*

loss ความสูญเสีย *khwaam sǔun sǐa*

lost (missing) หายไป *hǎi pai*

lost (can't find way) หลงทาง *lǒng thaang*

lot (a large amount) มาก, เยอะ *mâak, yér*

lotion โลชั่น *lohchân*

loud ดัง *dang*

love ความรัก *khwaam rák*

love (v.) รัก *rák*

lovely, cute, attractive น่ารัก *nâa-rák*

low ต่ำ *tàm*

low tide น้ำลงสุด *náam long sùt*

luck โชค *chôhk*

lucky โชคดี *chôk-dii*

luggage กระเป๋าเดินทาง *krapǎo doehn thaang*

luggage locker ที่เก็บสัมภาระ *thîi kèp sǎmphaará*

lumps (sugar) ก้อน *kâwn*

lunch อาหารกลางวัน *aahǎan klaang wan*

lungs ปอด *pàwt*

lyrics (words of song) เนื้อเพลง *néua phlehng*

M

madam แหม่ม *màem*

magazine วารสาร *waarásǎan*

mail (letters) จดหมาย *jòtmǎai*

mail (v.) ส่งจดหมาย *sòng jòtmǎai*

main road ถนนใหญ่, ถนนหลวง *thanǒn yài, thanǒn lǔang*

make, create สร้าง *sâang*

make an appointment นัด *nát*

makeshift ใช้ชั่วคราว *chái chûa khrao*

makeup ที่แต่งหน้า *thîi tàeng nâa*

man ผู้ชาย *phûu chaai*

manager ผู้จัดการ *phûu jàt kaan*

manicure การแต่งเล็บ *kaan tàeng lép*

manners (etiquette/behavior) มารยาท *maa-rá-yâat*

many มาก *mâak*

map แผนที่ *phǎehn thîi*

marble หินอ่อน *hǐn àwn*

March มีนาคม *mii-naa-khom*

margarine เนยมาร์การีน *noei maakaariin*

marina ที่จอดเรือ *thîi jàwt ruea*

marital status สถานภาพสมรส *sathǎana phâap sǒmrót*

market ตลาด *talàat*

Mass (go to) ไปร่วมพิธีในโบสถ์ *(pai rûam) phíthii nai bòht*

massage นวด *nûat*

mat (on floor) เสื่อ *sùea*

mat (on table) ที่รอง *thîi rawng*

match เข้ากัน *khâo kan*

matches ไม้ขีด *mái khìit*

mattress ที่นอน *thîi-nawn*

May พฤษภาคม *phrúetsaphaakhom*

maybe อาจจะ *àat jà*

mayor นายกเทศมนตรี *naayók-thêhtsamontrii*

me (female) ฉัน *chǎn*, (male) ผม *phǒm*

meal มื้อ *múeh*

mean ใจแคบ *jai khâehp*

measure วัด *wát*

measure out แบ่งวัด *bàeng wát*

measuring jug ถ้วยตวง *thûai tuang*

meat เนื้อ *núea*

medication การรักษาด้วยยา *kaan ráksǎa dûai yaa*

medicine ยา *yaa*

medium (not too much) ปานกลาง *paan-glaang*

meet พบ *phóp*

meeting, conference ประชุม *pra-chum*

melon แตง *taehng*

member สมาชิก *samaachík*

membership card บัตรสมาชิก *bàt samaachík*

memory card เอสดีการ์ด *es-dii káad*

mend ซ่อมแซม *sâwm saehm*

menstruate มีประจำเดือน *mii prà-jam duean*

menstruation การมีประจำเดือน *kaan mii prà-jam duean*

menu เมนู, รายการอาหาร *mehnuu, raikaan aahǎan*

merit (religious) บุญ *bun*

message ข้อความ *khâw khwaam*

metal เหล็ก *lèk*

meter (in taxi) มิเตอร์ *mítôeh*

meter (measurement) เมตร *méht*

middle, center กลาง *glaang*

migraine ปวดหัวอย่างหนัก *pùat hǔa yàang nàk*

mild (taste) รสอ่อน *rót àwn*

milk นม *nom*

millimeter มิลลิเมตร *millílméht*

million ล้าน *láan*

mince (meat/pork) สับ *sàp*

mind ใจ *jai*

mine (female) ของฉัน *khǎwng-chǎn*, (male) ของผม *khǎwng-phǒm*

mineral water น้ำแร่ *nám râeh*

ministry (government ministry) กระทรวง *krà-suang*

minute นาที *naathii*

mirror กระจก *grà-jòk*

miss (flight, train) ตกรถไฟ *tòk rót fai*

miss (loved one) คิดถึง *khít thǔeng*

missing หายไป *hǎi pai*

missing person คนหาย *khon hǎi*

mist หมอก *màwk*

mistake ความผิด *khwaam phìt*

mistaken เข้าใจผิด *khâo-jai phìt*

misunderstanding เข้าใจผิด *khâo-jaiphìt*

mobile phone โทรศัพท์มือถือ/โมบาย *thorasàp mue-thǔe/moo-bai*

modern art ศิลปะสมัยใหม่ *sǐnlapà samǎi mài*

moment เดี๋ยว *dǐao*

monastery วัด *wát*

Monday วันจันทร์ *wan jan*

money เงิน *ngoehn*

monk (a Buddhist monk) พระ *phrá*

monkey ลิง *ling*

month เดือน *duean*

moon ดวงจันทร์ *duang can*

mope ซึมเศร้า *suem sâo*

more than (comparative form of adjectives) มากกว่า *mâak-gwàa*

morning ตอนเช้า *tawn-cháo*

mosquito ยุง *yung*

motel โมเต็ล *mohten*

mother แม่ *mâeh*

mother-in-law แม่ยาย *mâeh yaai*

motorbike มอเตอร์ไซค์ *mawtoehsai*

motorboat เรือยนต์ *ruea yon*

mountain ภูเขา *phuu khǎw*

mountain climbing การปีนภูเขา *kaan piin phuu khǎo*

mouse หนู *nǔu*

(computer) mouse เมาส์ (คอมพิวเตอร์) *mao (khawm-phiu-tôeh)*

mouth ปาก *pàak*

movie หนัง *nǎng*

Mr./Mrs./Miss คุณ *Khun*

MSG (monosodium glutamate) ผงชูรส *phǒng chuu rót*

much มาก *mâak*

mud โคลน *khlohn*

muscle กล้ามเนื้อ *glâam núea*

museum พิพิธภัณฑ์ *phíphítthaphan*

mushroom เห็ด *hèt*

music ดนตรี *dontrii*

mustache หนวด *nùat*

N

nail (metal) ตะปู *tapuu*

nail (finger) เล็บ *lép*

naked เปลือย *plueai*

name ชื่อ *chûeh*

nappy, diaper ผ้าอ้อม *phâa âwm*

nation ชาติ *châat*

nationality สัญชาติ *sǎnchâat*

natural ตามธรรมชาติ *taam thammachâat*

nature ธรรมชาติ *thammachâat*

naughty ซน *son*

nauseous คลื่นไส้ *khlûehn sâi*

navy blue สีน้ำเงิน *sǐi-nám-ngern*

near ใกล้ *klâi*

nearby (here) แถวนี้ *thǎeo níi*

nearby (there) แถวนั้น *thǎeo nán*

necessary จำเป็น *jampen*

neck คอ *khaw*

necklace สร้อยคอ *sôi khaw*

necktie เน็คไท *nékthai*

needle เข็ม *khěm*

neighbour เพื่อนบ้าน *phûean bâan*

nephew หลานชาย *lǎan chaai*

never ไม่เคย *mâi khoei*

never mind ไม่เป็นไร *mâi-pen-rai*

new ใหม่ *mào*

news ข่าว *khàaw*

newspaper หนังสือพิมพ์ *nangsǔeh phim*

New Zealand นิวซีแลนด์ *niw-sii-laen*

next ต่อไป *tàw pai*

next to ถัดไป *thàt pai*

nice (pleasant) ดี ปลอดโปร่ง *dii,
plàwt pròhng*

nickname ชื่อเล่น *chêu-lên*

niece หลานสาว *lǎan sǎo*

night กลางคืน *klaang khuehn*

night duty เวรกลางคืน *wehn klaang
khuehn*

nightclothes ชุดนอน *chút nawn*

nightclub ไนท์คลับ *nái(t) kláp*

nine เก้า *gâo*

nineteen สิบเก้า *sìp-gâo*

ninety เก้าสิบ *gâo-sìp*

no ไม่ *mâi*

no entry ห้ามเข้า *hâam khâo*

no thank you ไม่เอา ขอบคุณ *mâi ao
khàwp khun*

noise เสียง *sǐang*

noisy/loud noise เสียงดัง *sǐang-dang*

non-smoking เขตปลอดบุหรี่ *khèet
plàwt burìi*

nonstop (flight) บินตรง *bin trong*

noodles ก๋วยเตี๋ยว *gǔay-tîaw tǐao*

noon เที่ยงวัน *thîang-wan*

no-one ไม่มีใคร *mâi mii khrai*

normal ปกติ *pàkàtì*

north เหนือ *nǔea*

nose จมูก *jamùuk*

nosebleed เลือดกำเดาออก *lûeat
kamdao àwk*

not ไม่ *mâi*

not at all ไม่เลย *mâi-loei*

notebook สมุดบันทึก *samùt banthúk*

notebook computer
คอมพิวเตอร์โน้ตบุ๊ค *khawm-phíu-tôeh
nóo-t-búk*

notepad สมุดฉีก *samùt chìik*

notepaper กระดาษจด *kradàat còt*

nothing ไม่มีอะไร *mâi mii arai*

November พฤศจิกายน
phrúetsacìkaayon

novice (Buddhist) เณร *nehn*

now ตอนนี้ *tawn-níi*

nowhere ไม่มีที่ไหน *mâi mii thîi nǎi*

number เบอร์, หมายเลข *boeh, mǎai lêhk*

nun แม่ชี *mâeh chii*

nurse พยาบาล *phayaabaan*

nuts ถั่ว *thùa*

O

object, thing สิ่งของ *sìng- khǎwng*

occupation อาชีพ *aachîip*

o'clock โมง *mohng*

October ตุลาคม *tulaakhom*

of, belong to ของ *khǎwng*

off (gone bad) เสีย *sǐa*

off (turned off) ปิด *pìt*

offer เสนอให้ *sanǒeh hâi*

office ที่ทำงาน *thîi tham ngaan*

often บ่อย *bòi*

oil น้ำมันเครื่อง *náamman khrûeang*

ointment ขี้ผึ้งทา *khîi phûeng thaa*

okay ตกลง *tòk long*

old (of persons) แก่ *kàeh*

old (of things) เก่า *kào*

old-fashioned, traditional โบราณ *boh-raan*

on (on top of) บน *bon*

on, at ที่ *thîi*

on (turned on) เปิด *pòeht*

on board ขึ้น, อยู่บน *khûen, yùu bon*

one หนึ่ง *nèung*

one hundred หนึ่งร้อย *nùeng-rói*

one thousand หนึ่งพัน *nùeng-phan*

one hundred thousand หนึ่งแสน *nùeng-săen*

one-day trip การเที่ยวไปเช้า-เย็นกลับ *kaan thîao pai cháw-yen klàp*

one-way ticket ตั๋วเที่ยวเดียว *tŭa thîao diao*

one-way traffic รถเดินทางเดียว *rót doehn thaang diao*

onion หอมใหญ่ *hăwm yài*

on the left ทางซ้าย *thaang sái*

on the right ทางขวา *thaang kwăa*

on the way กำลังมา *gamlang maa*

online shopping ซื้อของออนไลน์ *súeh khăwng awn-laai*

open เปิด *pòeht*

open (v.) เปิด *pòeht*

operate (surgeon) ผ่าตัด *phàa tàt*

operator (telephone) โอเปอเรเตอร์ *ohpoehrehtôeh*

opposite ตรงข้าม *trong khâam*

optician ช่างทำและขายแว่น *châang tham lâe khăai wâen*

or หรือ *rŭe*

orange (fruit) ส้ม *sôm*

order (command) คำสั่ง *kham sàng*

order (written) ใบสั่ง *bai sàng*

order (v.) สั่ง *sàng*

other อื่นๆ *ùehn ùehn*

other side อีกข้าง *ìik khâang*

our ของเรา *khăwng-rao*

outside ข้างนอก *khâang nâwk*

oven เตาอบ *tao-òp*

over there (yonder) ที่โน่น *thîi nôhn*

overpass สะพานข้าม *saphaan khâam*

overseas ต่างประเทศ *tàang prathêht*

overtake แซง *saehng*

ox วัว *wua*

P

pacemaker เครื่องกระตุ้นกล้ามเนื้อหัวใจ *khrûeng-kra-tûn klâam-núea hŭa-jai*

packed lunch ห่อ/กล่องอาหารกลางวัน *hàw/klàwng aahăan klaangwan*

page หน้า *nâa*

pain เจ็บปวด *jèp pùat*

painkiller ยาแก้ปวด *yaa kâeh pùat*

paint สี *sĭi*

painting รูป *rûup*

pair คู่ *khôu*

pajamas ชุดนอน *chút nawn*

palace วัง *wang*

panties กางเกงใน *kaangkehng nai*

pants กางเกง *kaangkehng*

pantyhose ถุงน่อง *thŭng nâwng*

papaya มะละกอ *malákaw*

paper กระดาษ *kradàat*

parasol ร่มกันแดด *rôm kan dàeht*

parcel พัสดุ *phátsadù*

pardon ขอโทษ *khăw thôht*

parents พ่อแม่ *phâw mâeh*

park, gardens สวน *sŭan*

park (v.) จอด *jàwt*

parking garage โรงรถ *rohng rót*

partner (business) หุ้นส่วน *hûn sùan*

party งานปาร์ตี้ *ngaan paatîi*

passable (road) รถผ่านสองคันได้ *(thanŏn) rót phàan săwng khan dâi*

passenger ผู้โดยสาร *phûu doeysăan*

passport หนังสือเดินทาง *năngsŭeh doehn thaang*

passport photo รูปพาสปอร์ต *rûup phâat-à-pàwt*

password รหัส *rahàt*

patient คนไข้ *khon khâi*

patient (personality) ใจเย็น *jai-yen*

pay จ่าย *jàai*

pay the bill จ่ายบิล *jàai bin*

peach พีช *phíit*

peanut ถั่วลิสง *thùa lísŏng*

pear แพร์ *phaeh*

pedal บันไดถีบ *bandai thìip*

pedestrian crossing ทางม้าลาย *thaang máa laai*

pedicure ทำเล็บเท้า *tham*

pen ปากกา *pàak gaa*

pencil ดินสอ *dinsăw*

penknife มีดพก *mîit phók*

people คน *khon*

pepper (black) พริกไทย *phrík thai*

pepper (chilli) พริกหยวก *phrík yùak*

performance การทำงาน *kaan tham ngaan*

perfume น้ำหอม *náam hăwm*

perhaps บางที *baang thii*

period (menstrual) ประจำเดือน *pracam duean*

permit ใบอนุญาต *bai anúyâat*

person คน *khon*

personal ส่วนตัว *sùan tua*

pet สัตว์เลี้ยง *sàt líang*

petrol น้ำมัน *náamman*

petrol station ปั๊มน้ำมัน *pám náamman*

pharmacy ร้านขายยา *ráan khăai yaa*

phone โทรศัพท์ *thohrásàp*

phone (v.) พูดโทรศัพท์ *phûut thohrásàp*

phone card บัตรโทรศัพท์ *bàt thohrásàp*

phone number หมายเลขโทรศัพท์ *măai lêhk thohrásàp*

photo รูปถ่าย *rûup thài*

photocopy สำเนา *sămnao*

photocopy (v.) อัดสำเนา *àt sămnao*

photo-editing การตัดต่อ-รูปภาพ *kaan tàt-taw rûup-phâap*

phrasebook หนังสือคำศัพท์ *nangsŭeh khamsàp*

pick up (come to) มารับ *maa ráp*

pick up (go to) ไปรับ *pai ráp*

picnic ปิคนิค *píkník*

pill (contraceptive) ยาคุมกำเนิด *yaa khum kamnòeht*

pills, tablets ยาเม็ด *yaa mét*

pillow หมอน *măwn*

pin เข็มหมุด *khĕm mùt*

PIN number รหัสส่วนตัว *rahàt sùan tua*

pineapple สับปะรด *sapparót*

pink สีชมพู *sĭi-chom-phou*

pipe (plumbing) ท่อ *thâw*

pipe (smoking) ไปพ์ *pái(p)*, กล้อง *klâwng*

pity สงสาร *sŏngsăan*

place of interest สถานที่น่าเที่ยว *sathǎan thîi nâa thîao*

plain (simple) ธรรมดา *thammadaa*

plain (not flavored) เปล่า *plào*

plan (map) แผนที่แสดงแนวราบ *phǎehn thîi sadaeng naew râap*

plan (intention) แผน *phǎehn*

plane เครื่องบิน *khrûeang bin*

plant (factory) โรงงาน *rohngngaan*

plant (vegetation) ต้นไม้ *tôn mái*

plastic พลาสติก *plaasatìk, plaastìk*

plastic bag ถุงพลาสติก *thǔng plaasatìk*

plate จาน *jaan*

play (drama) ละคร *lakhawn*

play (v.) เล่น *lên*

playful ขี้เล่น *khîi-lên*

play golf เล่นกอล์ฟ *lên káwf*

playground สนามเด็กเล่น *sanǎam dèk lên*

play sports เล่นกีฬา *lên gii-laa*

pleasant ดี *dii*

please ช่วย *chûai*

pleased ดีใจ *dii-jai*

pleasure ความยินดี *khwaam yindii*

plug (electric) ปลั๊กไฟ *plák fai*

plum ลูกพลัม *lûuk phlam*

pocket กระเป๋า *grà-pǎo*

point out ชี้ *chíi*

poisonous เป็นพิษ *pen phít*

police ตำรวจ *tamrùat*

police station สถานีตำรวจ *sathǎanii tamrùat*

pond สระน้ำ *sà-náam*

pony ม้าประเภทเล็ก *máa praphêht lék*

pop music ดนตรีป๊อป *dontrii páwp*

population ประชากร *prachaakawn*

pork หมู *mǔu*

port ท่าเรือ *thâa ruea*

porter (for bags) คนขนกระเป๋า *khon khǒn krapǎo*

possible เป็นไปได้ *pen pai dâi*

post (v.) ส่ง *sòng*

post, mail (n.) จดหมาย *jòt-mǎay*

postage ค่าส่งไปรษณีย์ *khâa sòng praisanii*

postbox ตู้ไปรษณีย์ *tûu praisanii*

postcard ไปรษณียบัตร *praisaniiyábàt*

post office ไปรษณีย์ *praisanii*

postpone เลื่อน *lûean*

pot (for rice) หม้อ *môr*

potato chips มันฝรั่งทอด *man faràng thâwt*

poultry ไก่ *kài*

powdered milk นมผง *nom phǒng*

power outlet ที่เสียบปลั๊ก *thîi sìap plák*

prawn กุ้ง *kûng*

precious metal โลหะมีค่า *lohhà mii khâa*

precious stone พลอย *phloi*

prefer ชอบมากกว่า *châwp mâak kwàa*

preference สิ่งที่ชอบมากกว่า *sìng thîi châwp mâak kwàa*

pregnant มีท้อง *mii tháwng*

prepare, make ready เตรียม *triam*

prescription ใบสั่งยา *bai sàng yaa*

present (here) อยู่นี่ *yùu nîi*

present (gift) ของขวัญ *khǎwng khwǎn*

press กด *kòt*

pressure ความกดดัน *khwaam kòt dan*

pretty สวย *sǔay*

price ราคา *raakhaa*

price list รายการราคา *raikaan raakhaa*

primary (school) ประถม *prà-thǒm*

print (picture) ภาพพิมพ์ *phâap phim*

print (v.) พิมพ์ *phim*

prize/reward รางวัล *raang-wan*

probably อาจจะ *àat jà*

problem ปัญหา *panhǎa*

profession อาชีพ *aachîip*

professor อาจารย์ *aa-jaan*

profit ผลกำไร *phǒn kamrai*

program โปรแกรม *prohkraehm*

promise สัญญา *sǎn-yaa*

pronounce ออกเสียง *àwk sǐang*

proud, to be ภูมิใจ *phoum-jai*

province จังหวัด *jangwàt*

pudding พุดดิ้ง *phútdîng*

pull ดึง *dueng*

pull a muscle กล้ามเนื้อตึง *glâam núea tueng*

pulse ชีพจร *chîiphajawn*

punctual/on time ตรงเวลา *trong-we-laa*

pure บริสุทธิ์ *bawrísùt*

purple สีม่วง *sǐi mûang*

purse (for money) กระเป๋าสตางค์ *krapǎo sataang*

push ผลัก *phlàk*

put on, wear ใส่ *sài*

puzzle ปริศนา *prìtsanǎa*

pyjamas ชุดนอน *chút nawn*

Q

quarrel (v.) ทะเลาะกัน *thá-láw gan*

quarter หนึ่งในสี่ *nùeng nai sìi*

quarter of an hour สิบห้านาที *sìp hâa naathii*

queen ราชินี *raachinii*

question คำถาม *kham thǎam*

quick เร็ว *reo*

quiet เงียบ *ngîap*

quit/give up เลิก *lôek*

quit/resign ลาออก *laa-àwk*

R

rabbit กระต่าย *grà-tàai*

radio วิทยุ *wítthayú*

railroad, railway ทางรถไฟ *thaang rót fai*

rain ฝน *fǒn*

rain (v.) ฝนตก *fǒn tòk*

raincoat เสื้อฝน *sûea fǒn*

raise, breed เลี้ยง *lîang*

rape ข่มขืน *khòm khǔen*

rapids น้ำเชี่ยว *náam chîao*

rash ผื่นคัน *phùen khan*

rat หนู *nǔu*

raw ดิบ *dìp*

razor blade ใบมีดโกน *bai mîit kohn*

read อ่าน *àan*

ready พร้อม *phráwm*

really จริงๆ *jing jing*

reason เหตุผล *hèht phǒn*

reasonable เหมาะสม *màw-sǒm*

receipt ใบเสร็จ *bai sèt*

receive รับ *ráp*

reception desk แผนกต้อนรับ *phanàehk tâwn ráp*

recipe สูตรอาหาร *sùut aahǎan*

recommend แนะนำ *náe-nam*

recover (from illness) หาย *hǎai*

red สีแดง *sǐi daehng*

red wine ไวน์แดง *wai(n) daehng*

reduce (lower) ลด *lót*

reduction ส่วนลด *sùan lót*

refrigerator ตู้เย็น *tûu yen*

refund เบิกคืน *bòehk khuehn*

regards (closure) นับถือ *náp thǔeh*

region ภูมิภาค *phuumíphâak*

registered ลงทะเบียน *long thabian*

regret (to feel sorry) เสียใจ *sĭa-jai*

relatives ญาติ *yâat*

reliable ไว้ใจได้ *wái jai dâi*

religion ศาสนา *sàatsanăa*

remember จำได้ *jamdâi*

remove (take off, clothes, shoes) ถอด *thàwt*

rent เช่า *châo*

rent out ให้เช่า *hâi châo*

repairs การซ่อม *kaan sâwm*

repeat ทำซ้ำ *tham sám*

reply/answer ตอบ *tàwp*

report (police) แจ้ง *jâehng*

request ขอ *khăw*

reserve ถนอม, สำรอง *thanăwm, sămrawng*

responsible รับผิดชอบ *ráp phìt châwp*

rest พักผ่อน *phák phàwn*

restaurant ร้านอาหาร *ráan aahăan*

restroom ห้องพักผ่อน *hâwng phák phàwn*

result ผล *phŏn*

return/go back กลับ *glàp*

return a call โทรกลับ *thoh-glàp*

return ticket ตั๋วไปกลับ *tŭa pai glàp*

reverse (car) ถอยรถ *thŏi rót*

rheumatism โรคปวดในไขข้อ *rôhk pùat nai khăi khâw*

rice (cooked) ข้าวสวย *khâao sŭai*

rice (grain) ข้าวสาร *khâao săan*

rice field นา *naa*

rich รวย *ruai*

ride(bicycle or animal) ขี่ *khìi*

ridiculous ไม่เข้าเรื่อง *mâi khâo rûeang*

riding (horseback) การขี่ม้า *kaan khìi máa*

right (side) ข้างขวา *khâng khwăa*

right (correct) ถูก *thùuk*

right here/there ตรงนี้ *trong níi*, ตรงนั้น *trong-nán*

right of way มีสิทธิ์ไปก่อน *mii sìt pai kàwn*

ring (jewelry) แหวน *wăen*

rinse ล้างน้ำ *láang náam*

ripe สุก *sùk*

risk เสี่ยง *sĭang*

river แม่น้ำ *mâeh náam*

road ถนน *thanŏn*

roadway ถนนหลวง *thanŏn lŭang*

rock (stone) หิน *hĭn*

roll (bread) ขนมปัง *khanŏm pang*

roof หลังคา *lăngkhaa*

roof rack ที่วางของบนหลังคารถ *thîi waang khăwng bon lăngkhaa rót*

room ห้อง *hâwng*

room service บริการถึงห้อง *baw-rí-gaan thŭeng hâwng*

rope เชือก *chûeak*

rose apple ชมพู่ *chom-phôu*

round trip (ticket) ไปกลับ *pai-glàp*

route เส้นทาง *sên thaang*

rubber (material) ยาง *yaang*

rubbish ขยะ *khà-yà*

rude ไม่สุภาพ *mâi suphâap*

ruins ของพัง *khăwng phang*

run วิ่ง *wîng*

run out of (something) หมด *mòt*

running shoes รองเท้าสำหรับวิ่ง *rawngtháo sămràp wîng*

S

sad เศร้า *sâo*

safe ปลอดภัย *plàwtphai*

safe (for cash) ตู้เซฟ *tûu séhf*

sail (v.) ล่องเรือ *lâwng ruea*

sailing boat เรือใบ *ruea bai*

salad สลัด *salàt*

salary เงินเดือน *ngoehn-duean*

sale ขาย *khǎi*

sale (reduced prices) ลดราคา *lót-raa-khaa*

sales clerk พนักงานขาย *phanákngaan khǎi*

salt เกลือ *kluea*

salty (taste) เค็ม *khem*

same เหมือนกัน *mǔeankan*

sandals รองเท้าแตะ *rawng tháo tàe*

sandy beach หาดทราย *hàat sai*

sanitary towel ผ้าอนามัย *phâa anaamai*

Saturday วันเสาร์ *wan sǎo*

sauce ซอส *sáws*, น้ำจิ้ม *nám cîm*

sauna อบไอน้ำ *òp ai náam*

say/speak พูด *phôut*

scald (injury) แผลน้ำร้อนลวก *phlǎeh nám ráwn lûak*

scales ที่ชั่งน้ำหนัก *thîi châng námnàk*

scanner เครื่องสแกน *khrûeng sa-kaen*

scarf (headscarf) ผ้าพันคอ *phâa phan khaw*; (muffler) ผ้าพันคอหนา *phâa phan khaw nǎa*

scary, frightening น่ากลัว *nâa-glua*

scenic walk ที่เดินชมวิว *thîi doehn chom wiu*

school โรงเรียน *rohng rian*

scissors กรรไกร *kankrai*

scolding, (verbal) abuse คำด่า *kham dàa*

Scotland สก็อตแลนด์ *sakàwtlaehn*

screen จอ *jaw*

scuba diving ดำน้ำลึก *dam náam lúehk*

sculpture รูปปั้น *rûup pân*

SD card เอสดีการ์ด *es-dii káad*

sea ทะเล *thaleh*

seafood อาหารทะเล *aa-hǎan-thá-le*

search for หา *hǎa*

seasick เมาเรือ *mao ruea*

season ฤดู *rúe-dou*

seat ที่นั่ง *thîi nâng*

second (in line) ที่สอง *thîi sǎwng*

second (instant) วินาที *wínaathii*

secondary (school) มัธยม *matthayom*

security ความมั่นคงปลอดภัย *khwaam mân-khong plàwt-phai*

sedative ยาระงับประสาท *yaa rangáp prasàat*

see เห็น *hěn*

sell ขาย *khǎi*

send ส่ง *sòng*

sentence (words) ประโยค *prayòhk*

separate แยกกัน *yâek kan*

September กันยายน *kanyaayon*

serious จริงจัง *jing jang*

service บริการ *bawríkaan*

service station ปั๊มน้ำมัน *pám náamman*

sesame oil น้ำมันงา *náamman ngaa*

set ชุด *chút*

several/many หลาย *lǎai*

sew เย็บผ้า *yép phâa*

shade ร่มเงา *rôm ngao*

shallow ตื้น *tûehn*

shame ละอาย *lá-ai*

shampoo แชมพูสระผม *chaehmphuu sà phǒm*

shark ปลาฉลาม *plaa chalǎam*

shave โกน *kohn*

shaver ที่โกน *thîi kohn*

she เขา *khǎo*

sheet ผ้าปูที่นอน *phâa puu thîi nawn*

shirt เสื้อเชิ้ต *sûea chóeht*

shoe รองเท้า *rawng tháo*

shop, store ร้าน *ráan*

shop (v.) ไปซื้อของ *pai súeh kǎwng*

shop assistant คนขาย *khon kǎi*

shopping center ศูนย์การค้า *sǔun kaan kháa*

short สั้น *sân*

short (height) เตี้ย *tîa*

short circuit วงจรสั้น *wongjawn sân*

shorts (short trousers) กางเกงขาสั้น *kaangkehng khǎa sân*; (underpants) กางเกงใน *kaangkehng nai*

shoulder บ่า *bàa*

shout ตะโกน *tà-gohn*

show แสดง, โชว์ *sadaehng, choh*

shower อาบน้ำฝักบัว *àap náam fàk bua*

shrimp กุ้ง *kûng*

shut, close ปิด *pìt*

shutter (camera) ชัตเตอร์ *thîi pìt*

shutter (on window) บานหน้าต่าง *baan nâatàang*

shy อาย *aai* (feeling), ขี้อาย *khîi-aai* (personality)

siblings พี่น้อง *phîi-náwng*

sick, ill ไม่สบาย *mǎi-sà-baai*

side ข้าง *khâang*

side-street ซอย *soi*

sieve กระชอน *krachawn*

sightseeing ชมทิวทัศน์ *chom thiuthát*

sign (road) ป้ายสัญญาณ *pâi sǎnyaan*

sign (v.) เซ็น *sen*

signature ลายเซ็น *lai sen*

silence ความเงียบ *khwaam ngîap*

silk ไหม *mǎi*

silver เงิน *ngoehn*

SIM card ซิมการ์ด *sim-gáat*

simple ธรรมดา *thammadaa*

sing ร้องเพลง *ráwng-phlehng*

single (only one) เดียว *diao*

single (unmarried) โสด *sòht*

single bed เตียงเดี่ยว *tiang dìaw*

single room ห้องเดี่ยว *hâwng dìaw*

single ticket ตั๋วเที่ยวเดียว *tǔa thîao diao*

sir เชอร์ *soeh*

sister (older) พี่สาว *phîi sǎao*

sister (younger) น้องสาว *náwng sǎao*

sit (be sitting) นั่ง *nâng*

sit down นั่งลง *nâng long*

size ขนาด *khanàat*

skiing การเล่นสกี *gaan lên sa-gii*

skillful, good at something เก่ง *gèng*

skin ผิว *phǐu*

skinny ผอม *phǎwm*

skirt กระโปรง *kraprohng*

skytrain (BTS) รถไฟฟ้า *rót fai fáa*

Skype สไกป์ *sa-kai-p*

sleep หลับ *làp*

sleeping pills ยานอนหลับ *yaa nawn làp*

sleepy ง่วงนอน *ngûang-nawn*

sleeve แขนเสื้อ *khǎehn sûea*

slippers รองเท้าแตะ *rawng tháo tàe*

slow ช้า *cháa*

slow train รถหวานเย็น *rót wǎan yen*

small เล็ก *lék*

small change เศษสตางค์ *sèht staang*

smartphone สมาร์ทโฟน *sa-máat fohn*

smell กลิ่น *klìn*

smile ยิ้ม *yím*

smoke (cigarette) สูบบุหรี่ *sùup burii*

smoke detector ที่ตรวจจับควัน *thîi trùat jàp khwan*

snack ขนม *khà-nǒm*

snake งู *nguu*

snorkel ท่อหายใจนักประดาน้ำ *thâw hǎai jai nák pradaa náam*

snow หิมะ *himá*

snow (v.) หิมะตก *himá tòk*

soap สบู่ *sabùu*

soap powder ผงซักฟอก *phǒng sák fâwk*

soccer ฟุตบอล *fút bawn*

social networking เครือข่ายสังคม *khruea-khàai sǎngkhom*

socket (electric) ที่เสียบปลั๊ก *thîi sìap plák*

socks ถุงเท้า *thǔng tháo*

sofa, couch โซฟา *soh-faa*

soft drink น้ำอัดลม *náam àt lom*

software ซอฟแวร์ *sawf-wae*

soldier ทหาร *thá-hǎan*

sole (of shoe) พื้นรองเท้า *phúehn rawng tháo*

someone บางคน *baang khon*

sometimes บางที *baang thii*

somewhere บางแห่ง *baang hàeng*

son ลูกชาย *lûuk chaai*

song เพลง *phleng*

soon เร็วๆ นี้ *reo reo níi*

sore (ulcer) แผลมีหนอง *phlǎeh mii nǎwng*

sore (painful) เจ็บ *jèp*

sore throat เจ็บคอ *jèp khaw*

sorry (regret) เสียใจ *sǐa jai*

sorry (apology) ขอโทษ *khǎw-thôt*

sound, noise เสียง *sǐang*

sour เปรี้ยว *prîao*

south ทิศใต้ *tit tai*

souvenir ของที่ระลึก *khǎwng thîi ralúek*

spanner, wrench กุญแจเลื่อน *kunjaeh lûean*

spare parts อะไหล่ *alài*

spare tire ยางอะไหล่ *yaang alài*

speak พูด *phôut*

special พิเศษ *phísèht*

specialist (doctor) หมอเฉพาะทาง *mǎw chapháw thaang*

specialty (cooking) อาหารจานพิเศษ *aahǎan jaan phisèht*

speed limit ความเร็วจำกัด *khwaam reo jamkàt*

spell สะกด *sakòt*

spices เครื่องเทศ *khrûeang thêht*

spicy เผ็ดร้อน *phèt ráwn*

spoon ช้อน *cháwn*

sport กีฬา *kiilaa*

sports center ศูนย์เครื่องกีฬา *sǔun khrûeang kiilaa*

sportsman/woman นักกีฬา *nák gii-laa*

spot (place) ที่ใดที่หนึ่ง *thîi dai thîi nùeng*

spot (stain) รอยเปื้อน *roi pûean*

spouse คู่สมรส *khûu sǒmrót*

sprain เคล็ด *khlét*

spring (season) ฤดูใบไม้ผลิ *rúeduu bai mái phlì*

spring (device) สปริง *sapring*

square (shopping plaza) ศูนย์การค้า *sǔun kaan kháa*

square meter ตารางเมตร *taaraang méht*

squash (game) เล่นสควอช *lên sakhwáwt*

stadium สนามกีฬา *sanǎam kiilaa*

stain รอยเปื้อน *roi pûean*

stairs บันได *bandai*

stamp แสตมป์ *sataehm*

stand (be standing) ยืน *yuehn*

stand up ยืนขึ้น *yuehn khûen*

star ดาว *daao*

starfruit มะเฟือง *má-fueang*

start เริ่ม *rôehm*

state รัฐ *rát*

station สถานี *sathǎanii*

statue รูปปั้น *rûup pân*

stay (remain) คงอยู่ *khong yùu*

stay (in hotel) พัก *phák*

steal ขโมย *khamoey*

steel เหล็กกล้า *lèk klâa*

stepfather พ่อเลี้ยง *phâw líang*

stepmother แม่เลี้ยง *mâeh líang*

steps ก้าว *kâo*

sterilize ฆ่าเชื้อ *khâa chúea*

sticking plaster พลาสเตอร์ *phlaasatôeh*

sticky rice ข้าวเหนียว *khâao-nǐaw*

sticky tape เทปเหนียว *théhp nǐao*

stink เหม็น *měn*

stir-fried ผัด *phàt*

stitches (in wound) เข็ม *khěm*

stomach (organ) ท้อง *tháwng*

stomach (abdomen) ท้อง *tháwng*

stomach ache ปวดท้อง *pùat tháwng*

stomach cramps ตะคิวที่ท้อง *takhiu thîi tháwng*

stools (feces) อุจจาระ *ùtjaará*

stop (halt) หยุด *yùt*

stop (cease) เลิก *lôehk*

stopover ค้างคืน *kháang khuehn*

store, shop ร้าน *ráan*

storey ชั้น *chán*

storm พายุ *phaayú*

stove เตา *tao*

straight ตรง *trong*

straight ahead ตรงไปข้างหน้า *trong pai khâng nâa*

straw (drinking) หลอดดูด *làwt dùut*

street ถนน *thanǒn*

strike (work stoppage) นัดหยุดงาน *nát yùt ngaan*

string เชือก *chûeak*

strong แข็งแรง *khǎeng raehng*

student (school) นักเรียน *nák-rian*, (university) นักศึกษา *nák-sùek-sǎa*

study เรียน *rian*

stuffing ยัดไส้ *yát sâi*

sub-district ตำบล *tam-bon*

subtitles บรรยาย *ban yaai*

succeed สำเร็จ *sǎmrèt*

sugar น้ำตาล *námtaan*

suit สูท *sùut*

suitcase กระเป๋าเดินทาง *krapǎo doehn thaang*

sum (calculate figures) คิดเลข *khít lêhk*

summer หน้าร้อน *nâa ráwn*

sun ดวงอาทิตย์ *duang aathít*

sunbathe อาบแดด *àap dàeht*

Sunday วันอาทิตย์ *wan aathít*

sunglasses แว่นกันแดด *wâen gan dàeht*

sunrise ดวงอาทิตย์ขึ้น *duang aathít khûen*

sunscreen ครีมกันแดด *khriim kan dàeht*

sunset ดวงอาทิตย์ตก *duang aathít tòk*

sunstroke เป็นลมแดด *pen lom dàeht*

suntan lotion โลชั่นกันแดด *lohchân gan dàeht*

supermarket ซูเปอร์มาร์เก็ต *suupôehmaakèt*

surcharge เงินเก็บเพิ่ม *ngoehn gèp phôehm*

sure แน่ใจ *nâe-jai*

surf เล่นโต้คลื่น *lên tôh khlûehn*

surface mail เมล์ธรรมดา *meh(l) thammadaa*

surfboard กระดานโต้คลื่น *gra daan tôh khlûehn*

surname นามสกุล *naam sakun*

swallow กลืน *kluehn*

swamp บึง *bueng*

sweat เหงื่อ *ngùea*

sweater เสื้อกันหนาว *sûea kan nǎo*

sweep (the room) กวาดบ้าน *gwàat-bâan*

sweet หวาน *wǎan*

sweet (dessert) ของหวาน *khǎwng-wǎan* swim ว่ายน้ำ *wâai náam*

swimming pool สระว่ายน้ำ *sà wâai náam*

swimming costume ชุดว่ายน้ำ *chút wâai náam*

swindle โกง *kohng*, หลอกลวง *làwk luang*

switch สวิทช์ *sa-wít*

symptom อาการ *aa-gaan*

synagogue สุเหร่าของยิว *suràw khǎwng yiu*

syrup น้ำเชื่อม *náam chûeam*

T

table โต๊ะ *tó*

tablemat ผ้ารองจาน *phâa rawng jaan*

tablespoon ช้อนโต๊ะ *cháwn tó*

table tennis ปิงปอง *ping pawng*

tablet PC แท็บเล็ท พีซี *tháeb-lét phii sii*

tablets ยาเม็ด *yaa mét*

tableware ชุดทานอาหาร *chút thaan aahǎan*

take (medicine) กิน *gin (yaa)*

take (photograph) ถ่ายรูป *thàai rûup*

take (time) ใช้เวลา *chái wehlaa*

take off ถอด *thàwt*

talk พูด *phûut*

tall สูง *sǔung*

tampon ผ้าอนามัยแบบสอด *phâa anaamai bap sâwt*

tanned สีน้ำผึ้ง *sǐi nám phûeng*

tap ก๊อก *káwk*

tape measure สายวัด *sǎai wát*

taste รส *rót*

taste (v.) ชิม *chim*

tasty อร่อย *à-ròi tax* ภาษี *phaasǐi*

tax-free shop ร้านปลอดภาษี *ráan plàwt phaasǐi*

taxi แท็กซี่ *tháeksîi*

taxi stand ป้ายรถแท็กซี่ *pâi tháeksîi*

tea ชา *chaa*

tea (black) ชาดำ *chaa dam*

tea (green) ชาเขียว *chaa khǐao*

teaspoon ช้อนชา *cháwn chaa*

teat (bottle) จุกนม *jùk nom*

teeth, tooth ฟัน *fan*

telephone โทรศัพท์ *thoh-rá-sàp*

telephoto lens เลนส์ส่องทางไกล *len sàwng thaang klai*

television ทีวี *thii wii*

telex เทเล็กซ์ *thehlèk*

tell (someone) บอก *bàwk*

temperature (heat) อุณหภูมิ *unhàphuum*

temperature (to have a) มีไข้ *mii khâi*

temple วัด *wát*

temporary filling อุดฟันชั่วคราว *ùt fan chûa khraao*

ten สิบ *sip*

ten thousand หมื่น *mùen*

tender, sore ช้ำ *chám*

tennis เทนนิส *thehnnít*

tent เต็นท์ *téhn*

terminus สถานีปลายทาง *sathǎanii plaai thaang*

terrace (houses) บ้านห้องแถว *bâan hâwng thǎeo*

terrible แย่มาก *yâeh mâak*

textbook หนังสือเรียน *nǎng-sǔeh rian*

texting ส่งเอสเอ็มเอส *sòng es-em-es*

Thai (language) ภาษาไทย *phaa-sǎa-thai*

Thailand ประเทศไทย *prà-thêt-thai*

thank ขอบคุณ *khàwp kun*

thank you, thanks ขอบคุณ *khàwp khun*

thaw ละลาย *lálaai*

theater โรงหนัง *rohng nǎng*

theft การขโมย (ของ) *kaan khamoey (khǎwng)*

then แล้วก็ *láew-gâw*

there ที่นั่น *thîi nân*

there is/there are มี *mii*

thermometer (body) ปรอท *paràwt*

thermometer (weather) เทอร์โมมิเตอร์ *thoehmohmítôeh*

they เขา *khǎo*

thick หนา *nǎa*

thief ขโมย *khamoey*

thin (not fat) ผอม *phǎwm*

thin (not thick) บาง *baang*

think (ponder) คิด *khít*

think (believe) เชื่อ *chûea*

think of คิดถึง *khít-thǔeng*

third (1/3) หนึ่งในสาม *nùeng nai sǎam*

third (place) ที่สาม *thîi sǎam*

thirsty หิวน้ำ *hǐu náam*

this afternoon บ่ายนี้ *bàai níi*

this evening เย็นนี้ *yen níi*

this morning เช้านี้ *cháo níi*

thread ด้าย *dâai*

throat คอหอย *khaw hǒi*

thunderstorm พายุ *phaayú*

Thursday วันพฤหัสบดี *wan pharúehàt (sabawdii)*

ticket (admission) บัตร *bàt*

ticket (travel) ตั๋ว *tǔa*

ticket office ที่ขายตั๋ว *thîi khǎai tǔa*

tidy เรียบร้อย *rîap rói*

tie (necktie) เน็คไท *nék thai*

tie (v.) ผูก *phùuk*

tights (thick) ถุงน่องหนาๆ *thǔng nâwng nǎa nǎa*

tights (pantyhose) ถุงน่อง *thǔng nâwng*

time (occasion) เวลา *wehlaa*, ที *thii*

times (multiplying) คูณ *khuun*

timetable ตาราง *taaraang*

tin (can) กระป๋อง *krapǎwng*

tin opener ที่เปิดกระป๋อง *thîi pòeht krapǎwng*

tip (gratuity) ทิป *thíp*

tired, exhausted เหนื่อย *nùeay*

tissues กระดาษเช็ดปาก *kradàat chét pàak*

tobacco ยาสูบ *yaa sùup*

today วันนี้ *wan níi*

toddler เด็กวัยหัดเดิน *dèk wai hàt doehn*

toe ปลายเท้า *plaai tháo*

tofu/soyabean เต้าหู้ *tâo-hôu*

together ด้วยกัน *dûai kan*

toilet ห้องน้ำ *hâwng náam*

toilet paper กระดาษชำระ *kradàat chamrá*

toiletries เครื่องใช้ในห้องน้ำ *khrûeang chái nai hâwng náam*

tomorrow พรุ่งนี้ *phrûng níi*

tongue ลิ้น *lín*

tonight คืนนี้ *khuehn níi*

too/also ด้วย *dûay*

tool เครื่องมือ *khrûeang mueh*

tooth ฟัน *fan*

toothache ปวดฟัน *pùat fan*

toothpaste ยาสีฟัน *yaa sǐi fan*

top up เติม *toehm*

torch, flashlight ไฟฉาย *fai chǎai*

total ทั้งหมด *tháng mòt*

tough ยาก *yâak*

tour ทัศนาจร, ทัวร์ *thátsanaajawn, thua*

tour guide มัคคุเทศก์ *mákkhúthêht,* ไกด์ *kái*

tourist information office สำนักงานข้อมูลนักท่องเที่ยว *sǎmnák ngaan khâw muun nák thâwng thîao*

tow ลาก *lâak*

towel ผ้าเช็ดตัว *phâa chét tua*

tower หอคอย *hǎw khoi*

town เมือง *mueang*

toy ของเล่น *khǎwng lên*

traffic การจราจร *kaan já-raa-jawn*

traffic jam รถติด *rót-tìt*

traffic light ไฟจราจร *fai já-raa-jawn*

train รถไฟ *rót fai*

train station สถานีรถไฟ *sathǎanii rót fai*

train ticket ตั๋วรถไฟ *tǔa rót fai*

train timetable ตารางรถไฟ *taaraang rót fai*

translate แปล *plaeh*

travel เดินทาง *doehn thaang*

travel agent เอเย่นขายตั๋ว *ehyên khǎai tǔa*

traveler นักเดินทาง *nák doehn thaang*

traveler's check เช็คเดินทาง *chék doehn thaang*

treatment การรักษา *kaan ráksǎa*

tree ต้นไม้ *tôn-mái*

trim (hair) เล็ม *lem*

trim (haircut) ตัดผม *tàt phǒm*

trip การเดินทาง *kaan doehn thaang*

truck รถบรรทุก *rót banthúk*

true จริง *jing*

trustworthy ไว้ใจได้ *wái jai dâi*

try on ลอง *lawng*

Tuesday วันอังคาร *wan angkhaan*

tuna ปลาทูน่า *plaa thuunâa*

tunnel อุโมงค์ *ùmohng*

turn left เลี้ยวซ้าย *líaw-sáay*

turn right เลี้ยวขวา *líaw-khwǎa*

turn off ปิด *pit*

turn on เปิด *pòeht*

turn over พลิก *phlík*

TV ทีวี *TV*

TV guide รายการทีวี *raikaan thii wii*

tweet ทวีท *tha-wíit*

tweezers แหนบ *nàehp*

twenty ยี่สิบ *yîi- sìp*

Twitter ทวีทเตอร์ *tha-wít-toeh*

two สอง *sǎwng*

typhoon ไต้ฝุ่น *tâifùn*

tyre, tire ยางรถ *yaang rót*

U

ugly น่าเกลียด *nâa klìat*

ulcer แผลเปื่อย *phlǎeh pùeai*

umbrella ร่ม *rôm*

uncle ลุง *lung*

uncomfortable ไม่สบาย *mâi-sà-baai*

under ใต้ *tâi*

underpants กางเกงใน *kaangkehng nai*

underpass ถนนลอดใต้สะพาน *thanǒn lâwt tâi saphaan*

understand เข้าใจ *khâo jai*

underwear เสื้อกางเกงใน *sûeakaangkehng nai*

undress แก้ผ้า *kâeh phâa*

unemployed ว่างงาน *wâang ngaan*

uneven ไม่เรียบ *mâi rîap*

unfortunate โชคร้าย *chôhk-ráai*

university มหาวิทยาลัย *mahǎawítthayaalai*

unleaded ไร้สารตะกั่ว *rái sǎan takùa*

unmarried เป็นโสด *pen sòht*

up ขึ้น *khûen*

upload อัพโหลด *ap-lòod*

upright ตั้งตรง *tâng trong*

upstairs ข้างบน *khâng bon*

urgent ด่วน *dùan*

urine ปัสสาวะ *patsǎawá*

use ใช้ *chái*

username ชื่อผู้ใช้ *chûeh phûu chái*

used to เคย *khoei*

usually มักจะ *mák cà*

V

vacant ว่าง *wâang*

vacate ปล่อยให้ว่าง *plòi hâi wâang*

vacation วันหยุด *wan yùt*

vaccinate ฉีดวัคซีน *chìit wáksiin*

valid ใช้ได้ *chái dâi*

valley หุบเขา *hùp khǎo*

valuable มีค่า *mii khâa*

valuables ของมีค่า *khǎwng mii khâa*

van รถตู้ *rót tûu*

vase แจกัน *jaehkan*

vegetable ผัก *phàk*

vegetarian มังสวิรัติ *mang-sà-wí-rát*

vegetarian (Chinese) กินเจ *kin-jeh*

vein หลอดเลือดดำ *làwt lûeat dam*

vending machine เครื่องขายของ *khrûeang khǎi khǎwng*

venomous มีพิษ *mii pít*

venereal disease โรคที่ติดต่อทางร่วมเพศ *rôhk thîi tìt tàw thaang rûam phêht*

vertical แนวตั้ง *naeo tâng*

very, very much มาก *mâak*

via โดยทาง *doey thaang*, ผ่าน *phàan*

video camera กล้องวิดิโอ *klâwng widii-oh*

view ทัศนะ *thátsaná*, วิว *wiu*

village หมู่บ้าน *mùu bâan*

villager ชาวบ้าน *chaaw bâan*

visa วีซ่า *wiisâa*

visit เยี่ยม *yîam*

visitor (guest) แขก *khàek*

vitamins วิตามิน *wítaamin*

voice/sound เสียง *sǐang*

volcano ภูเขาไฟ *phuu khǎo fai*

volleyball วอลเล่ย์บอล *wawllêhbawn*

vomit อาเจียน *aa-jian* (formal), อ้วก *ûak* (informal)

W

wait รอ *raw*, คอย *khoi*

wait a moment (informal) รอเดี๋ยว *raw-dǐew*

waiter บริกร *bawríkawn*, คนเสิร์ฟ *khon sòehf*

waiting room ห้องนั่งรอ *hâwng nâng raw*

waitress บริกรหญิง *bawríkawn yǐng*

wake up ตื่น *tùehn*

walk (n.) การเดิน *kaan doehn*

walk (v.) เดิน *doehn*

wall กำแพง *kamphaehng*

wallet กระเป๋าสตางค์ *krapǎo sataang*

want, need ต้องการ *tâwngkaan* (formal), อยาก *yàak* (informal)

want (to get something) อยากได้ *yàak-dâi* (informal)

wardrobe ตู้เสื้อผ้า *tûu sûea phâa*

warm อบอุ่น *òp ùn*

warn เตือน *tuean*

warning คำเตือน *kham tuean*

wash ล้าง *láang*

wash clothes ซักผ้า *sák-phâa*

wash dishes ล้างจาน *láang-jaan*

wash face ล้างหน้า *láang-nâa*

wash hair สระผม *sà-phǒm*

wash hands ล้างมือ *láang-mue*

washing machine เครื่องซักผ้า *khrûeang sák phâa*

watch เฝ้า *fâo*

water น้ำ *náam*

waterfall น้ำตก *náam tòk*

waterproof กันน้ำ *kan náam*

water-skiing สกีน้ำ *sakii náam*

way (direction) ทาง *thaang*

way (method) วิธี *wíthii*

we, us เรา *rao*

weak อ่อนแอ *àwn aeh*

wear ใส่ *sài*

weather อากาศ *aakàat*

weather forecast พยากรณ์อากาศ *phayaakawn aakàat*

website เว็บไซต์ *web-sái*

wedding งานแต่งงาน *ngaan tàeng ngaan*

Wednesday วันพุธ *wan phút*

week สัปดาห์ *sàpdaa*

weekday วันทำงาน *wan tham ngaan*

weekend วันสุดสัปดาห์ *wan sùt sàpdaa*

weigh ชั่ง *châng*

welcome ยินดีต้อนรับ *yindii tâwn ráp*

well (good) ดี *dii*

well (for water) บ่อน้ำ *bàw náam*

well (skillful) เก่ง *gèng*

well-cooked/well-done สุก *sùk*

west ตะวันตก *ta-wan tòk*

wet เปียก *pìek*

what? อะไร *arai*

what time? กี่โมง *gìi-mong*

wheel ล้อรถ *láw rót*

wheelchair เก้าอี้มีล้อเข็น *kâo-îi mii láw khěn*

when? เมื่อไร *mûearai*

where? ที่ไหน *thîi nǎi*

which? อันไหน *an nǎi*

white ขาว *khǎao*

who? ใคร *khrai*

why? ทำไม *thammai*

widow แม่ม่าย *mâeh mâai*

widower พ่อม่าย *phâw mâai*

wife เมีย, ภรรยา *mia, phanyaa* (formal)

Wifi (wireless connection) วายฟาย *waai-faai*

wind ลม *lom*

window (in room) หน้าต่าง *nâatàang*

window (to pay) เคาน์เตอร์ *khaotôeh*

windscreen, windshield กระจกหน้ารถ *gra-jòk nâa rót*

windscreen wiper ที่ปัดน้ำฝน *thîi pàt nám fǒn*

wine ไวน์ *wai(n)*

winter หน้าหนาว *nâa nǎo*

wire ลวด *lûat*

with กับ *gàp*

withdraw (money) ถอนเงิน *thǎwn-ngoehn*

woman ผู้หญิง *phûu yǐng*

wonderful ยอดเยี่ยม *yâwt yîam*

wood ไม้ *mái*

wool (cloth) ผ้าขนสัตว์ *(phâa) khǒn sàt*

word คำ *kham*

work งาน *ngaan*

work (v.) ทำงาน *tham-ngaan*

working day วันทำงาน *wan tham ngaan*

world โลก *lôhk*

worn (used) ใช้แล้ว *chái láehw*

worn out ขาดแล้ว *khàat láehw*

worried กังวล *kangwon*

would like/may I have? ขอ *khǎww*

wound บาดแผล *bàat phlǎeh*

wrap ห่อ *hàw*

wrench, spanner กุญแจปากตาย *kunjaeh pàak taai*

wrist ข้อมือ *khâw mueh*

write เขียน *khǐan*

write down จดลงไป *jòt long pai*

wrong ผิด *phìt*

Y

yarn (thread) ด้าย *dâai*

year ปี *pii*

yellow สีเหลือง *sǐi lǔeang*

yes (that's right) ใช่ *châi*

yes (female speaking) ค่ะ *khâ*

yes (male speaking) ครับ *khráp*

yes, please (female) เอาค่ะ *ao khâ*

yes, please (male) เอาครับ *ao khráp*

yesterday เมื่อวานนี้ *mûeawaan níi*

yoga โยคะ *yoo-khá*

you คุณ *khun*, (intimate) เธอ *thoeh*, (respectful) ท่าน *thâan*

youth เยาวชน *yao-wachon*

Z

zebra ม้าลาย *máa-laay*

zero ศูนย์ *sǒun*

zip ซิป *síp*

zoo สวนสัตว์ *sǔan sàt*

"Books to Span the East and West"

Tuttle Publishing was founded in 1832 in the small New England town of Rutland, Vermont [USA]. Our core values remain as strong today as they were then—to publish best-in-class books which bring people together one page at a time. In 1948, we established a publishing outpost in Japan—and Tuttle is now a leader in publishing English-language books about the arts, languages and cultures of Asia. The world has become a much smaller place today and Asia's economic and cultural influence has grown. Yet the need for meaningful dialogue and information about this diverse region has never been greater. Over the past seven decades, Tuttle has published thousands of books on subjects ranging from martial arts and paper crafts to language learning and literature—and our talented authors, illustrators, designers and photographers have won many prestigious awards. We welcome you to explore the wealth of information available on Asia at **www.tuttlepublishing.com**.

Published by Tuttle Publishing, an imprint of Periplus Editions (HK) Ltd.

www.tuttlepublishing.com

Copyright © 2019 Periplus Editions (HK) Ltd

ISBN 978-0-8048-4687-5

First edition
26 25 24 23   8 7 6 5 4 3 2
2304MP

Printed in Singapore

TUTTLE PUBLISHING® is a registered trademark of Tuttle Publishing, a division of Periplus Editions (HK) Ltd.

Distributed by
North America, Latin America & Europe
Tuttle Publishing
364 Innovation Drive
North Clarendon, VT 05759-9436 U.S.A.
Tel: 1 (802) 773-8930
Fax: 1 (802) 773-6993
info@tuttlepublishing.com
www.tuttlepublishing.com

Japan
Tuttle Publishing
Yaekari Building, 3rd Floor, 5-4-12 Osaki
Shinagawa-ku, Tokyo 141 0032
Tel: (81) 3 5437-0171
Fax: (81) 3 5437-0755
sales@tuttle.co.jp
www.tuttle.co.jp

Asia Pacific
Berkeley Books Pte Ltd
3 Kallang Sector #04-01
Singapore 349278
Tel: (65) 6741 2178
Fax: (65) 6741 2179
inquiries@periplus.com.sg
www.tuttlepublishing.com